Roy Hattersley is a politician turned [...] Parliament in 1964 and served in each of Harold Wilson's governments and in Jim Callaghan's Cabinet. In 1983 he became deputy leader of the Labour Party. He has written 'Endpiece', his *Guardian* column, for twenty years, and before that was a columnist for *Punch* and the *Listener*. For two years he was television critic of the *Daily Express*. As well as contributing to the *Daily Mail*, and *The Times*, he has written fifteen books – including the much acclaimed *Fifty Years On*, the classic *A Yorkshire Boyhood*, three novels (*The Maker's Mark*, *In that Quiet Earth* and *Skylark's Song*), and *Blood and Fire*, a biography of William and Catherine Booth, the founders of the Salvation Army. His latest book is *John Wesley: A Brand from the Burning*. He has been Visiting Fellow of Harvard's Institute of Politics and of Nuffield College, Oxford.

'*Who Goes Home?* is a glorious conglomeration of self-deprecating anecdotes, razor-edged character sketches of defenceless ex-colleagues and frivolous *aperçus* about the nature of parliamentary politics in general and Labour politics in particular'

Ian Aitken, *New Statesman & Society*

'What makes this book such a joy is that it explains what so often baffles outsiders: why it is that, despite the buffetings, the public disdain, the long, unrewarding hours in disputatious committees and half-empty halls, people get so hooked on the vocation, trade, pastime and game which is political life'

David McKie, *Guardian*

'It is a superb book, possibly one of the funniest and most self-deprecatingly candid ones ever committed to print by a major politician'

Manchester Evening News

'Hattersley caused me to laugh out loud in a public place'
Peter Hennessy, *Financial Times*

Also by Roy Hattersley

Non-fiction

Nelson: A Biography
Goodbye to Yorkshire
Politics Apart
Endpiece Revisited
Press Gang
A Yorkshire Boyhood
Choose Freedom: The Future for Democratic Socialism
Between Ourselves
Fifty Years on
Buster's Diaries
Blood and Fire
John Wesley: A Brand from the Burning

Fiction

The Maker's Mark
In That Quiet Earth
Skylark Song

WHO GOES HOME?

Scenes from a Political Life

ROY HATTERSLEY

An *Abacus* Book

First published in Great Britain in 1995
by Little, Brown and Company
First published in paperback by Warner Books in 1996
This edition published by Abacus in 2003

A CIP catalogue record for this book
is available from the British Library.

ISBN 0 349 11692 X

Typeset by
Hewer Text Composition Services, Edinburgh
Printed and bound in Great Britain by
Clays Ltd, St Ives plc

Abacus
An imprint of
Time Warner Books UK
Brettenham House
Lancaster Place
London WC2E 7EN

www.TimeWarnerBooks.co.uk

FOREWORD

The Prime Minister's invitation was both a surprise and an embarrassment. I had not spoken to Tony Blair since the 1997 general election campaign and nothing that I knew about his reaction to my criticisms of New Labour's 'project' suggested that he had missed my company. I had, however, been a member of Jim Callaghan's cabinet. So honour required my name to be included on the guest list for the Downing Street celebration of his ninetieth birthday. At first I thought that honour also obliged me to decline with the usual thanks. Then friends – with an understanding of etiquette which was far greater than mine – explained that, although Tony Blair was the host, it was Jim Callaghan's party. I owe a great deal to Jim. He was a good Prime Minister and, given a second term, might well have become a great one. So I drew a deep breath and went through that famous door for the first time since the valedictory cabinet meeting in 1979.

The Waterloo Room was so crowded that I felt safe from sudden exposure to the trademark grin and the self-deprecating, shrugged shoulders. All the survivors of Callaghan's cabinet were there – including the four apostates who had left the Labour Party to form the SDP. David Owen and I were telling each other that we must meet for lunch, with neither of us expecting anything to come of it, when the assembled guests parted like the Red Sea and the Prime Minister – who, unlike Moses, entered into the promised land but left his most progressive followers behind – confronted me. Swinging his foot in a way that suggested diffident embarrassment, Tony Blair told me: 'You never come to see me these days'.

Prime Ministers possess the power to make me feel guilty. Thirty years ago, after I had waited a week by the telephone, Harold Wilson had prefaced his eventual invitation to join the government with the complaint that he had searched for me in vain for seven days. I apologised not because it seemed polite or expedient but because, for a moment, I believed him. Five years later, when I was at last in the Cabinet, Jim Callaghan had called a special meeting to threaten the dismissal of whoever had leaked secrets of Common Market policy to the *Financial Times*. As he looked around the table, I felt sure that I was the primary suspect – even though, not being a regular *FT* reader, I was not even sure what the leaked policy-paper contained. As Callaghan warmed to his theme, I got very near to offering my immediate resignation.

Tony Blair's inconsequential greeting had exactly the same effect. For a moment I felt as though, for five long years, he had regularly asked my advice, frequently sought my company and constantly hoped for my friendship. And that I had always turned him down. Fortunately I sufficiently recovered my composure to stutter a reply which was both suitably sycophantic and placed the blame for our estrangement where it properly belonged. 'You have', I said, 'been very busy'.

For a few minutes we talked about the 'old days' when we had been close. Then Tony Blair moved on with the promise, 'We will be in touch'. Of course, the usual courtesies having been completed, I expected to hear no more and the next morning I hurried off to my office to describe the previous night's experience to my PA. Before I had time to say 'good morning', she announced, 'Downing Street has telephoned. The Prime Minister wants you to go for tea. I assumed you would want to accept'.

Of course, I wanted to accept. But, like so many invitations, it grew increasingly unattractive as the date approached. It would, I knew, be neither sensible nor polite to arrive with a list of errors and omissions. 'Prime Minister, I thought I ought to point out some of your failures and mistakes.' And what I had learned of Tony Blair's character over the years left me in no doubt that he would not initiate a discussion on the theory and practice of socialism. I was not worth the effort. Nothing I had said or written had deflected him one inch from his chosen path. I would be no more influential in the future than I had been in the past. The Prime Minister's only motive was kindness. I had been invited to Downing Street for ten minutes of inconsequential chat. Then the duty of a dimly remembered friendship would be done.

I was wrong. The inconsequential chat lasted for almost an hour. And during that time, I came genuinely to regret that so much stood between us. Throughout that afternoon we never even mentioned the secret assault of comprehensive schools, the creation of a two-tier health service or the mistaken belief that private investment improves the efficiency of the public sector. At one stage the Prime Minister suddenly said, 'It's my view on equality that bothers you, isn't it?' and I answered, 'Yes'. Then, by instinctive agreement, we both chose not to pursue the argument. Perhaps I should have launched into an exposition of John Rawls' 'difference principle' or offered a modernised version of R. H. Tawney's 'frog and tadpole' analogy. But I let the moment pass. I left Downing Street feeling guilty, not that I had missed my chance to change history, but that I had so often publicly attacked such an engaging man. As I walked out into Whitehall, I wondered if I would be able to renew the assault in my column during the following week. My doubts lasted for about five minutes.

Roydie from Airedale Road in Sheffield – the boy who first delivered Labour leaflets on the afternoon of his eleven-plus examination – would have found it hard to believe that one day he would have tea with the Prime Minister in Downing Street. His delight at the prophecy would have been moderated by awe and wonder. As the policeman on the gate gave me a half salute, I felt a deep sense of resentment that fate and political philosophy prevented me from recapturing those emotions. But much had happened since my discovery of the Labour Party. What had begun as the infatuation with an activity had become an obsession with an idea. I would have liked to have been a regular and welcome visitor to Downing Street, basking in the warm glow of reflected glory and endorsing every detail of Tony Blair's policy. I am an insider by instinct. But the fifty years that had gone before made that impossible.

CHAPTER

1

It all began in 1945 – 'The Year of Victories', when the Allies won the war, the Labour Party won the general election and I won a scholarship to the City Grammar School. Technically speaking, scholarship was not quite the right word. Sheffield had anticipated the Butler Education Act by almost twenty years. So my aptitudes and abilities were assessed and I was adjudged suitable for an academically orientated syllabus. But we called it the scholarship – a name which properly emphasised the drama of the occasion, even for candidates like me who (having been ill the year before) took the eleven-plus when we were twelve.

That half day's examination – choosing the appropriate adjective, nominating the right number and selecting the relevant shape – more or less set the pattern of our lives for ever. So it was assumed that by lunch-time we would be exhausted by the emotional effort of trying to join the elite fifteen per cent of the city's pupils who were taught French and Latin, entered for the School Certificate and, perhaps most important of all, entitled to wear the distinctive caps and blazers of the selective schools. A compassionate City Council gave us the afternoon off to recover.

No doubt I hoped to spend the free half day playing cricket in the road outside my house. But my mother had other ideas. I was taken by bus and tramcar to Shalesmoor – a huddle of run-down terrace houses which had been built for the industrial poor of Victorian England when they deserted the hill farms of the West Riding to work in the forges and foundries of the industrial revolution. The front doors opened straight out on to the road and, since it seemed unlikely that the occupants would receive much correspondence, they were not fitted with letter boxes. Fortunately for my mother and me – if not for the families of Shalesmoor – a hundred years of Pennine rain and wind had shrunk and warped the cheap wood. So there were gaps above the top step, gaps down the side of the jamb and gaps below the lintel. Into those gaps I pushed the first Labour Party leaflets that I ever delivered.

There were a dozen of us when the work began, but only eleven when the job was finished. I was sent home – not, as you might imagine, because of bad behaviour, but in order to protect my moral welfare. Halfway through the afternoon, we ran out of leaflets. When new supplies arrived, they were not the sheets of closely printed and carefully reasoned argument which we had expected. They were a simple message illustrated with a strip cartoon. And not any strip cartoon. The character who proclaimed the wisdom of supporting the Labour Party was Jane, a *Daily Mirror* fantasy who had delighted the troops with escapades which always involved losing her skirt, tearing her blouse or being caught unawares while bathing.

I cannot recall the message which, on that occasion, she endorsed. But I remember that she was portrayed cycling, with her skirt scandalously above her knees. I have an even more vivid memory of our agent, Councillor Albert Ballard, holding the leaflet at arm's length between thumb and finger. He would, he assured my mother, make an immediate protest to the Trades and Labour Council who had supplied the pornographic pamphlet, but the delivery must continue. For in the fight to build a new Jerusalem not even a tarnished sword could sleep in our hand. However, it would be quite wrong for a boy of my age to handle such corrupting material. I was put on the next tramcar home. But not without protest. I had been introduced to political campaigning and it was love at first sight.

Ours was one of those Labour parties which, in the hallowed phrase, owed more to Methodism than Marx. Unlike the heathens of Birmingham, who came into my political life almost thirty years later, Sheffield socialists never canvassed on Sunday mornings. Respect for the Sabbath was a practical necessity, for most of our councillors and key party workers were non-conformist local preachers who spent the day of rest in their best suits, spreading the Word of the Lord. Their piety was endorsed and supported by even the few agnostics amongst the membership. Knocking on doors on Sunday was not respectable. And we were an absolutely respectable Labour party. When in my late teens I borrowed Winifred Holtby's *South Riding* from the local branch of the municipal library, and read about the councillors of East Port 'furtively fumbling' young waitresses behind the Town Hall, I never even wondered if my City Fathers did the same.

Our Member of Parliament was A. V. Alexander, First Lord of the Admiralty in both Churchill's wartime coalition and Attlee's post-war government. He wore what was called – at least when the elders were not listening – a 'come to Jesus' collar; starched stiff, winged and much favoured by Congregationalist Ministers. It was claimed, but never proved, that towards the end of one pre-war speech his false teeth flew out of his mouth and that, catching them with the agility of a Yorkshire slip fielder, he returned them to their proper place without interrupting his peroration. It was forty years before I discovered what those initials – A. V. – stood for. He was always 'Mr Alexander' to his faithful followers, and it was not for the likes of me to enquire about an MP's Christian name. But I always felt that he was in my debt. I had no doubt that, on 5th July 1945, he was re-elected as a direct result of my leaflet deliveries.

Three months after Mr Attlee formed the first majority Labour government, I became a candidate myself. I began to boast about my political experience as soon as I got to the City Grammar School and shamelessly demanded to stand in the mock election which Form I held that autumn. The spirit of 1945 was upon us and nobody was prepared to accept the Conservative nomination. No doubt in retribution for the political airs and graces which I had affected, I was forced to become the Tory standard bearer. My only consolation was that, like so many Conservatives that year, I did not receive enough votes to save my deposit.

My father – always sympathetic and supportive – had helped me make an election poster. For the sake of authenticity, it was based on a Union-Jack motif, which my mother angrily insisted was not the personal property of the Tory Party. She also made some initially incomprehensible references to my father 'knowing all about' Conservative propaganda. I subsequently discovered that she was rattling the political skeleton in his cupboard. Ten years before the war ended, he had voted for Commander Gurney Braithwaite, the Tory candidate for Hillsborough who, in 1931, had actually beaten our Mr Alexander during the Ramsay Mac-Donald National Government landslide.

My father had an excuse, of sorts, for his brief apostasy. He had attended the opening meeting of Commander Braithwaite's 1935 campaign – no doubt for the same reason that he attended HMV record demonstrations, archaeology lectures in the City Museum and Salvation Army recitals at the local citadel: it was free, and therefore one of the few forms of entertainment which were open to the unemployed. Perhaps, as he always claimed, my father did go to the meeting only to scoff. He remained, if not to pray, at least to be seduced by the eloquence of the guest speaker. The star of the evening was Jimmy Thomas – sometime leader of the railway union, Cabinet Minister in the 1929 Labour government and one of the traitors who had deserted the Party with Ramsay MacDonald and taken office in the National Coalition. Thomas spoke emotionally about his son Leslie (a young man of outstanding ability, unimpeachable virtue and immense promise) and confided to the meeting that if Labour won the election, he would persuade the only comfort of his declining years to emigrate to Australia. Parting would break his heart. But in a socialist Britain it would be impossible for a youth of talent to realise his full potential. Moved by the remarkable expression of paternal affection, my father decided that – since I was too young to emigrate – he would do the next best thing. He would protect my infant interest by voting for Gurney Braithwaite and keeping Labour out.

Jimmy Thomas was already one of my mother's villains – the man who had betrayed the miners in 1926 and destroyed her hero, A. J. Cook. So, my father could not have chosen a worse excuse for his treachery. That single indiscretion caused one of the few disagreements in my parents' fifty-year partnership. My father was reminded of his political infidelity with remorseless regularity. If he failed to push the rusty mower over the grass we called a lawn, or left scraps of leather in front of the living room fire after he had mended our shoes, she would add, at the end of her complaint, 'And you voted for Gurney Braithwaite in 1935.'

When I became a Member of Parliament in 1964, Sir Leslie Thomas was still in the House. Other MPs just thought of him as Jimmy's son or the man who, according to folklore, wrestled Dick Crossman to the ground after he overheard a slighting reference to his father. But I always felt that we had a special relationship. I was often tempted to approach him and ask if he had any idea how much trouble he had caused my family during the years which followed the war.

During those years, I received my elementary political education in and around the grocery store owned by 'The Brightside and Carbrook' – one of the three Sheffield Co-operative Societies which, although dedicated to the ideal of working together, could not be persuaded to amalgamate. Most of my lessons were learned in a dilapidated brick hut which gloried in the name of the Old Cobblers' Shop. Cockney rhyming slang had not reached the north, so nobody thought it an unsuitable place from which to preach the gospel of democratic socialism. Under its leaky roof I became treasurer of the local Labour League of Youth and argued with my elders and betters about policy which I did not understand. For reasons which I cannot now even imagine, I was particularly enthusiastic for the nationalisation of the land. But in those days, political ideas were far less attractive than political activity. Strange how, after almost half a century, the relationship has gone into reverse.

My great joy, when at last I was judged old enough to be let loose without supervision, was canvassing. Elections, I was assured, were won 'on the doorstep'. And, since we had Labour's majority on the City Council to sustain, we knocked on doors on Friday nights throughout the year. A foreman called Syd Osgathorpe taught me how the job was done. 'Don't waste time arguing. Just ask politely if we can expect their vote. If there's any doubt, put 'em down against.' Nearly fifty years after he taught me that first lesson, I presented Syd Osgathorpe with what, in Labour's old-fashioned way, we still call the Merit Award – a cross between the Distinguished Service Order and a good conduct medal. He asked me if I still went canvassing on Friday nights.

Between the ages of twelve and eighteen, I performed the young socialist's full repertoire, with the single exception of regular attendance at Socialist Sunday School. I went to a couple of their special services – held, I suppose, on radical feast days and the anniversaries of the martyrs whose life blood dyed the red flag's every fold. I enjoyed the hymns.

> When will thou save the people,
> Oh God of Mercy, when?
> The people, Lord, the people
> Not Crowns and Thrones but men.

I was not, however, a regular worshipper. Unlike the Wadsley Church Bible Class, the Socialist Sunday School did not have an associated youth club with cricket and football teams and table tennis every Tuesday night.

For although I grew up in the strange world of the Labour Party, I wanted to do most of the things that are natural to more normally nurtured adolescent boys. And my parents – who had a proper horror at the idea that I might really want to devote my life to politics – encouraged what they regarded as 'ordinary' behaviour. My father regarded 'ordinary' as life's most desirable condition – no risks, no anguish and, above all, no anxiety. So, during the years of the great Attlee government, I played football and cricket with more enthusiasm than talent and read the sports pages of the morning papers before I turned to the political news. I attended church on Sunday evenings in the hope of taking a girl for a walk on Wadsley Common afterwards, watched Sheffield Wednesday in winter and Yorkshire in the summer, spent Saturday evenings at the local cinema and persuaded my parents to let me buy a pair of crepe-soled shoes. But the Labour Party was always looking over my shoulder – reassuring, protective, demanding.

That is why, although parties were no more my style then than they are my style now, I went with my parents to the celebrations that marked Labour's two greatest achievements – the creation of the National Health Service, and independence for India and the new state of Pakistan. We cycled to Cortonwood – the nearest pit to where we lived – just for the joy of seeing the notice that had been nailed to the gate: 'This colliery is Managed by the National Coal Board on Behalf of the People.' My joy was wholly tribal – the victory of my side over their side in a contest which in 1947, at the age of thirteen, I did not understand. I make no apology for that. When, in the early eighties, it looked as if the Labour Party was going to sink, it was that tribal loyalty – mixed with gratitude – which made me decide that, if the worst came to the worst, I would go down with the ship.

I was in the City Grammar School's sixth form before I worked out why I was Labour. There had, however, been glimmerings of

understanding along the way. I had learned from the hard
experience of my crippled grandmother's chronic illness that
constant doctors' bills were the terror of working families. And
even on the glorious September day when I turned up to reap the
rewards of 'passing the scholarship', I could tell the difference
between the 'proper' bottle-green blazers bought from the
'official suppliers' and the cheap substitutes supplied to boys
with 'clothing allowance'. Halfway through that first term,
Mr Shields – my form master whom I much admired because
he still wore his Royal Artillery captain's trenchcoat – announced
that, from the following Monday, mid-morning milk would be
free. Every boy in Ix indicated a wish to receive a bottle. 'Which
of you', asked Mr Shields, 'did not order milk this week?' A dozen
hands went up. 'These boys', our friendly form master announced, 'are having it because they don't have to pay.' Looking
back on that incident, I feel surprise that I grew up to be a
moderate.

In the sixth form, Mr Walker (games), Mr Goodfellow (history)
and Mrs Potter (English) – the three teachers of whom I saw the
most – were all open in their allegiance to the Labour Party. But,
because of either their obligations to impartiality or their desire to
concentrate my attention on the General Certificate of Education
(Advanced Level), they did little or nothing to improve my
ideological understanding. I became so desperate for philosophical debate that I even joined the Student Christian Movement
and attended its summer conferences, where I had a bad-
tempered argument with George Macbeth – then a lordly prefect
at Sheffield's one posh grammar school but soon to become a
distinguished poet. Thirty years later, I read Mr Macbeth's
boyhood reminiscences in the hope of finding a description of
our adolescent dispute. It was not mentioned. But disappointment quickly turned to envy. According to his biography, he
rarely went out into South Yorkshire – moors, woods or fields –
without being seduced by a middle-aged lady. It never happened

to me. Perhaps I was paying the penalty for having lost my political virginity so early in life.

In the year that Labour lost office, I was a 'scrutineer' at the Hillsborough count and stood eyes glazed and mouth open watching the ballot papers being separated into the rival heaps and making sure that none of 'ours' was given to 'them'. George Darling, who had succeeded A. V. Alexander, signed a copy of his election address and told me that it was 'another landslide like 1945'. I discovered that he was wrong next morning in the City Grammar School's prefects' room when the news bulletin – straight from Conservative Central Office – broadcast the carefully rehearsed spontaneous reaction of Lord Wootton, the Tory Party Chairman. 'After five years, we've beaten the socialists.'

I tried to submerge my sorrow under the knowledge that I was on nodding acquaintance with an MP and the glorious news that, having applied to read English at all of what were then called the Northern Universities, I had been offered a place at Leeds. Professor Bonamy Dobree, a man who took literary criticism seriously, had accepted my application despite my interview turning into a fiasco. Arnold Kettle – the world's greatest authority on *Bleak House* – had asked me about humour. I confessed that I had never found Falstaff funny. Toby Belch, I said, was much to be preferred. He made me laugh. And what was more, as well as wenching and drinking, he was (unlike fat Sir John) prepared to fight. I think that Mr Kettle, who was certainly a Communist, was also a pacifist. Whatever his reason, he snorted with disapproval and asked me about Mr Pickwick. 'Not funny either,' I said. But I had read, and much admired, *Modern Prose Style* by Bonamy Dobree and I knew that the 'pleasure of criticism lies in its function of making distinctions, of getting things clear, of enabling you to see your way through the crowd'. That got me my place.

In the early summer of my last year at school, I was sitting in the reference room of the Sheffield City Library when George

Darling came in on an official tour. I abandoned both the pretence of reading *The Harvest of Tragedy* and my real occupation – staring at the girls behind the desk – and smiled demurely at the man I had helped to make a Member of Parliament. He congratulated me on the news that I had won a place at Leeds and asked me, in his Cambridge way, if that red-brick university had a good economics department. Even MPs make mistakes. So I politely explained that I was going to read English. He was incredulous. 'I thought', he stuttered through his astonishment, 'that you wanted to go into politics.'

That single remark was enough for me. I wrote to all the Northern Universities saying that I was an economist at heart and begging them to let me pursue my passion by giving me the chance to study for their BAs and BSc(Econ)s. Not even the BCom was beneath my interest. First to reply with an unconditional offer was Hull. I spent three years by the side of Andrew Marvell's Humber reading George Eliot and Jane Austen, hidden inside copies of Marshall's *Principles* and Keynes's *General Theory*.

Before I left Sheffield, I made a farewell appearance at the General Management Committee of the Hillsborough Constituency Labour Party. It was an evening of celebration – not because I was leaving but because George Darling had been made parliamentary private secretary to the joint parliamentary secretary to the Board of Trade. It was not so much a foot on the ministerial ladder as the chance to get a long-distance view of the bottom rung. But, strangely for a constituency which had been represented by a Cabinet Minister, we were profoundly impressed. A resolution of congratulations was carried unanimously – but not without amendment.

A. V. Alexander, despite his many virtues, had not been the most assiduous of what are now known as 'constituency MPs'. Perhaps, when he was First Lord of the Admiralty, he believed that he ought to concentrate his energy on defeating the Germans. And he was part of that pre-war generation of Members of

Parliament who thought that they were elected to represent their electors in Westminster, not Westminster to their electors. So, to put it more crudely than I would have dared at the time, 'A. V.' was an absentee member. I recall the irritation I felt during an election meeting at Wisewood School when Sir Knowles Edge – the Tory candidate and proprietor of Dolly Dies Ltd – had expressed the fear that, if elected, George Darling would follow in his predecessor's negligent footsteps. No doubt George Darling felt irritated too. For, before the campaign was over, he made a solemn promise. When he became Hillsborough's MP he would return to the constituency every three months and, during the Saturday of his visitation, make himself available for advice and assistance.

Our gratitude was boundless. But when we heard that he had been appointed PPS, we felt guilty about the exacting under-taking which we had accepted. So the resolution of congratulations was amended to include a sentence which made our position clear. 'Furthermore, whilst expressing our full support for the Member's wish to serve this constituency to the best of his ability, we appreciate that the office to which he has been appointed may make it impossible for him to fulfil the onerous obligation of continual visits.' For more than thirty years – including four as a Cabinet Minister – as I held my Sparkbrook Advice Bureaux on the second and fourth Friday evenings and Saturday mornings of each month, I remembered the demands made by Hillsborough on George Darling. And I began to understand what was meant by the good old days.

On the day that I left for Hull, I promised my father – the cautious member of the family – that I would not get involved in politics. On the first morning of the Freshers' conference, I joined the Socialist Society. I was immediately plunged into the world of bewildering initials which has confused me ever since. Having confessed to being a paid-up member of the real Labour Party, I was warned that SocSoc was affiliated to the IUS, a Communist-front organisation, and I was recruited into the campaign to move its allegiance to the IUSY – the youth wing of Socialist International and an organisation which (despite bearing a name that was redolent of continental Marxism) was the proper parent body for democratic socialist parties. We staged a coup. The name was changed to Labour Club, the affiliation was changed to IUSY and the Communists were kicked out. The purge was long and bitter, and it consumed weeks of my time which should have been occupied in more creative activities. During the long campaign against Militant, I often thought how wrong the philistines were to claim that a university education was not a preparation for life in the real world.

I became chairman of the new respectable Labour Club and, eventually, chairman of the National Association of Labour Student Organisations – beating, by a single vote, my Scottish rival. My success was built on a mistake. As NALSO treasurer I had to present the annual accounts. Unfortunately they had not been audited. The accountant who should have performed the task (naturally free of charge) was the chairman of the Woodcraft Folk – the co-operative boy scouts. And on his way to Hull to inspect my books, he had fallen off his tricycle. I reported this sad fact to the conference to explain my failure to comply with Standing Orders, but the delegates – particularly those who spent their time in either the Oxford or the Cambridge Unions – believed that I was being madly witty. The delegates from both the ancient universities supported me solely because of my sense of humour.

My successor as NALSO chairman was an earnest young man known as Citizen Walden, who spoke with his hands clasped before him, as if in prayer. It was generally agreed that Brian had a great political future. My predecessor – like Walden, an Oxonion – was Christopher Price, who subsequently won (and then lost) two marginal seats in Parliament. For the next forty years Price played an intermittently influential part in my life – not always to my advantage. But, during my time in student politics, he was my constant benefactor. He persuaded me, rather against my will, to make my first visit to Rome, a city with which I am now infatuated. I suppose that my fascination began during that visit in 1954. At the time, however, my experiences seemed to have little in common with Audrey Hepburn's *Roman Holiday* – my only previous experience of the Eternal City. The Student Bureau of IUSY met in the Hotel California – from which we escaped minutes before the origins of a typhoid outbreak were traced to its fetid swimming pool and the residents placed under an unhappy compromise between house arrest and quarantine. Late one night, at my insistence, we visited St Peter's Square in company with our fellow delegate, Will Fancy of Exeter. Mr Fancy had a Lenin beard, a Trotsky haircut and opinions to go with his appearance. He believed, and said with some force, that St Peter's ought to be demolished and replaced by old people's flats. The Vatican, he insisted, should be converted into a public park and children's playground. Next day, Giuseppe Matteoti – general secretary of the Partito Socialisto Italiano and son of the man whom Mussolini murdered after the March on Rome – addressed the assembled cream of socialist youth. He spoke in Italian for two hours. Will Fancy kept awake from start to finish.

A month later, in Cologne, I was elected student representative on the IUSY Executive. Price, to my surprise and against my will, nominated me to contest the vacancy against a German who had the support of all the big battalions. The French, Swedish, Austrian, Indian and Israeli students all cast their votes for my opponent. Then Christopher Price took the proxies out of his pocket – all of them provided by the phantom organisations which had headquarters (but, as far as I could make out, no members) in London. My triumph was secured when I received the support of the Azerbaijan Social Democrat Students in Exile.

Labour student business took me to London on the day that Hugh Gaitskell was elected leader of the Labour Party. Chris Price and I went into the House of Commons in the hope that we would somehow be associated with the historic event. We were hanging about the Central Lobby when Hugh Gaitskell passed through on his way to the meeting at which the result of the Parliamentary Party's ballot was to be announced. No doubt he already knew the result, but he was entitled to be preoccupied. Yet when he saw Price – who had been his host a couple of months earlier at the Oxford Labour Club – he left his posse of rejoicing henchmen and crossed the lobby to where we were standing, transfixed, beside a statue of William Ewart Gladstone. He asked us if he could get us tickets for the gallery. From then on, I was a Gaitskellite.

By then I had developed what I believed to be a clear theory of socialism – by R. H. Tawney out of Matthew Arnold. Through sheer good fortune, I read the authorised texts in the proper order. First Arnold himself because I had read the poetry – starting with 'The Forsaken Merman' – and after 'The Scholar Gypsy' I knew that I would enjoy anything that he wrote. After *Culture and Anarchy* came Tawney's *Equality*, Cole, Hobhouse and Durbin. So I was ready for Tony Crosland's *The Future of Socialism* and prepared for John Rawl's *Theory of Justice*. Everything I read, like everything I saw about me, confirmed my belief in equality. Discrepancies in wealth and power seemed unreasonable as well as immoral. They still do. It was life, not art, that nurtured my conviction. During my last summer at Hull, I delivered milk – naturally enough for the Brightside and Carbrook Co-operative Dairy. It was my second choice of vacation jobs, for I had hoped to dig holes in the Hull roads. But rather a milk round than nothing. My experiences gave me enough confidence to deal with a left-wing trade union leader who, when I became deputy leader of the Labour Party, objected to my parliamentary candidature being sponsored by the Shop, Distributive and Allied Workers. Anyone who has never tried to get a handful of coppers out of a dirty milk bottle on a cold morning is in no position to talk about the class struggle.

My days on the back of the Co-op milk float also provided an example of why, in Matthew Arnold's words, we should 'choose equality and flee greed'. My milk round was in Shalesmoor, the scene of my political baptism, and there were, amongst our regular customers, a number of women who, by the end of the week, could not afford the price of a pint. The regular milkman believed that he could distinguish between the deserving and undeserving poor and he had invented a way of helping what he described as 'genuine cases'. He would carefully remove the tin-foil top from a full bottle and pour the milk, free of charge, into the virtuous pauper's jug. Then, the top being replaced with equal delicacy, he would smash the bottle and enter it in his records as 'a broke'. I was full of admiration for both his compassion and his ingenuity. But I believed it to be far too selective. Much as I detested smoking, it seemed wrong that anyone with a packet of Woodbines on the sideboard was disqualified from help. At the other, more salubrious, end of the city nobody was expected to choose between milk and smoked salmon, milk and their golf club subscription or milk and dinner in one of Derbyshire's country hotels. I had become a class warrior. I also became – more or less absent-mindedly – a graduate.

Since, as well as a BSc (Econ), I also possessed a charcoal-grey suit and a cricket club tie, the University Appointments Board came to the dubious conclusion that I should embark on a career in industry. I agreed for the very good reason that I had to live on something until politics came along. I survived my first interview with ICI and was then invited to visit their head office in Smith Square – close by, indeed cemented on to, Transport House, then the headquarters of the Labour Party. Certain that I had made a fool of myself in my formal interview by talking about my parliamentary ambitions, I went to find solace and comfort with my old friends next door. I also talked to the national agent about including my name on Labour's B-List of Parliamentary Candidates – persons virtually unknown who were prepared to fight hopeless seats.

A week later, ICI offered me a job. By the same post, I received a letter from the Labour Party. I was not, in the national agent's opinion, ready to be a candidate. It was, he rightly said, years since I had been active in a real constituency party. To him, the triumphs of Rome and Cologne could not make up for my persistent failure to knock on doors. I wrote back to ICI, declining their offer with thanks. I was, I told them, hoping for a job in the steel industry. When I said steel, I thought of home – the place where I had spent my adolescence 'on the doorstep'. I had decided that, if I was to win my parliamentary spurs, they would be stamped 'Made in Sheffield'.

Industrially speaking, I was not a great success. My six months in the Fuel and Efficiency Department of a Sheffield steelworks ended during the Suez crisis when – because of the shortage of oil – the company became suddenly as short of fuel as it had always been of efficiency. What we patronisingly called 'hourly paid' workers were put on half time. In the staff canteen, feelings ran very high against Colonel Nasser who had stolen our canal, the Americans who had stopped us taking it back and traitors who were always on the side of Britain's enemies. I was granted asylum in the Workers' Educational Association, and spent a couple of years organising lectures for enthusiastic miners and bored housewives.

At about the same time I offered myself as a candidate in the municipal elections and was nominated for Crookesmoor, a ward which had elected a Labour councillor every year since 1945. Shalesmoor had come back into my life. It made up one of the polling districts in which the majority was built up.

On the May morning when I took my seat, Albert Ballard – sometime Labour agent and election leaflet censor – was made Lord Mayor of Sheffield. In his acceptance address, he spoke of the working men and women who, thirty years before, had taken over the municipal government of the city. Some of them were there to hear him – sitting high on the Aldermen's Bench and still firmly in charge of Sheffield's destiny. They ran the city with a combination of discipline and democracy which was often onerous, sometimes ridiculous, but which always worked.

The monthly Council Agenda – the 'Summons' as it was confusingly called – amounted to no more than the minutes of innumerable committees which, before the decisions could be implemented, had to be confirmed by a full meeting of the 'Corporation'. On the last Monday evening of each month the Labour caucus, known by the more acceptable name of the Labour Group, considered the agenda line by line. No item was too trivial for discussion. No principle was too great to be challenged. Even the most junior councillor could, without offence, 'move the reference back' of the most exalted alderman's cherished plans to close a library, open a health centre or build a road. But once a committee's proposals were approved, they became holy writ. I have no idea what the punishment would have been for opposing an agreed minute in open council with the Tories present. For in my time nobody ever thought of doing it.

A couple of weeks after I arrived – full of enthusiasm for municipal socialism – the Labour Group met late into Monday night to consider a proposition of the Lord Mayor's Advisory Committee. For as long as anyone could remember, the Council had been provided with a buffet tea, available from three thirty to five for any councillor or alderman who left the chamber and wandered into the banqueting suite. The contentious minute which we discussed that night proposed that the buffet should be replaced by a sit-down tea at precisely four o'clock. At first I could only guess why Alderman Ballard wished to change the time-hallowed arrangement. I assumed that the Lord Mayor – scrubbed pink, and as precise in dress as he was in speech – was offended by the discourtesy and indiscipline of council members leaving their seats during debates on the future of the municipal abattoir and the historic plans (constantly revised but never realised) for a Sheffield airport. No doubt he regarded buffets as untidy. And, for a certain sort of Workers Educational Association socialist, tidiness was next to godliness.

When the tea debate got under way I realised that buffets were a class issue. A sit-down tea took time. And the Tories – impatient to return to their offices and boardrooms – much preferred a quick cucumber sandwich eaten during one of the many *longueurs* in the Council's proceedings. Labour members, on the other hand, were working men who had taken a whole afternoon off work in one of the city's great factories or were trade union officials with time on their hands. The longer the Council meeting went on, the greater Labour's already overwhelming majority became.

The socialist case against set teas was argued by the couple of solicitors, the cutlery manufacturer, the office machine salesman and the headmaster from a school outside the city who made up the middle-class element in the Labour Group. After a fierce and prolonged rearguard action, the buffet brigade were beaten. The discussion then moved on to an almost equally important issue of what time tea should be served. On the following Wednesday afternoon, every Labour councillor and alderman voted, apparently with good heart, for a sit-down tea which was to begin at half past four precisely and last until five o'clock. All amendments – covering the buffet itself and both the time and the duration of the formal alternative – were defeated by the same unanimous vote of the Labour Group.

During my nine years on the City Council – the last two of them as a virtual absentee in Westminster – there was only one rebellion. And that came about because events moved so quickly that the Labour Group could not be consulted before decisive action was taken in their names. One morning in the magistrates' court, two defendants, who had been charged with multiple burglaries, suddenly tore off their shirts to reveal huge weals across their backs. They had, their solicitor claimed, been beaten with a rhino-whip from the 'black museum' at the central police station. One of the men said – with a terrifying eloquence which gave his story veracity – 'We're professional thieves. We expect a bit of bashing about, but this was sheer brutality.'

The two CID officers who had interviewed them were suspended. So was the probationary constable who acted as turnkey that night. Before the day was out, the Home Office had concluded that the head of CID and the Chief Constable himself had tried to cover up the assaults. The City of Sheffield Watch Committee – then a virtually autonomous authority – suspended them both. We expected a revolt from the Masons. It came from Alderman Sydney Dyson – a twenty-stone, virtually blind, profoundly impoverished, full-time Labour Party agent. He rebelled not because of funny handshakes and secret oaths, but because natural justice had been denied – and the proper procedures of the Labour Party, as laid down in the Standing Orders, had not been carried out. The chairman of the Watch Committee had acted without the approval of the Labour Group. And the Standing Orders made no exception for emergencies.

The experience taught me nothing that I did not already know about the Party's love of fair play and obsession with procedure. But I did learn something about how the police behave and both why and when they behave badly. The circumstances in Sheffield that summer made an attempt to pervert the course of justice almost inevitable. The crime figures were bad – the number of offences was increasing rapidly and the conviction rate was deteriorating fast. The police in general and the CID in particular were undermanned. Press and public were echoing each other's demands for a 'crack down on crime'. The police arrested two men who they *knew* had committed a series of robberies, but there was not enough evidence to guarantee a conviction. So two junior and overworked detectives decided to obtain a confession. That is how it always happens. Shortcuts towards doing what is right lead to doing what is wrong.

I enjoyed the rigid discipline of the Sheffield City Council – which I thought of, not entirely incorrectly, as a solidarity which requires personal vanities to be sacrificed for, and submerged within, the collective wisdom of seventy-odd genuine comrades. I prospered within the Labour Group because I felt a natural part of that strange institution and because the elder aldermen who led it had sensed that it was time for them to go. Like wise elders of any tribe, they were anxiously looking for young warriors to carry on the battle. I thought of my progress as spectacular. Within a couple of years, I had become vice chairman of the Philharmonic Committee – a remarkable achievement for a young man who hated classical music. I spent two whole winters inventing reasons for not attending Hallé concerts in the City Hall.

My heart was, of course, set on Westminster. I had been short-listed to fight the hopeless seat of Bridlington but – in one of those quirks of fate that look like tragedy but turn out to be triumph – I missed the Saturday morning train to York. I suspect that the East Coast Labour Party knew at once that the telephone message about an accident in the steelworks was a lie. They selected from the prospective candidates who condescended to submit themselves for selection. But, a year before the 1959 election, I was invited to Sutton Coldfield and – rather to my surprise – was selected as the Labour candidate.

I nursed the seat for two years, driving from Sheffield to the West Midlands every Sunday morning in an ancient Sunbeam Talbot which had been brought back from the dead with 'cannibalised' parts from a derelict Humber Hawk that an enterprising mechanic had found on a bomb site. Those were the days before motorways cut their way through middle England, so I made slow and eccentric progress through Derby and Burton-upon-Trent. But I nursed the constituency with a passion which would have been appropriate to a marginal seat on which the fate of a general election hung. As a result of my hard work, the Conservative majority would increase from seventeen to twenty-one thousand.

My agent in Sutton Coldfield was a young man who had recently lost his job in a Northampton shoe factory. We employed him for the month of the campaign out of sympathy after he explained that, 'We knew things were bad in the company when the managers told us to take the cardboard out of the windows and use it for inner soles.' He played a wind-up gramophone from the moment that he arrived at the Committee Rooms early in the morning, until the time when he left late at night. Unfortunately, he only had one record. In the years which followed I was much admired in more folksy Labour circles because of my ability to sing *Joe Hill* from start to finish. During the election campaign, I heard Paul Robeson's version of the American trade union anthem on average twenty times a day.

We held a workers' rally on the last Sunday night of the campaign. Had we been a normal constituency we would have gathered together for mutual inspiration and in order to lay our plans for the final week. Our meeting was called, on the instructions of Labour Party headquarters, in order to tell my supporters that they must not waste their time working for me. It was their duty to go out into the marginal seats which had to be saved and won. I prepared my speech with every intention of doing my duty and making the almost supreme sacrifice for the greater glory of socialism. But, in my heart, I hoped that the party activists of Sutton Coldfield would rise up in loyal revolt and insist on sticking by me.

The meeting never reached the item on the agenda in which tactics would have been discussed. Indeed, the assembled enthusiasts found some difficulty even in concentrating on my inspirational address. The Committee Room walls were lined with complicated charts and diagrams. What appeared to be giant bingo cards were spread out on tables at the back of the room. Huge piles of note pads – with sheets of carbon paper between their leaves – were stacked in one corner. Sutton Coldfield Labour Party had never fought a fierce campaign before and the potential shock troops could not wait to be up and at 'em. My peroration was hardly over when somebody shouted a question about the purpose of the exciting stationery. The agent explained that chapter ten of the campaign handbook was explicit. To operate what he knowledgeably called 'The Mikardo System', it was necessary to set out the paraphernalia which was essential to its success during the weekend before polling day. 'And what', the same enthusiast asked, 'do we do with it?' There was a long pause before the agent answered. 'That is on page twenty-one of the handbook. I've only got to page seventeen.' The meeting broke up in disappointed chaos. At least, I thought, they did not all agree to go and work in marginal constituencies.

On election night, I got to the Sutton Coldfield Town Hall about an hour after the poll closed. The votes were quickly counted and I prepared a speech of which I felt immensely proud – theoretically thanking the returning officer for his well-paid efforts. I decided to follow the pious concession that the people had spoken and democracy had been the true victor by making the best of a humiliating defeat: 'The local papers have said throughout this campaign that the real battle was for second place. Labour has won that battle decisively.' I was so pleased with the brave face that I intended to assume, that I could not wait to counterfeit my satisfaction. But the returning officer refused to declare the result.

The Right Honourable Geoffrey Lloyd was, he told me, still at dinner. A message had been sent to his house explaining that we were ready for him to reclaim his kingdom. But according to his butler, it would be some time before he had finished. We had no choice but to await his pleasure with humility and patience.

When the victor condescended to arrive, he could not have behaved with greater courtesy. It took him a while to identify me and, even then, he mistook me for the Liberal candidate – despite my giant red and yellow rosette. But once he realised who I was, he told me that he had done almost as badly himself when he had fought George Lansbury in Poplar during the 1935 election. He assured me that the damage to his career had only been temporary.

It was not only Geoffrey Lloyd who swept back into power in 1959. Back in my lodgings, the radio was broadcasting Hugh Gaitskell's concessionary speech from Leeds Town Hall. 'The flame of democratic socialism still burns bright.' The results that were flashing across the flickering television screen suggested that, in Birmingham, the fire had almost gone out. Labour had lost All Saints, Yardley and a seat of which I had never heard called Sparkbrook. I put away my huge red and yellow rosette without feeling very much confidence that I would ever wear it in a winning campaign. I wore it – win or lose – in nine general elections. I have just put it away for the last time.

CHAPTER
2

The sixties – which no doubt swung in London – rarely moved out of the vertical in Sheffield. All I can remember of those rebellious times is an angry demonstration outside a dress shop which was exhibiting a topless evening gown, and a visit to Chesterfield Repertory Theatre to see the local company's production of John Osborne's *Look Back in Anger.* There was not an angry young man in the house. Indeed, the only emotion expressed all evening was the rapture which followed an announcement made by Jimmy Porter after the final curtain came down. 'Don't forget, folks. We've got something special for you next week – Agatha Christie's *Murder on the Orient Express.*'

For me, next week was always the search for a winnable seat. I chased every shadow – sometimes with more enthusiasm than discretion. Dan Wood, an official of the bricklayers' union who had been the chairman of the Sutton Coldfield Party, invited me to a social evening in Aston with the assurance that the sitting member, Julius Silverman, had been diagnosed as suffering from a mysterious terminal illness. I spent the evening cultivating influential Party members and watching Silverman for signs of imminent death. The illness was more mysterious than Wood realised. Shortly after the premature attempt to make me his successor, Julius married. We served together in the House of Commons from 1964 to 1983. He now lives in healthy retirement and I gave the first of the Silverman Lectures – an occasion invented to celebrate his long life of service. I tried not to feel ashamed of how I had behaved in 1960.

Even when there was a vacancy, I rarely got much nearer to becoming a candidate. Sometimes I reached the final selection conference before I was rejected. Usually I could not find a ward or trade union branch which was prepared to throw my hat into the ring. In three years I was rejected by Derby North, Middlesbrough East, Middlesbrough West, Newcastle East, Sunderland, Bradford North, Bradford West, Derbyshire South-East, Pontefract, Birmingham Small Heath, Hull North, Hull West, Doncaster, Cleveland, York, Keighley, Colne Valley, Brighouse and Spenborough, Rotherham, Huddersfield West, Ilkeston, Halifax, and Hartlepool – twice. In the most desirable seats – Middlesbrough East, Birmingham Small Heath and Rotherham – I did not receive a single nomination. Perhaps it was as well. For it avoided the invariable anxiety and occasional humiliation of proceeding further. Not surprisingly, I made most progress in the north.

I was short-listed at Hull West. When I arrived at the Sunday afternoon selection conference, I was greeted at the door by Jim Johnson, the eventually successful nominee. Mistaking me for a delegate, he handed me a printed invitation for the party which had been arranged to celebrate his triumph. I returned home determined to prepare the ground at Hartlepool as carefully as Johnson had cultivated Hull. I had real hopes of Hartlepool. For I had contacts in the constituency.

Once upon a time, the Labour Party employed full-time local agents. It was a hard life and, even in the sixties, a precarious occupation. So men and women with a vocation to draft leaflets and keep canvassing records up to date were forced to move from constituency to constituency, as one local party ran out of money and another started up a sweepstake or a lottery and raised enough cash to employ for a year or two an enthusiast who was willing to work on near starvation wages. Ted Eldred had started his working life as a plaster's labourer. But he had left his secure employment to become a political organiser in Lancashire. We became friends when he was appointed the paid secretary of the Sheffield Co-operative Party. Then the pay ran out and he moved on to Belper to take charge – in so far as anybody could – of George Brown. It was his appointment which brought the deputy Party leader into my life and, in consequence, caused me endless embarrassment. At some point during his Party travels, Eldred had organised in Hartlepool. He determined to use his contacts in order to secure the seat for me.

In those days prospective candidates did not pursue nomination with the professional determination which is employed today. Indeed, technically speaking it was a breach of rules to do anything more than turn up on the appointed day, make a speech, answer a few questions and hope. But – profiting from Jim Johnson's example in Hull and Ted Eldred's contacts in Hartlepool – I made regular visits to the north-east. I always drove there and back in the day because – although the A1 wound through Boroughbridge, Wetherby and a dozen other crowded market towns – I could not afford either rail ticket or hotel room. One frosty Sunday, I arrived home to find that a note had been pushed through my letter box by Councillor Cecil Johnson of the Plumbers' Trade Union. The Derby Branch of the PTU were holding a meeting that night in the Woodman Hotel. If I paid them court, they would almost certainly nominate me for the by-election which was to be held in that city. I drove straight off into the snowy night. It took me some time, in the blizzard, to find the Woodman. The landlord told me that the plumbers, being unable to afford the rent, no longer met in his public house. I drove home, telling myself that Hartlepool would be mine.

Not surprisingly, in the light of my hard work, I was short-listed. By then there was a candidates' circus which rotated round the selection conferences. On the day of the selection conference, I greeted Maurice Foley and Harold Walker like old friends. They had both failed with me before. There was also a local man called Ted Leadbitter. I should have guessed that things were going wrong when I answered a question on the NEDC and was hissed by the audience. Apparently the same thing happened to Foley and Walker. Like me they had spoken about the National Economic Development Council – the political talking point of the moment. Leadbitter, the local man, had been greeted with cheers when he emphasised the importance of giving more power to the North Eastern Development Committee. I suppose that, in the circumstances, I was lucky only to lose by one vote on the head count.

One of the candidates complained about malpractice. I was neither the culprit nor the complainant. We believed that the objection had been raised by Maurice Foley – soon to win the West Bromwich by-election – who had remarked, even before the formal proceedings began, that something fishy was going on. Perhaps we misjudged our man. But we had no doubt who the complaint was about. Eddie Leadbitter was accused of arranging transport to carry elderly and infirm Party members to the meeting. These days, a selection conference candidate who failed to provide such a service would be penalised for negligence. In the early sixties, it was regarded as sharp practice. The contest was rerun and I made my speech, confident that – since I had only lost by one vote before – I would easily win this time round. I lost by twenty-three votes. I turned my attention, with some reluctance, to the Middlesbrough West by-election.

It was clear enough to me that Labour would not win Middlesbrough and, keen though I was, the idea of resigning my job with the health service for nothing more than a month's frustrating campaign had little charm. But George Brown, the

Party's deputy leader, forced me into offering myself for what *Beyond the Fringe* had described that year as a pointless sacrifice. Appropriately enough, George had come to Sheffield on the night of the Great Wind – a gale which blew the roofs off countless council houses. He came to the Town Hall to show concern for the homeless, but had to spend much of his time listening to my concern about finding a constituency which would send me to Parliament. As it turned out, I was exactly what he was looking for. George Brown had discovered that the candidate most likely to carry Labour's colours on Teesside was the secretary of something called the Young Workers – an organisation which he took for granted was a Communist front. It was, in fact, the Young Catholic Workers. But, by the time that George Brown found out, he was committed to me.

The man whose loyalties George Brown had so cruelly misjudged was Maurice Foley, and before the selection conference began we reminisced about Hartlepool. Neither of us was chosen, but whilst Foley went off happily to West Bromwich – and, although he did not know it at the time, a parliamentary secretaryship in George Brown's ministry after Labour won the 1964 election – I drove home with no immediate prospect except the need to tell the deputy leader that I still needed his help.

I put off telling him the bad news for as long as I could. But as six o'clock approached, I knew that if he did not get the news from me, he would get it from the BBC. Labour was winning by-elections all over the country and it was assumed that the long list of victories was a prelude to a change of government. So even the selection of an unknown candidate to fight an obscure northern constituency got a mention on the national bulletins. I had to force myself to tell my patron that the nominee with whom he had become publicly associated had been turned down.

It took an effort of will to pull up at an AA box just north of Wakefield and even greater courage to push button A and admit, 'It's Roy Hattersley.' George Brown, in a voice higher pitched and even more agitated than usual, simply said, 'Yes.' There was a long pause. Then I told him, 'I didn't get it. Jeremy Bray won.' The second pause was even longer than the first. I realise now that George felt humiliated by the defeat of his favourite and that his disappointment was even greater (and far more difficult to disguise) than mine. But at twenty-eight – and with my own sadness to accommodate – I made no allowance for his sensitive nature and volatile temperament. I regarded his reply as absolutely indefensible. 'Congratulations, brother,' he shouted. 'In half a day, you've set yourself back five years.' There were times, as the general election got nearer and nearer, when I began to fear that George was right.

Sometimes the Labour Party rubbed salt into my wounds. I had real hopes of Colne Valley and Pontefract – both of which were just down the road from where I lived. But neither Yorkshire seat wanted me. Within weeks of deciding that I was not a suitable candidate to fight the Pontefract by-election, I was asked to speak at the eve of poll meeting. My task was to fill in between Joe Harper, the man who had beaten me for the nomination, and the star of the evening, Harold Wilson. Harper was brief and Wilson was late and I had to speak for something like an hour. Harper had not been chosen because of his oratory and Wilson, as is the habit of senior politicians who are obliged to speak to small audiences, read a text prepared for a quite different meeting and read it badly.

A couple of weeks later I read in the diary column of *The Times* that Joe Harper had been one of the guests at a Polish embassy reception which was held to congratulate the British finalists in the competition for the Chopin Prize. According to the newspaper's story, Harper – impatient for the action to begin – edged his way towards the piano on which the virtuosi were to perform, slid onto the stool and began to vamp boogie-woogie. When, the next Saturday, I saw Fred Mulley – MP for Sheffield Park, a member of Labour's National Executive and a constant source of good, though often unwelcome, advice – I told him that it was time for the Party to devise a way of selecting decent candidates. Fred replied that it was the Harpers (content on the back benches), not the Hattersleys (constantly aspiring to the front), who made the House of Commons work. I changed the topic of conversation to our usual weekend preoccupation, football.

Having, as I believed, been rejected by national politics, I sublimated my disappointment by throwing myself into local government. For more than a year I had been chairman of the Public Works Committee – a vast construction company that competed against all Wimpeys, Tersons and Laings and often won the contracts. 'Direct Labour' was an immensely potent notion in the Labour Party. But, paradoxically, despite its ideological associations, the Public Works Department did not offer its political head the slightest opportunity to take political decisions. Everything was decided by quantity surveyors. When I was moved to the chairmanship of the Housing Committee there were enough political decisions to satisfy half a dozen sensible councillors. There were also at least two crises every week.

When at last I got my seat in Parliament, I left with relief, gratitude and a permanent memorial in Park Hill, the giant blocks of flats which dominated the Sheffield skyline. True to its traditions – it was inspired by Quarry Hill Flats in Leeds, which were built after that city's fathers visited Marseilles and saw how the Communist mayor was rehousing the workers – the opening ceremony, performed by Hugh Gaitskell, included the unveiling of a vast marble commemorations panel far too large to be called a plaque. Amongst the names engraved upon it was Councillor R. S. G. Hattersley, JP, BSc(Econ). By the time that Hugh Gaitskell pulled the string and revealed my municipal memorial, JP was a distinction which I did not deserve. I was a magistrate for only two months before I decided that I did not enjoy sitting in judgement. But although outdated, my name was carved in stone.

I used to think of little boys asking, 'Who was he, Dad?' and their fathers replying, 'I haven't got the faintest idea.' It seemed a sort of immortality.

My principal task as chairman of the Housing Management Committee was the reconciliation of the Sheffield Labour Party's two irreconcilable aims – to build the best houses in Europe and charge the lowest rents in Britain. Sheffield had a noble housing tradition. Between the wars it had boasted England's most extensive slum clearance programme. The political inheritance was my greatest problem. I felt like the heir to a noble, but troubled, dynasty who was unable to face the problems of the future because of the legacies of the past. After months of argument I was allowed to make a modest rent increase. But I was refused permission to provide rebates for poorer families, since charging poor families less than the better off was too reminiscent of the pre-war means test which drove working sons out of the homes of their unemployed fathers and forced applicants for Poor-Law relief to sell their furniture. My request to prune the waiting list – thirty-six thousand names, some of which were also carved on tombstones – was treated with almost as much hostile contempt as my suggestion that a points system, giving houses to the people who needed them most, was a better way to allocate tenancies than first come first served. Despite the vicissitudes, I loved it.

In those days – when councillors were more than administrators of central government policy – local government offered a pleasure which Whitehall and Westminster could never provide. It was possible to watch ideas turn into reality. This year's committee minutes became next year's changes in the life and work of Sheffield. The Housing Committee decided where its next 'comprehensive redevelopment' would be, bought the land (often by compulsory purchase order), approved the plans, opened the tenders, awarded the contracts and visited the site when the first tenant moved in. I still think of the houses which were built in the early sixties as 'mine'.

There are not as many of them about as there used to be. In those days we built high, wide and not very handsome – great terraces of concrete, which rose twenty storeys into the sky and, according to the City Architect, 'reproduced the best features of the old terraces'. They also contained water-borne refuse disposal systems, central heating and parquet floors. For a decade or more the people loved them. Then the mood changed. Instead of waiting years for a high-rise flat, families in urgent need of a decent house said that they would only accept the key to something that was semi-detached. Half of the tower blocks were knocked down. What I still cannot understand is how the Luddite councillors – who were so wrong about rent levels and waiting lists – knew that we ought to forget about architectural prizes which we were awarded in every European capital from Rome to Stockholm. It was the ancients of the Trades and Labour Council – the men (no women played a noticeable part) who rejected every sort of reform – who said that, in the end, we would regret not building what they called 'workmen's cottages'. I should have realised that the City Architect misunderstood the needs of the city when, in preparation for building the Hackenthorpe Estate, he showed the committee a slide of St Mark's Square in Venice to prove that it was possible for 'a variety of designs to blend into an aesthetically acceptable whole', and expressed his regret that for this development we would have to abandon the 'gutsy concrete' which had become a feature of Sheffield's housing policy.

At the time, I was immensely proud of what we had achieved – not least because, in a variety of ingenious ways, we had overcome the difficulty of building on Sheffield's hilly terrain. So when Dick Crossman, chairman of the Labour Party, came to visit the city, I naturally wanted to show him our award-winning houses. Crossman stayed with Alderman Isadore Lewis, cutlery manufacturer, chairman of the Finance Committee and one of the few members of the Labour Group with a house which was worthy to accommodate a member of the National Executive and sometime Fellow of New College, Oxford. I joined Crossman for breakfast at the Lewises' just before half past eight. He emerged from his bedroom just before ten o'clock. By eleven, Crossman was ready to begin his tour. But he hoped that, on his way to inspect our remarkable achievement, he could fulfil a long-standing ambition. Harold Laski had told him that Sheffield was deplorable in all but two respects – Ward's bookshops and Wyming Brook, a valley which ran across the moors south of the city boundary. Could he at least see the bilberries and broom, the massive stone tors and the silver stream before we moved on to the modular-constructed, systems-built, low-cost housing which was waiting his inspection? Of course, I agreed.

Having seen Wyming Brook from the road, Crossman wanted to climb down to the path that ran by the stream and, having reached the path, he wanted to walk to at least the foot of the first hill. Crossman was the sort of man to whom hills are irresistible and he announced that he proposed to toil to the top and look out over all Derbyshire. In the Peak District, hills hide behind each other. The landscape promises that the next summit is the ultimate horizon, but the promise is always broken. So we toiled onwards and upwards and, for the first time, I listened to the calculated, but reckless, indiscretions which, for thirty years, made up one of the most enjoyable parts of my political life. Crossman talked scurrilously of all the great figures in the Labour Party and he talked as if I knew them. Wilson 'could not be trusted an inch', Barbara Castle was impossible 'when she got a bee in her bonnet', Hugh Gaitskell 'had no real intellectual grasp'. At Oxford, Crossman said, 'my friends were poets and philosophers. He went ballroom dancing.' I deeply resented the attack on Gaitskell, but I walked on, enthralled. At twelve o'clock we turned back. At half past one, when we climbed into my car, it was time for Crossman to return to London and for me to make my way to the football match. Three years later, when Crossman became Minister of Housing and Local Government, he declined an invitation to Sheffield with the explanation that he had seen all that the city had to offer when I took him round at the beginning of the decade.

Crossman's stories of Westminster and Whitehall certainly reawakened my dormant longing for a seat in Parliament. And whenever I chaired a committee meeting in the Town Hall's Committee Room Number Two, I stared at the portrait of James Arthur Roebuck and imagined the glories of representing Sheffield, or anywhere, in the House of Commons and perhaps, like him, becoming 'the hardest man in England'. But for most of the time, I was content to devote my political life to local government and hope to become the Labour equivalent of Sir Harold Jackson, the Tory leader who had served on the Council for fifty years. Indeed, I had every chance of beating Sir Harold's record. I was first elected at the age of twenty-three and, as critics of the Council's waste disposal service constantly pointed out, I was younger than some of the Cleansing Department's refuse disposal vehicles. I was just getting to like the idea of becoming a City Father when the Labour Party was convulsed by one of its periodic spasms of self-destruction and, for the first time, I acted under the compulsion of a sincerely held belief which was as arrogant as it was unjustified. I thought that the Labour Party needed me.

It was the year in which the Labour Party conference voted in favour of unilateral nuclear disarmament and Hugh Gaitskell promised 'to fight, and fight and fight again to save the party we love'. Nothing I had ever heard or seen had moved me as much as that speech. Indeed in the thirty-three years since it was made, there have been only a couple of moments when I have felt the same desperate elation. I think that I feared the case for a sensible defence policy was lost. But, since it was to be death rather than retreat, I wanted to fight with the rearguard. Now, I can only feel embarrassed by my presumption. But, moved by a combination of love and duty, I renewed my search for a winnable seat in Parliament.

Hugh Gaitskell died in January 1963. His death was announced on the Friday evening and, on a Saturday morning now clouded in my mind with the memory of grief, two events stand out in the gloom. A neighbour, Anita Hirston by name, stopped me on the road to say that her ideological objection to joining the Labour Party had been removed and that she would be grateful for my advice about where to obtain a membership application form. Instead of abusing her as she deserved, I burst into tears. And it should have been a day of joy. For there flopped through my letter box a long buff envelope, postmarked Birmingham 11, containing one of the bright yellow forms which had become well known to me. The Fox Hollies ward of the Sparkbrook Constituency Labour Party had nominated me for consideration as prospective parliamentary candidate.

I was the beneficiary of a local civil war. Sparkbrook, which had been Labour since 1945, had been won by the Conservatives in 1959 on a swing of votes which was unusual even by West Midland standards. Fox Hollies – the superior end of the constituency in so much as it was made up of pre-war council houses rather than slum terraces and once prosperous villas that had been turned into squalid flats – blamed the defeat on the candidate, Jack Webster. Jack was the favourite son of the two northern wards and an undoubted eccentric who, shortly after his nomination, was converted to militant atheism – an attribute which did not endear him to the many Irish Catholics who then voted in the constituency. The Fox Hollies Labour Party refused to work in the 1959 campaign and men and women who should have been canvassing and addressing envelopes toured the West Midlands, attending other constituencies' public meetings in the pretence that they were contributing to the national campaign. For reasons which it is difficult to understand and impossible to justify, they spent the eve of poll in the Sutton Coldfield Town Hall, where they heard me booed and hissed by a number of middle-aged ladies in fur coats. Four years later, they remembered.

Jack Webster had certainly been an unusual candidate. Like me he was a city councillor and chairman of the Housing Committee. But the legends which surrounded him always concerned his attendance at other meetings. In Birmingham, they still talk of his historic intervention in the Planning Committee's deliberations. He had arrived late and embroidered his apology with the explanation that he had been forced to divert from the most direct route to the Council House when he discovered that 'the cast iron toilet' – a relic of Victorian Birmingham which was much admired by heritage organisations – had been removed from Camp Hill. His extended journey had been further prolonged by the need to search, in increasing discomfiture, for the nearest alternative. The chairman expressed his sympathy and moved on to consideration of the plans for an underpass at one of the road junctions on Smallbrook Ringway.

Each contribution to the discussion was punctuated by Jack Webster's complaints about the shortage of public lavatories and the Council's failure to meet the needs of regular patrons. After the six or seventh intervention, the chairman warned him that if he persisted in discussing a subject which was not on the agenda, he would be asked to leave the meeting. Jack turned his attention to the plans for the underpass. 'Why', he asked, 'is there so much space on each side of the north-bound carriageway?' He was told that it was needed for cleaning and maintenance. 'Is it', Jack asked, 'wide enough to accommodate a toilet?' The planning officer nodded. 'I don't want it there,' the councillor replied. 'I want it on Camp Hill.' The Fox Hollies Ward were determined that Councillor Webster should not fight Sparkbrook at the next election.

By a combination of logical argument, crude blackmail and sharp practice, the Fox Hollies modernisers – ahead of their time

in their determination to make the Labour Party respectable –
managed to keep Jack Webster off the short list from which the
candidate would be selected. I was included, but so – as part of
the 'block Webster' stratagem – was Frank Beswick, a junior
minister in the Attlee government who had lost his seat in the
1959 landslide. I looked forward to the selection conference
with mixed feelings. I desperately wanted to be candidate for
Sparkbrook. But I did not want to be rejected again. Then South
Leeds came into my life.

South Leeds had been Hugh Gaitskell's seat and, when one
of its union branches nominated me to contest the candidature,
I knew that destiny had chosen me to be his successor. I was
equally sure that it was fate that had saved me from selection
from all those other – infinitely less desirable – constituencies. I
believed that Gaitskell's inheritance was no more than I
deserved. Had I not – after his unilateral defeat – persuaded
every well-known Sheffield socialist to sign a letter of support
and, when it was published in the *Sheffield Telegraph*, had I not
faced and defeated a motion of censure at the monthly meeting
of the Trades Council? What was more, I had sent an offensive
letter to Harold Wilson when that perfidious upstart had
challenged Gaitskell for the Labour leadership. Our names
were chiselled on the same marble slab at Park Hill. He had
spoken to me on the day that he succeeded Clem Attlee. I was
his heir by right.

I decided that it was best to pull out of the Sparkbrook
selection altogether – just to make sure that it did not stand in
Leeds' way. But Reg Underhill, Labour's West Midlands regional
organiser and a man of whom I stood in awe, convinced me that to
behave with such presumption in Birmingham would rightly
prejudice my chances of being chosen in Yorkshire. I suspected, rightly or wrongly, that he would denounce my arrogance
to his counterpart in the West Riding. After I told him that, as a
sign of grace, I would go through with the Sparkbrook formalities,

he added – totally gratuitously, I thought – that I need not worry. The seat was undoubtedly destined for Frank Beswick.

I set out for Birmingham cursing the waste of time and energy. But I can never take part in any contest without wanting to win. So I did my best. Strangely enough, it turned out to be good enough for the Sparkbrook Constituency Labour Party and I, not Frank Beswick, became their prospective candidate. It was wonderful to be wanted and, in the elation of my unexpected victory, I felt nothing but joy until I was half-way home. Then I remembered South Leeds.

Sparkbrook was a Tory-held seat in Birmingham that I had to win for Labour whenever the general election came. Leeds offered a solid majority of almost twenty thousand votes, a by-election in six weeks' time and a lifelong political home in Yorkshire. What was more, I would have walked in Hugh Gaits-kell's footsteps.

Early next morning, I telephoned the Labour Office in Leeds with the news that they had lost me. They were depressingly undepressed. Then, after a long pause, John Anson, the long-time regional secretary, added almost as an aside, 'It's just as well. We didn't like to tell you but you wouldn't have got it. It's all sewn up for a young man called Merlyn Rees.'

No doubt John Anson thought that it was anger, resentment or embarrassment that made me end the telephone call without a word of thanks. In fact I was too weak to hold the receiver to my ear. All I could think about was how near I had come to squandering my last chance of a seat in the next Parliament. As I began my slow recovery I felt increasingly grateful to the constituency which had wanted me and, as is often the case, gratitude turned into affection. It was the beginning of a love affair – with Sparkbrook not with Birmingham – that has lasted for more than thirty years.

All that stood between me and the House of Commons was a Tory majority of 886. And I had no doubt that, when the great day came, it would be swept aside. In the weeks which followed my selection, Labour's lead on the opinion polls – fifteen per cent when Hugh Gaitskell died – began to fade. But that was only to be expected. Throughout the spring and summer of 1963, Harold Wilson, his successor, captured the national mood with a series of speeches which said exactly what the frustrated British wanted to hear. The traditional virtues of the British people – as characterised by the glories of the industrial revolution – were being undermined by a selfish and effete ruling class. The world would be made fit for heroes of commerce and industry to live in and the work would be done by Labour ministers who stood astride the two cultures of science and arts. It was all summed up in the speech that the new leader made to that year's Party conference. 'The white heat of the technological revolution' would transform the country. We all believed it. Science would make us rich and Labour would use the wealth to build a more equal society.

It was – I now confess – not the vision of slide rules and valve-driven computers that inspired me. I was moved by Wilson's apparent determination to turn Britain's back on the class system which had prejudiced the national prospect for so long. That system was, he claimed, personified by the choice of Alec Douglas-Home as successor to Harold Macmillan as Tory leader. 'At a time when even the MCC has ended the distinction between amateurs and professionals, the Conservative Party has chosen to be led by a gentleman, not a player.' As 1963 came to its end, it seemed to me that Labour was irresistible.

And so it was and continued to be right through the spring and summer of 1964 – which is why the Tories postponed the general election until the autumn of that year. Harold Wilson called it 'the last humiliating moment'. For me it was very nearly the last straw that broke not my back, but my heart. For victory in Sparkbrook very nearly slipped away. We spent the first fortnight of August at Holt on the Norfolk coast and every morning one newspaper or another carried an opinion poll. Breakfast after breakfast was enlivened with the news that the Labour lead was disappearing. In London, when the holiday was over, I had dinner with Tony Howard, who had just resigned as political correspondent of the *New Statesman* in order to become Whitehall correspondent of the *Sunday Times*. He did nothing to improve my confidence. I was enormously impressed by his detailed knowledge of how Harold Wilson's first Cabinet would be constructed. His apparent status as one of the next Prime Minister's closest confidants made me all the more apprehensive about his concern that I had wasted, in East Anglia, two whole weeks which might have been spent canvassing in the West Midlands. After an uncertain start to our relationship, Howard and I have become close friends. But he remains candid. He still thinks that I behaved irresponsibly during the summer of 1964.

I remember very little about the national campaign. The infantry, up to its knees in the mud of the trenches, has no way of making a judgement about how the battle is progressing on other fronts. From our tactical headquarters – a filthy room above a derelict Co-operative furniture shop – we worried about advancing in our own small sectors. I was vaguely aware that somewhere in London strategic decisions were being taken. But my time was filled by such mundane preoccupations as making sure that my election address was printed in time for it to be distributed in the free post. Only once did I feel part of the great national debate.

Back in 1964 the political parties held genuine rallies. The sophistication of the carefully vetted, all-ticket audience was still ten years away. In Birmingham that year, both Alec Douglas-Home and Harold Wilson spoke in the old Bull Ring covered market and had to fight to make themselves heard above the noise of organised heckling.

The Prime Minister was destroyed when the crowd which swayed in front of his platform opened to reveal something which its creators called a Homosaurus. The cardboard monster had the body of a prehistoric reptile and the face of Sir Alec. It had been

made, much against my will, by a group of students who had
attached themselves to my campaign. My objection to their
enterprise had nothing to do with the denial of free speech. I
was perfectly happy to see the Tory rally disrupted and Alec
Douglas-Home's speech drowned under a typhoon of derisive
laughter. But I wanted the saboteurs to come from another
constituency. For it did not seem to me that trying to paint green
scales on old packing cases was as important as knocking on doors
with the announcement and enquiry that I hoped would be
repeated outside every house in Sparkbrook: 'I'm calling on
behalf of Roy Hattersley, the Labour candidate in the forth-
coming general election. Can we rely on your support?'

The night after Sir Alec's humiliation, the *Birmingham Post*
predicted that when Harold Wilson spoke in the Bull Ring the
Young Conservatives would undoubtedly respond in kind. Having provoked a riot, the paper naturally dissociated itself from the
consequences of its self-fulfilling prediction with a homily on the
importance of the democratic process. We candidates told each
other that Harold would be more than a match for a mob of
adolescent Tories whose real political experience was limited to
beetle-drives, treasure hunts and dinner dances. But when, on the
early evening of the rally, we assembled to greet him at Snow Hill
Station, we secretly wondered if he would survive the night.

We lined up like a football team before the start of the Cup
Final and Roy Jenkins, who introduced us one by one, played
captain to Harold Wilson's queen. I very nearly bowed. But
deference turned to envy when I noticed that Brian Walden,
the candidate on my left, greeted the Party leader with an easy
familiarity which obviously came from earlier acquaintance. As
they talked, like old friends, about the progress of the campaign, I
began to understand the awful truth. Brian was going to speak at
the rally immediately before Harold Wilson.

He was the obvious choice to represent young candidates – not
least because he was the best platform speaker of his generation.

But he was also my age, my friend and the candidate in the marginal seat next to mine. I have no talent for disguising my feelings and I imagine that the jealousy showed. But, whatever his reason, Roy Jenkins asked me the fateful question. 'Would you like to add a word or two when Harold has finished?' It was not the sort of invitation that aspiring politicians decline. Indeed, when I accepted the suggestion, I felt positively enthusiastic about providing 'the two minutes' worth' that I had been offered.

It was not until the cavalcade sped off into the night that I realised the awful consequences of the changes to the evening programme. The rally would begin with an elegant welcome from Roy Jenkins. Julius Silverman – the local, long-serving and much loved Member of Parliament for Aston – would then warm hearts, moisten eyes and bring lumps to throats before Brian Walden, boy orator, introduced the Party leader. One way or another, Wilson was certain to be a sensation. He might vanquish his critics with his eloquence or he might be subdued into embarrassed incoherence by the volume of their heckling. Either way it was not a speech to be followed by anyone's 'two minutes' worth'. And I had nothing to say. Walden – whose brilliant impromptu performances were, I knew, always produced by days of hard work – had, no doubt, spent the day practising in front of the mirror. I decided that all I could do was echo, as if to emphasise, whatever Harold said and thank him for coming.

The rally began just as I had anticipated. The Young Tories booed Roy Jenkins. Brian, between the Party leader and me, sat impressively calm as the audience was promised 'one of the young candidates who is certainly going to make his mark in the next Parliament'. For a second, even when I heard my name, I did not realise that I had to speak next. I wasted a further ten seconds wondering which of us had made a mistake, Roy Jenkins or me. In 1964, there were no special effects or complicated lights. I could see a thousand faces looking up at the platform and all I could think of was the message on a wayside pulpit which I had read earlier that day. 'To build a new world, we first need new men: Charles Wesley.' So I said it. Then I said it again. I said that the moral and the message applied to that rally, our Party, this country, the whole world. I did not care if they thought that by 'new men' I meant me, not Harold. For at least I had something to say and, rather to my surprise, I was saying it. At one point there was loud applause. So I decided that my two minutes were up, said it again and sat down.

Walden's bravura performance followed. He ended by reminding those members of the audience who had forgotten their ancient history that the great orators of Greece could persuade the people of Athens to pause, think and march in turn, and claimed – rather implausibly, I thought, even at the time – that Wilson had the same effect on the British audiences which he addressed. At first the subliminal persuasion seemed to have worked. For the initial passages were received in respectful silence. Then the heckling started. But, tragically for the hecklers, they chose to take him on one by one. Harold shot each sniper dead – even if not always straight between the eyes. A florid lady in the front row shouted, 'You're a liar.' Harold grinned, almost affectionately, in her direction. 'Say that again and I'll mention Henry Brooke.' Even the ranks of Edgbaston could scarce forbear to cheer. That autumn Harold Wilson produced hysteria all over the country simply by pronouncing the name of the accident-prone Home Secretary. But that night in Birmingham, as the platform was engulfed in the first wave of laughter, the alarm on his wristwatch began to ring. Wilson held up both arms in a majestic call for silence before he gripped the edge of the podium and, staring straight ahead, began to give a solemn warning about the state of the economy. Ninety seconds of the rally were being broadcast live on the nine o'clock news.

When the rally was over, I joined the Sparkbrook contingency in the Mulberry Tavern. 'Great speech by Wilson,' I said. 'Great speech,' they all agreed. 'And a great speech by Brian Walden,' somebody added. Then we went back to discussing the opinion polls.

Next morning there was a message waiting at my committee rooms. Would I like to join Roy Jenkins in an audience with Harold Wilson? I hurried to the Albany Hotel. Inevitably, Brian Walden was in the foyer. We travelled together up to the penthouse suite. Jenkins was already in the vestibule pawing the ground like an impatient horse. It was a mannerism which I came to know well. That morning, his irritation was directed at a portly, middle-aged man in an electric blue suit. The man's name was Alf Richmond. His real job was general factotum for Mirror newspapers but, for the period of the general election, he was plying his trade with the leader of the Opposition. He had just told Roy Jenkins that there would be some time before Harold Wilson was ready to receive him. I distinctly heard him say, 'There's a bit of Marcia trouble.'

No doubt, the sophisticated Brian Walden understood. But I believed that 'Marcia' was a code word for some catastrophe which was to be kept from the likes of me. The Tories had surged ahead in the opinion polls, the pound had slumped to a value barely above two and a half dollars or George Brown had committed some awful gaffe. In fact, Marcia was Marcia Williams, Harold's hugely able and immensely strong-willed political secretary. On the previous night, whilst I was quoting Wesley in the Bull Ring, Quintin Hogg (now Lord Hailsham) had been speaking in Plymouth. Labour rowdies, knowing that he had a low flash point, had shouted at him about the Profumo scandal. His reply had been angry, but oblique. 'Don't tell me that there are no adulterers on the Opposition front bench.' Marcia had taken the riposte as the intentional implication that she was having an affair with Harold. And she wanted to sue for libel.

Her interpretation of Hogg's remark was understandably if not necessarily justified. At every election in which Harold Wilson led the Labour Party, Tory canvassers whispered to floating voters that he was unfit to be Prime Minister because he slept with his secretary. No doubt some of the more excitable Conservative workers believed the allegation to be true. And Quintin Hogg was very excitable indeed. Of course, Harold knew what was being said and what Hogg meant. But he had more sense than to issue a writ which would have turned a cheap aside into front page news. But, as we waited outside the leader's suite, Marcia argued with passion that her good name could not be left besmirched. She also argued for the best part of an hour. As I waited for what turned out to be a more perfunctory handshake than the one which I had received the night before, Roy Jenkins gave his remarkably accurate estimation of what was going on behind the fumed-oak door. I was profoundly grateful that I had been spared the humiliation of Brian Walden letting me in on the secret.

There should have been one more public meeting before polling day – Sparkbrook's own eve of poll rally in Hartfield School. It did not take place because nobody except the speakers turned up. I cannot remember or imagine why I was not de-pressed to the point of despair. But I woke up next morning feeling so cheerful that not even the pouring rain dampened my optimism. I spent a damp day persuading reluctant old ladies that, if we drove them to the polling station in one of our motor cars, we would not leave them to walk home when they had done their democratic duty. A Beverley Sister – then married to a local dentist – toured the streets of Sparkbrook in an open Rolls-Royce which was decorated with 'Vote Hattersley' slogans. At half past nine – dry, bathed and in the Hector Powe suit which had been tailor-made for the spring election – I was on my way to the count in the City Museum.

One by one, the ballot boxes were brought in, opened and emptied out on the long trestle tables. My 'scrutineers' peered over the shoulders of the tellers and, as the voting papers were checked and counted out into bundles of a hundred, pretended that they could calculate how many were marked with a cross against my name. I have been a candidate in ten general elections. Not once have the 'scrutineers' been able to give an accurate forecast of the outcome. On the night of 16th October 1964, they did not even try. Each bundle, they complained with a deplorable lack of perception, seemed to contain five for me and five for Leslie Seymour, my Conservative opponent.

When the returning officer was finally convinced that every vote that had been cast in Sparkbrook lay before him, the count really began. The rival bundles were spread out along the trestle tables, which had been moved so that they stood side by side, to heighten the impression that a neck and neck race was taking place. For almost two hours it was impossible to guess who would win. Sometimes, I edged in front. Often, so it seemed, Seymour surged ahead, leaving me to agonise as my ballot papers slowly caught up. At one moment between midnight and one o'clock, the Tories were so far ahead that I tried to prepare for defeat. It was more easily said than done. We had gambled everything on winning – old house sold, new house bought, and Sheffield jobs resigned. Defeat would – was about to – leave our lives in chaos.

Then, at about half past one on the morning of Friday 16th October, my line of bundles suddenly sprinted into the lead and stayed there until there were no more votes to count. I had won Sparkbrook for Labour by 1,254 votes. I made a modest, but barely comprehensible acceptance speech and rushed back to the old army hut that we called the Labour Club, hoping to be in time to see 'Labour Gain' – the most rewarding of all captions – slowly move across the television screen over my picture. I was too late.

The Irishmen who ran the Sparkbrook Labour Party in those days lifted me shoulder high and hit my head on one of the wooden beams which kept the walls more or less vertical. I spent the rest of the night in a daze. I felt much the same when I awoke the next morning. The dream had come true. I was a Member of Parliament. The great adventure had begun.

CHAPTER
3

I got off to a flying, if slightly disreputable, start. At the end of the meeting of the Parliamentary Labour Party, which preceded the State Opening of Parliament, Christopher Mayhew, Minister for the Navy and Gaitskellite die-hard, invited me to become his parliamentary private secretary. I accepted with astonished gratitude and, on the following day, Mayhew took the MP's oath of allegiance and I – 'his loyal Sancho Panza' – affirmed in the manner appropriate to a Dissenter. Then, Peggy Herbison, Minister for Pensions and National Insurance, suggested – strangely for a woman of such undoubted rectitude – that I should desert Mayhew in her favour.

Even then, I was essentially a domestic politician and it seemed sensible to follow my inclinations and interests. Mayhew – the most agreeable of men – was hurt but understanding. He warned me that Peggy Herbison and I were not soul mates. And so it proved. During the debate on the Termination of Pregnancies Bill, Andrew Faulds (a passionate supporter) referred to Norman St John Stevas (an opponent) in language which, though both colloquial and obtuse, left me in no doubt that it questioned Mr Stevas's enthusiasm to become a father. Peggy asked me what

Faulds meant, and, like a good PPS, I told her. 'I have never', she
replied, 'heard that word used before. I trust you will never use it
in my presence again.' Despite such cultural differences – which
were manifested at every meeting – I became an affectionate
admirer. She was, and remains, one of those genuinely upright
women whose piety is wholly natural. She resigned from the
government when she believed that the social security budget
was being mismanaged, and declined a peerage when she left the
House. She wrote to me with the news that her successor was to
be 'a young advocate called John Smith' and asked me to do all
that I could to help him. At John's funeral, she sat almost
unnoticed in the sixth row of pews.

I worked for almost a week on my maiden speech, which I
planned to give during the debate on the new housing subsidies
bill, the one subject in the world about which I could claim to be
an expert. But, in the second week of the Queen's Speech debate,
the Chief Whip told me that he needed a new MP to speak, next
day, on race relations. The two obvious candidates were Brian
Walden and me, but Brian was being kept for Friday – a
notoriously dull day which they believed he would enliven.
The time had come for one good man to come to the aid of
the Party. I agreed and started to prepare my notes.

It was my first public association with the topic which was to
dominate thirty years of my political life. Until I was elected for
Sparkbrook, I knew nothing of the problems faced by the Black
and Asian British. I did not even know – indeed I had barely met –
a member of either community. But it is impossible to represent a
Birmingham constituency without understanding the hideous
consequences of double deprivation – being poor and being
unable to escape from poverty because of the racial prejudices
that still afflict our society. I suppose that my understanding of the
problem – and my belief in the radical solution of affirmative
action – grew with the number of Black and Asian people whom I
represented. Soon more than half the voters in Sparkbrook will be

from families which are Asian in origin. One of the lessons which they have taught me is that there is an unintentional racism in discussing all the minorities as if they are the same. I claim to know a little about Sikhs and Muslims from Kashmir and Pakistan.

Strangely enough, my maiden speech went well – not least because I was obsequious and Geoffrey Lloyd, my old Sutton Coldfield adversary who had preceded me, was kind. I was fortunate to be followed, on the Labour side, by Michael Foot. I think that he honestly liked the speech. But show Michael a sparrow and he describes it as either an eagle or a vulture. Luckily enough I soared – at least temporarily – in his estimation. Iain Macleod noted in his diary that *The Times* had added the magic words 'cheers' after its precis of what I had said. He wondered what would become of me. A year later, in our only conversation, he was to change the course of my life.

In the weeks that followed my maiden speech, the idea of preferment was put into my mind. Paul Johnson, then editor of the *New Statesman*, wrote that I would do well if I moved to the left of the political spectrum. Newspapers – almost always ignorant diary editors rather than well-informed political correspondents – had decided that I would soon be a member of the government. And I was foolish enough to believe them. I was not, however, foolish enough to believe that it would happen without my assistance. I decided to subject the Prime Minister to a political version of saturation bombing – speeches, parliamentary questions, articles and as many radio and television broadcasts as I could get.

It was Robert Mitchum who said – Peggy Herbison forgive me – everybody wants the new girl in the whorehouse. And, for a few months in 1964 and early 1965, new Labour MPs were in fashion – particularly Brian Walden, Ivor Richard (now Labour's leader in the House of Lords), Shirley Williams, Christopher Rowland and me. An early evening television news magazine called *Tonight* invited one of us to appear almost every evening. In those days, young MPs did not possess a House of Commons telephone which they could call their own. So it was easy for the BBC to leave four identical messages – each of which said that the recipient was the producer's first choice for that evening's broad-cast – without being accused of anything more reprehensible than a determination to make the programme a success. The actual process of deciding which of the favoured four took part in the discussion was very similar to the method by which stevedores were once chosen to unload grain ships. The first prospective employee to volunteer was assumed to be the most eager for work and signed on. We were all desperate to appear on *Tonight*, so we would wander the corridors of the House of Commons hoping to meet a Badge Messenger bearing an invitation. Without pausing to offer thanks, we would then all race to the Members' telephone – a row of kiosks next to the men's lavatory. I must have been more fleet of foot in those days. For I appeared on *Tonight* quite often. I at least caught the attention of Sir Gladwyn Jebb, until the previous year Her Majesty's ambassador in Paris. He recruited me as a paid employee of the branch of the European Movement that campaigned for a political community. My pleasure was only slightly reduced by the discovery that Brian Walden had turned the job down.

I have no way of knowing if Harold Wilson was impressed with my continual television appearances. He only spoke to me once during those first frantic six months. And even then, he only addressed me together with the other nine of the ten youngest Members of the Parliamentary Labour Party who had invited him to dinner. All that I recall him saying on that occasion is, 'Life in London is full of delights for new MPs. Avoid them.' When he spoke to me directly, during the autumn of 1965, he was in a less benevolent mood. I still put it down to bad luck.

I had been invited to join the 1963 Club, a collection of irreconcilable Gaitskellites who met each month over dinner to remind each other how much better life would have been had the lost leader survived. One evening we discussed Harold Wilson's determination to press ahead with the nationalisation of steel, despite the possibility that two Labour rebels, Woodrow Wyatt and Desmond Donnelly, would vote with the Conservatives and, by reversing Labour's slim majority, bring the government down. When I spoke it was the Woodcraft Folk story all over again. My heartfelt comments about my own experiences in the industry – particularly my impassioned complaint about the way young talent had been wasted – was taken to be a brilliant satire on the Prime Minister's obsession with modernisation and technical advance. No doubt the Yorkshire accent and cheerfully truculent manner helped to create the illusion of caricature. Whatever the reason, I briefly became the man who made the 1963 Club laugh at Harold Wilson's expense. Fortunately, I told myself, the discussions at our dinners were absolutely confidential. Less than a week later I realised that, in the PLP, no meeting of more than two people is leak-proof.

I discovered how far my fame as a humorist had spread when Harold Wilson spoke to the West Midlands Group of Labour MPs on the following Wednesday evening. His speech began with an expression of gratitude for the loyal support which he had always received from the West Midlands – in the past. By way of a bridging passage, he expressed his confidence that, coming as we did from the industrial heart of England, we would need no reminding of the absolute necessity to re-nationalise the steel industry. He then said, 'However . . .' I have learned, over the years, that when a Prime Minister says 'However', it is time to duck. What followed was entirely directed at me. I was never mentioned by name. That would have been to afford me a distinction which I did not deserve. But the Prime Minister stared at me, without blinking once, as he began to satirise himself with a skill which I could not have matched at the 1963 Club – even if I had been trying. He knew that some comrades had reservations about steel nationalisation, knew that they were prepared openly to express them and knew that they had done so 'in one of the private dining rooms on the terrace corridors'. The loyal comrades of the West Midlands Group – with the exception of Denis Howell, who had been a witness to the act of treachery – tutted in disbelief. Harold warmed to his theme. He knew who had been present when the reprehensible speech had been made, knew what was on the menu and knew what wine the apostate had drunk. The wine did it. I began to giggle.

When Denis Howell – my older and worldly-wise neighbour in Small Heath – told me he knew how the Prime Minister had found out about my treachery, I did not, at first, believe him. He blamed George Wigg, the ex-regular soldier whose official title was Paymaster General but whose real role was Prime Minister's nark. Denis insisted that Wigg paid the House of Commons waiters to repeat the secrets of the private dining rooms. The idea seemed totally implausible until one evening, in the summer of 1966, when Wigg confronted me in the Aye Lobby whilst a vote of some sort was taking place. 'Tell me, my dear sir,' said Wigg, speaking, as always, in the manner of a Victorian villain, 'where were you last Saturday afternoon?' Saturday 30th July 1966 was an important date in the life of the whole nation and, naively, I assumed that Wigg was talking about the subject which had dominated the newspapers during the intervening three or four days. I gave a straight answer to his apparently straightforward question. 'I couldn't get a ticket. I had to watch it on television.'

Wigg first looked blank and then contemptuous. 'Do you, my dear sir, take me for a complete idiot?' I assured him that I did not and repeated that I had watched England's World Cup victory from home. 'I will', said Wigg, sounding more and more like a banana republic policeman in a bad pre-war film, 'give you one more chance to tell me all about it.' I was tempted to say that England won after extra time, but something in his manner suggested that it was not the right moment for comedy. So I just shrugged my shoulders. The Inquisitor General tried a different approach. 'Then tell me, my dear sir, does the name Anne Fleming mean anything to you?' It meant nothing at all and I told him so. My denial that I had ever met, or even heard of, the lady, was taken as conclusive proof that I had been part of a cabal, which had met at the house of Ian Fleming's widow, to plot the overthrow of Harold Wilson. It was not until I read Roy Jenkins' memoirs, almost a quarter of a century later, that I discovered that the meeting had really taken place. It still amazes me that grown men spent time on such an obviously fruitless activity when they could have been watching the live television broadcast of English football's finest hour.

I realise now that by the summer of 1966 Wilson – and more emphatically his henchmen – regarded me as a thoroughly bad lot. Certainly, I was infatuated by Roy Jenkins. But my real offence was talking too much and finding too much of parliamentary life a pompous joke. Only once did I knowingly behave in a way which entitled me to be regarded as any sort of a rebel. Looking back, I think that I should have rebelled more often. My one conscious act of disloyalty was committed in a good cause and, from my own point of view, had completely beneficial results.

Between the 1964 and 1966 elections, Harold Wilson was the hero of the popular press. Later he was to be portrayed as the comic villain. But during his early years in Downing Street, he was almost always described as the political genius who had led Labour out of the wilderness which we called Thirteen Wasted Years. My admiration for Hugh Gaitskell had not died with him and I felt that somebody ought to remind Harold's reverential public of the debt which he owed to his predecessor. I wrote an article with the admittedly inflammatory title, 'Where Credit is Due'.

It was not a very good article and its theme – which, at least by implication, diminished Harold Wilson – was highly unfashionable. I sent it to every national newspaper. None of them replied.

So I sent it to every magazine I thought might possibly be interested. No doubt I left *Woman's Own* and *Practical House-keeping* off my list. But it certainly went to *Tribune* and the *Spectator* – neither of which, for rather different political reasons, was likely to publish a eulogy of Hugh Gaitskell. In the end I was driven back on to the *Sheffield Telegraph* which, during my local government years, had published my uninformed views on international relations and the state of the British economy. No doubt somebody showed it to Harold Wilson and confirmed his worse suspicions. But thank heavens I wrote it.

One day, before I accepted that the article was only good for a provincial readership, Iain Macleod stopped me as I was walking along the library corridor of the House of Commons. 'Are you Hattersley?' he asked. Tory grandees spoke to young Members like that in those days. 'Yes, Mr MacLeod,' I replied. That was how young Members addressed Tory grandees. 'I've seen your article about Gaitskell.' My heart leaped up. For as well as being a contender for the Conservative leadership, Iain Macleod was editor of the *Spectator* and I did not know of the personal antipathy which he felt towards my dead hero. 'Don't want *that*,' he said. I mistook the emphasis and, believing it to indicate his general contempt for my work, I prepared to slink away, wondering why he had gone out of his way to cause me so much offence. Then, he said, 'Would you like to write for the *Spectator* regularly?' At first, I could not believe that my enzymes were carrying the correct message from ear to brain. Then, when I realised that I was not hallucinating, I felt like a composite of the heroines from *Forty-Second Street*, *On Your Toes* and *All About Eve*. 'Did you say "Give up, Baby?" This is Broadway, You never give up.'

I never spoke to Iain Macleod again – save for one embarrassing occasion in a motorway service station where we had, by coincidence, both stopped for petrol. He did not recognise me. But for almost two years I worked for the *Spectator*, providing for J. W. M. Thomson – Macleod's deputy and eventually the editor at the

Sunday Telegraph – two distinct sorts of contribution. Some weeks I wrote *A View From the Left*, a column intended as a counterweight to the paper's Conservative inclination. On other Fridays I contributed to *Endpiece*. When, in 1979, I became a *Listener* columnist, I stole the title. I have written an *Endpiece* for one newspaper or another ever since. God bless Iain Macleod.

It was my nascent attempts to become a metropolitan journalist that brought me into head-on collision with *Private Eye*. Now we seem to have become more or less reconciled to each other. Indeed, it was at one of their lunches in 1994 that Paul Foot told me of the reasons for our earlier estrangement. As I well knew, in the mid-sixties, he had thought of me as one of the better milk-and-water libertarians who made up the modern Labour Party. He had applauded my views on race relations and we had actually considered co-operating in the production of a television series which we thought of as a sort of local government version of *Z-Cars*! Our association had been sufficiently close to justify my invitation to one of the more celebrated *Private Eye* lunches of the 1960s. I sat next to Albert Finney, who was told that I was a millionaire bookmaker from Huddersfield. The whole two hours were occupied by his demands to be told tips for races of which I had never heard and his increasing anger at my 'pretence' that I was not a bookmaker but a Member of Parliament. Unfortunately, the days of blissful irresponsibility did not last. I wrote a critical review of Foot's book on the politics of race and became first Hatterjee, 'the youngest Pakistani immigrant in the government', and then the regular luncher whose eating habits were reported to *Private Eye* with a reward of five pounds for every sighting.

The 'Hatterjee' joke, if joke it was, filled me with delight. For, believing that notice was next to promotion, I was desperate to be noticed. I was warned against such confusion of shadow and substance by Tony Crosland who, in the most extraordinary way, became my friend. It was not the friendship of equals. Tony would not have tolerated any nonsense of that sort for a minute.

But it was, nevertheless, one of the most rewarding relationships of my life.

My earliest memory of Tony Crosland is seeing him striding down the esplanade at Scarborough, step-by-step with Roy Jenkins, on his way to the 1963 Labour Party conference. My second recollection is more characteristic. He walked out of a dinner of the 1963 Club, with the announcement that he was prepared to support Harold Wilson and prepared to plot against Harold Wilson but he was not prepared interminably to talk about Harold Wilson's shortcomings without having the nerve to do anything to remedy his failures of leadership.

We met, in a formal sense, in the Division Lobby of the House of Commons – thus vindicating Herbert Morrison's view, expressed in his book on parliamentary government, that the importance of constant votes in Parliament is the opportunities which they provide for the meek to rub shoulders with the mighty. I was talking to Dick Crossman about a visit he proposed to make (as Housing Minister) to Birmingham, when Tony asked me to spare him a moment. I replied, 'Of course, Mr Crosland!' So the first few minutes of our conversation were taken up with a cross-examination about why I was so formal with him when I treated other Cabinet ministers with proper disrespect. Dissatisfied with my explanation, he moved on to the topic he had originally intended to discuss with me.

After Patrick Gordon-Walker's double defeat – first in the 'nigger for a neighbour' election in Smethwick and then at the Leyton by-election – Michael Stewart had been promoted from Secretary of State for Education and Science to Foreign Secretary. Roy Jenkins had been offered Education, but had chosen to stay at Aviation, outside the Cabinet. Tony Crosland, Education Secretary by intellect and instinct, had been Harold Wilson's second choice. That night, as we voted, he wanted to talk to me about why Sheffield had come so belatedly to comprehensive education. On the following evening there was a 'running three-line whip' which confined us all to the House. We would – it was a statement, not an invitation – have dinner together in the Members' Dining Room.

I was reluctant to refuse. But my father was in London and, on the following day, I was booked to have dinner in the Strangers' Dining Room with him. I told Crosland of my problem, hoping that he would accept my apology and understand that I would have had dinner with him if it had been possible. He understood, but he did not accept. We would all have dinner together. It was, he said, a unique opportunity. For he knew that my father was a major figure in local government. It in fact was my mother who was city councillor, committee chairman and future Lord Mayor of Sheffield. But, in that mood, there was no arguing with Tony. Reluctantly – and riddled with something that can only be described as stage fright – my father and I had dinner with the Secretary of State for Education and Science. Tony ignored me completely and asked my father – a very junior councillor who had only stood for election because it was the only way of spending his retirement with my mother – complicated questions about the reorganisation of Sheffield secondary schools. I think that was the night when Tony Crosland entered into my pantheon. It was certainly the moment when my father felt that he had become somebody in the Labour movement. Five years later, when he became a governor of Sheffield Polytechnic, he would tell anybody who would listen that he knew Tony Crosland, the inventor of the new 'binary system' of higher education.

Tony Crosland became my friend, whilst Roy Jenkins – without my knowledge and with virtually no social contact – became my patron. He confirmed my suspicions of his help twenty years later after I had reviewed his autobiography. Jenkins, I wrote, constantly gave the impression that he was challenging Wilson for the leadership, and when the newspapers reported his rivalry, he 'did nothing to calm the Prime Minister's jangling nerves'. Roy sent me a postcard which expressed his thanks for 'a generally favourable review. The biggest argument we ever had was over my suggestion that you should be promoted. It may not have done much for Wilson's jangling nerves, but it calmed yours.' Jenkins had first suggested that I should join the government after the 1966 election. Harold Wilson was not impressed. So, during the weekend which followed Labour's electoral triumph, I was not invited to Downing Street. Several of the 1964 intakes were – Shirley Williams, Peter Shore and David Ennals amongst them.

Early on the Monday morning, whilst I was still licking my wounds, Tony Crosland telephoned to ask my advice. Should he appoint Christopher Price (my old friend and a new MP) as his PPS or should he stick with the Welsh stalwart who had served him faithfully and well? After a few minutes' discursive discussion it became plain to me that he was not remotely interested in who would become his parliamentary private secretary and I began to wonder why he had bothered me with the call. Then he said, 'By the way, don't think that yesterday's appointments were any sort of pecking order. At least not any pecking order of merit. The important thing is not to make a fuss or feel down-hearted. Your time will come.'

We met that evening for a drink and Tony suggested that we should have it in his new room in the upper ministerial corridor. There was a small neat package on the desk and nearby a small sheet of House of Commons notepaper overprinted with the name of the elderly contender for the job of Tony's aide. 'Look,' said Tony. 'He left me a welcome present.' He tore open the tissue paper and revealed a set of false teeth. Chris Price got the job.

My time came, as Tony Crosland promised. But I had to wait until January 1967. The newspapers knew that a reshuffle was sched-uled for that day and I sat by my telephone anxiously awaiting the Prime Minister's call. It did not come until almost midnight and I have never been able to work out if that made me an afterthought or someone who could not be trusted to keep my good news from the next day's papers. Next morning, I parked my car in the House of Commons before walking across to Downing Street and, outside the Members' Entrance, literally collided with Ray Gunter, the Minister of Labour. 'I'll give you a lift to St James's Square,' he said. I looked bewildered. 'Do you mean that you haven't seen him yet?' 'Just on my way,' I told him. Ray Gunter pretended to look nervous. 'Act surprised. You're coming to me but act surprised.'

I did as I was bidden – not that Harold Wilson would have noticed if I had acted suicidal. He asked how old I was and, when I told him thirty-three, said that he had been promoted to the Cabinet when he was two years younger. Since I remained delighted by his news, he went on to explain what a problem it was being promoted so early. 'In twenty years' time, when you're barely fifty, people will say, "how long is that old has-been going to hang around?"' At that moment, it did not seem much of a problem. 'You do believe that we are going to be in for the next twenty years?' Harold asked in a challenging sort of way. When I assured him that I did, I spoke with absolute sincerity.

That night – before the announcement had been made – Professor Anthony King and his wife came out to dinner at our house in Chislehurst. When I heard their car draw up on the road outside, I called ecstatically from the window, 'I'm in. I'm in.' That moment of infantile joy was subsequently extended into the stories of a flushed and tousled figure running across Blackheath shouting, 'I'm a minister. I'm a minister.' It contributed to the mythology of my insatiable ambition. I have given up trying to decide whether or not the myth – as distinct from the stories of the incident – was a calumny.

Next day the newspapers were full of stories about the New Men. Two of the four of us were rather elderly. Both Harold Lever and Ernest Fernyhough were older than the usual run of recently promoted parliamentary secretaries and had served in the House throughout the wilderness years of Conservative government. But Reg Freeson and I were Class of '64. Perhaps that is why the newspaper pictures were mostly of him and me. I was featured by the *Financial Times* in a photograph which was headed 'Appointed Junior Minister' and disconcertingly captioned 'Formerly Mrs Shirley Williams'. On my second day in office, I fulfilled one of Shirley's engagements. Recklessly, she had agreed to address a dinner of small clothing retailers.

In 1967, the Labour government was unpopular with anything industrial or commercial which might be described as small, for we were said to have heaped innumerable bureaucratic burdens upon them. With retailers, we were not so much unpopular as detested. Selective Employment Tax inconvenienced everybody – since even manufacturing companies to which the levy was returned with advantages had to make the initial payment. But firms in the 'service sectors', as they were called, paid and were not reimbursed. That is what made the tax selective. So the small clothing retailers – as well as paying a training board levy and filling in complicated forms concerned with safety at work and other trivial topics – had to subsidise the large clothing manufacturers from whom they bought their merchandise. Selective Employment Tax was administered by the Ministry of Labour. The association's dinner was an ideal baptism of fire for me.

The hostility hung so heavily in the air that I turned to the guest who sat on my right, a director of Aquascutum, and – having ingratiated myself by telling him that I sometimes shopped in his store – asked him a favour. 'I am desperately in need of a joke,' I said. 'Just to break the ice.' He agreed with my assessment of the audience in a way which did nothing to improve my self-confidence. 'Do you mind if I say that it is not every night that you come out to dinner and find yourself sitting next to your tailor?' There was a long pause whilst he contemplated his answer. Then he replied, 'That's fine as long as you make it clear that's not one of our suits you're wearing tonight.' I repeated the whole story to my assembled tormentors and they laughed so much they had no breath left to hiss or boo. Since then I have told the story several hundred times in the hope of making critical after-dinner audiences think, 'He may be a bloody socialist but at least he can laugh at himself.' During my last year in the Cabinet, my over-fastidious private secretary – wrongly fearing that I would be embarrassed by imposing the story on colleagues who had heard it before – would pass me a note before I got up to speak. 'Permanent Secretary four times, PPS seven. Advisers six or seven each. Me, lost count but it doesn't matter.' Having done what he regarded as his duty, he would sit back and pretend to laugh.

I managed to get into more trouble almost immediately. On my second day as joint parliamentary secretary, it was the Ministry of Labour's turn to answer oral questions in the House of Commons. Naturally enough, Ray Gunter dealt with the more contentious subjects. But I was allowed to reply to a couple of innocuous enquiries about industrial training – one of the areas of my ministerial responsibility and a policy area which, for all its importance to the future of the economy, has all the political excitement of the prayers which precede each day's parliamentary sitting. I spent all morning studying the anodyne responses which civil servants had prepared for me. I have never blamed them for failing to prepare me for the supplementary question which I was asked by the excitable Bernard Braine.

Mr Braine (as he then was) had put down a question about the Shipbuilding Industry Training Board. The prepared reply, which I read out verbatim in the prescribed fashion, gave a brief résumé of the Board's work, and I waited – confident in the knowledge that I had spent the morning studying background notes – for the 'supplementary', which I thought may even congratulate the government on the progress which it had made. At first I believed that Bernard Braine was having a fit. He swayed from side to side, waved his arms in the air and

struggled to speak. When, after the supreme effort had been
rewarded, he managed to articulate his fury, he described my
answer as 'wholly unsatisfactory'. It had omitted all mention of
fibre-glass – the material on which the future of shipbuilding
depended. I thought that his behaviour was self-evidently ridiculous and assumed that he was driven to counterfeit fury by the
need to defend a constituency interest. And, since I had nothing
much else to say, I offered him my opinion of his performance.
'Appropriate', I said, 'that there should be so much synthetic anger
about a synthetic material.' Mr Braine had a second seizure and took
spluttering refuge in a parliamentary procedure of which I had not
previously heard. 'In view of the unsatisfactory nature . . .'

To be frank, I felt rather pleased with myself, and when Ray
Gunter asked me to travel back to the Ministry in his car, I half
expected him to congratulate me on my maiden performance. His
first words to me were, 'Never do that again.' I knew, at once,
what he meant. 'We just have to get through question time', he
said, softening a little, 'with as little trouble as possible. No fine
words. Nothing clever. Above all, no jokes.' In fact, Gunter's
entire parliamentary technique was a single joke on which he
relied with constant success. It was based on clearly bogus
humility. 'Don't ask me that,' he would reply to taxing interventions. 'I've got enough troubles of my own.' It never failed.

Although I was temperamentally incapable of affecting such a
self-depreciative defence, I determined to treat every parliamentary occasion absolutely seriously. Even then, I did not always
satisfy the demands of my elders or betters. In those days, debates
on the Finance Bill went on all night. And in the early hours of
one morning, I replied – in meticulous detail – to an amendment
on Selective Employment Tax. I sat down after my twenty
minutes' tour de force and Jim Callaghan, then Chancellor of
the Exchequer, offered me his frank opinion of my performance.
'For God's sake,' he implored me, 'stop addressing the issues. We
all should be home in bed. There's no point in rebutting the

criticism, point by point.' Years later – when I became a member of his Cabinet – I reminded him of that early advice. He told me that it had all been said in jest. I did not believe him.

My responsibilities at the Ministry of Labour never involved me in the industrial disputes which were a constant feature of the nation's life. Although both conciliation and arbitration appeared prominently on my job description, it was almost always Ray Gunter himself who distributed the tea and sympathy. On his appointment, he had famously described the Ministry of Labour as a 'bed of nails', but he loved every minute that he spent arguing with recalcitrant trade unions. So, no matter how trivial the dispute, the Minister himself dealt with it. He did very little else.

He naturally expressed his relief that, when the Prime Minister set up a Statistical Affairs Committee, it was composed exclusively of junior ministers. The Ministry of Labour collected the employment statistics and the data which eventually became the Retail Price Index. The first meeting of the new committee provided the occasion of my first meeting with Thomas Balogh – Hungarian economist and, at that time, special adviser to the Prime Minister. Towards the end of the meeting, he called me a 'bloody fool'. I do not remember the exact nature of my foolishness. But I do recall his strange apology when the meeting was over. 'A Labour Member of Parliament', he said, for no reason which I have ever been able to discover, 'can be lazy, sexually deviant, financially corrupt or on the right of the Party – but only one of those things.'

I have only ever been accused of one of those offences, and even to that charge – being on the right of the Party – I plead not guilty. My right-wing reputation was based largely on my un-doubted enthusiasm for European Union and undisguised irrita-tion at the insular and sentimental posturing of the Campaign for Nuclear Disarmament. Neither of those issues is concerned with the nature of society and, in consequence, does not provide a test of ideological commitment. I am also guilty of never having resigned. I should have done so in February 1968, when the Commonwealth Immigration Bill was rushed through the Commons in seven days.

The bill had one purpose: to prevent East African Asians coming to Great Britain. It was necessary, in the judgement of the Cabinet, because the governments of Kenya, Uganda and Tanganyika were 'Africanising' their countries and driving out the Asian citizens who had made such a contribution to the welfare and prosperity of their adopted countries. In Uganda – where Idi Amin was in power – lives as well as jobs were at risk. I had no doubt that Britain had more than a moral obligation to welcome the refugees to the mother country. We had promised them refuge at the time of East African independence. The bill broke that promise.

On every night of the extended Committee Stage, Shirley Williams (then Minister of State at the Department of Education) and I agonised about whether we should go or stay. We took the wrong decision. Twenty-five years later she told me that she had few regrets, for she had privately persuaded the Home Secretary to introduce the Special Voucher Scheme by which the East African Asians came gradually to Britain. It has been very gradual. Some are still waiting.

Despite the several setbacks in my early ministerial career, within a year of becoming joint parliamentary secretary to the Minister of Labour, I was appointed Under Secretary of State for Employment and Productivity. It was exactly the same job. But my original boss, Ray Gunter, was exiled to the Ministry of Power. His successor, Barbara Castle, was dignified with the title of First Secretary of State and the small fish, who swam along behind her, all had their titles suitably upgraded.

I almost went out as she came in. In her diaries, Barbara recalls how Harold Wilson warned her that I was a dangerous subversive who wanted to overthrow the legitimate government and install

Roy Jenkins in Downing Street. Barbara replied that she was prepared to risk an enemy agent in her department but – according to her account of Harold Wilson's conduct – he insisted that my loyalty must be tested. Barbara is notorious for telling the truth. So, incredible though it seems, we must believe that the Prime Minister and First Secretary of State wasted their time devising a scheme to determine whether an insignificant junior minister – on the very bottom rung of government – could be trusted. I have no idea what form their test of loyalty took, for I was unaware that anything so foolish was going on. But I assume that I passed, because Barbara Castle came to St James's Square and I stayed.

On the Friday of the reshuffle – hoping against hope that I would be promoted to Minister of State – I tried to calm my nerves by visiting the galleries in the streets around Pall Mall. One of them was filled with minor Post-Impressionists and I wandered inside for no better reason than I had nothing else to do and stood in front of a green and blue French landscape. I no longer recall the artist's name. But I do remember that the picture was priced at five hundred pounds – a parliamentary secretary's gross monthly salary. The proprietor, working on the principle that works so well for pet shop owners, suggested that I took it home to see if I liked it. I walked down Whitehall with it under my arm.

I hung the picture over my drawing room mantelpiece just before the six o'clock news announced the full details of the reshuffle. It looked magnificent. I never even aspired to own it, but I did hope to keep it for a few days. The cautious half of the household had other ideas. What about the insurance? It might be stolen, burned or damaged as it fell from the hook which, since it had been hammered in by me, would certainly not remain on the wall for long. I succumbed to common sense and, as promised, took it back the following day. I parked my car in St James's Square and was just lifting the Post-Impressionist out of the boot when a cavalcade of black limousines drew up at the opposite pavement. Barbara Castle was about to enter into her kingdom.

Speed of recognition had always been one of Barbara's virtues. On that morning she displayed a peripheral vision which would have done credit to an international centre-forward. Rushing across the road, she thanked me for turning up on a Saturday morning to celebrate her arrival at her new department. Then she saw the picture. 'What', she asked, 'is that?' Because it was the simple truth, I told her. 'It's a minor Post-Impressionist that I had at home on approval. I'm taking it back. That's why I'm here.' I suppose that it must have confirmed her worst suspicions about my Jenkinsite inclinations. But, much to her credit, she waited for the outcome of my loyalty test and, when she discovered that I was innocent of all charges, treated me with the same cheerful lack of consideration that characterised her relationship with left-wing junior ministers.

Barbara Castle was a star. And she possessed all a star's disadvantages as well as a star's virtues. She added a frenzied excitement to everything that she did – often when excitement of any sort was disastrous to the cause which she supported. One of her tasks at the Department of Employment and Productivity was the re-invigoration of the government's prices and incomes policy. I doubt if she supported the suppression of wages before she moved to St James's Square. Indeed, it is unlikely that she even knew the details of the complicated procedures by which pay increases were prevented. But, once she was responsible for making a policy work, she became its greatest enthusiast and it became the essential ingredient in the success and survival of the whole government.

Until 1967, prices and incomes policy had been administered by the Department of Economic Affairs – George Brown's ministry which was supposed to react against Treasury economic orthodoxy with new ideas in order to provide creative tension. By 1968, the result was all tension and no creation. So the job of preventing pay increases became our job – Barbara's and mine. Especially mine. The Prices and Incomes Act which we were required to administer was hugely democratic and totally impractical. Every time the government wanted to prevent a wage rise, there had to be a debate in the House of Commons. It was always my job to justify the government decision to deny each group of deserving workers the pay increase which they had agreed with their employers. I began by asking Parliament to freeze the earnings of the limb-fitters at the Roehampton Orthopaedic Hospital. At ten o'clock one Tuesday night, I began solemnly to explain why men who made artificial arms and legs should not earn an extra few pence an hour. Naturally enough, everybody shouted at me.

I loved it. Facing an unsympathetic House of Commons is like batting against an aggressive fast bowler. Each intervention – like each ball – has to be played on its individual merits. When you are almost caught out, you cannot afford to brood about it. You just get on with the game – except that in the House of Commons the contest has deadly serious consequences. The workers who had their wages held down certainly thought so. Over the years I have grown increasingly impatient with parliamentary sport – the points of order, early day motions and procedural arguments. The more interested I have grown in political ideology, the less attractive I have found political theatre. During those innumerable debates on incomes policy, however, I joined in the spirit of the place. It helped that I believed in incomes policy. But I admit that I relished the conflict and the confrontation and, because of that, my speeches were well received – even by people who did not agree with a word of what I said. Funny place the House of Commons.

I was still with Barbara Castle when, in January 1969, she published the White Paper, *In Place of Strife* – the first attempt to confine industrial relations within a framework of law. I was in her presence when she announced its title to startled civil servants who had agonised for days about what it should be called. She gave the creative credit to her husband, Ted. Both of the Castles had been devoted to Aneurin Bevan and they judged that an adaptation of *In Place of Fear* (the title of Bevan's personal testimony) both represented the future which Barbara had planned for industrial relations and paid proper tribute to the man whom she had admired more than any other politician. The association with Labour's old hero did nothing to endear her proposals to the trade union movement.

For a couple of weeks the Cabinet and the Parliamentary Labour Party were in turmoil and there was much talk of Harold Wilson either resigning or being deposed. Early one Saturday morning in Birmingham, I decided that I must give Roy Jenkins the benefit of my advice. It was an unfortunate decision for two reasons. Firstly, my two tickets for that afternoon's Rugby League Cup Final were at home on my desk in London. So when I abandoned my hopes of a sporting afternoon I sacrificed my guest's pleasure as well as my own. Secondly, Roy Jenkins' lofty refusal even to contemplate deserting Barbara Castle and *In Place of Strife* both dashed any hope I had of him becoming Prime Minister and made my suggestion of a premature strike for Downing Street seem profoundly squalid. We sat in the garden of his house in East Hendred and tried to outdo each other with stories about how other putative Prime Ministers had behaved at the crucial moment of decision. 'Such a position', said Tom Young, Lord Melbourne's valet, 'was never held by any Greek or Roman.' At the time, instead of thinking about the absurdity of that comment, I simply regretted that it would never be held by Roy Jenkins. I tried in vain to encourage him by continuing the quotation, 'If it only lasts three months it will be worth while.' On the way home, I heard on my car radio that it had been the greatest Rugby League Cup Final of all time. Wigan, in the last minute of the game, missed a penalty which would have given them victory. My deserted guest was very good about it.

Now, it is very difficult to understand why Barbara Castle's essentially modest proposals raised so much passion. But politicians of undoubted common sense and impeccable moderation – Jim Callaghan, Douglas Houghton and I amongst them – believed that industrial relations should be regulated by good intentions, enlightened self-interest and the occasionally flexed muscle, not the law. I had the unhappy duty of pronouncing the virtual quietus on the policy when I reported to Barbara that Douglas Houghton – the chairman of the Parliamentary Labour Party – had urged Labour MPs to rise up against *In Place of Strife*. Her rage against both the message and the messenger was terrible to behold and so violent that I thought I would be lucky to get away with only my hand cut off. But I think that my clear association with the Luddites helped to secure my release. A week after Harold Wilson announced that *In Place of Strife* would be abandoned, I was – at Denis Healey's suggestion – promoted to Minister of Defence for Administration. At my farewell party, Barbara kissed me, wished me well and assured me that I would not enjoy my new job with anything like the pleasure which I had found in working for her.

CHAPTER
4

When Denis Healey told me that I was about to become his deputy at the Ministry of Defence, I did not believe him. I had no doubt that he wanted me for the job and that he had told the Prime Minister that I was his choice. It was even possible that Harold Wilson – when pressed by the ebullient Healey – had agreed to promote me. But the more I thought of the process which, all being well, would follow Denis's early warning – summons to Downing Street, interview in Cabinet Room, newspaper headlines and triumphal arrival at new ministry – the more fantastical the idea sounded. For I had already gone through one phantom promotion.

During the summer of 1968, Dick Crossman – Secretary of State for Health and Social Security – had cornered me after a meeting of a Cabinet sub-committee and asked if I would like to become Minister of State at his department in succession to Stephen Swingler, who had died a couple of days before. I said that I would like it very much indeed. Dick thought that Harold 'being very proper about these things', would want a decent time to pass before the replacement was announced, so I should not expect the call to Number 10 until after the funeral.

After the decent interval had lasted for almost a fortnight, I began to wonder if something had gone wrong. Pride and reticence combined to prevent me from telephoning Crossman to ask what had happened. A couple of times, during the weeks of waiting, we passed each other in the corridors of the House of Commons. But, as is the strange custom of the place, we barely nodded. I told myself that if Dick had changed his mind – or had it changed for him by the Prime Minister – he would have at least sent me a message. Then I read in the *Evening Standard* that a new Minister of State had been appointed. The name in the headlines was not mine.

Twenty-five years later – at a dinner given by the Shadow Cabinet to mark the end of the Kinnock-Hattersley leadership – Gerald Kaufman, who was proposing my health, revealed why my hopes of running the health service had not been realised. At the time of Stephen Swingler's death, Kaufman was Harold Wilson's political press officer and he had actually been with his chief when Dick Crossman (true to his word and his character) burst in and announced that he had promoted me on his own initiative. Harold – not the man to stand on his dignity with an old friend – had overlooked the fact that it was the Prime Minister's job to form the government and endorsed Dick's decision. All thought of decent interval ignored, he was on the point of calling me to Downing Street when he was reminded that I was a Jenkinsite. Gerald refuses to tell me who jogged the Prime Minister's memory, but I have always blamed Marcia Williams – now Lady Falkender and then Harold's political secretary. Whoever it was brushed aside Crossman's suggestion that my political loyalty had little relevance to junior doctors' pay and prescription charges. With the insistence that the wages of political sin were death not promotion, alternatives were then considered. The search was long and, at first, inconclusive. A list of parliamentary secretaries was examined. None of them was acceptable to Crossman. Commons back-benchers were considered. Those whom Wilson liked, Crossman despised and *vice versa*. Then the names of peers were dropped into the hat. My detractor – let us call her Marcia for convenience – was particularly keen on one baroness who, quite rightly as it turned out, was extolled as a woman of judgement and, above all, loyalty. The Prime Minister confessed that he knew nothing about her. 'At least', said the formidable Ms Williams, 'she isn't Hattersley.' Gerald Kaufman told the Shadow Cabinet that the incident confirmed my unique place in political history. 'Many ambitious young men have been passed over for somebody. He is the only one, in my experience, who has been passed over for anybody.'

It was the death of Gerry Reynolds – a stalwart of the London Labour Party – which left Denis without a deputy. Perhaps by the time that he died the Prime Minister's advisers had run out of trustworthy peers. It may have been that Gerry was so closely identified with George Brown that replacing him with a Jenkins-ite seemed like promoting a friend. Whatever the reason, a week after Gerry's funeral, I became Minister of Defence for Admin-istration. Mrs Reynolds gave me all of her husband's ceremonial clothes – white tie and tails, morning dress with both striped and sponge-bag trousers, tropical dinner jacket and undertaker-type top coat. Although I was at least four inches taller than Gerry, I wore his bequest, as necessary, throughout my time in the Ministry of Defence. It was supplemented by a bowler hat which I bought for myself – having been told by my ADC, a captain in the Blues and Royals, that it was absolutely necessary for taking salutes. Trilbies are hard to get on and off. Caps were of course unthinkable.

Gerry had been one of the principal bit part players in the farce which accompanied George Brown's resignation from the govern-ment. On the night of the 1968 sterling crisis, Harold Wilson had made a late-night dash to Buckingham Palace to observe the rituals which were necessary for the closure of the stock exchange on the following day. George – then Foreign Secretary – believed that he should have been one of the Privy Councillors who joined the Prime Minister at the audience. Downing Street's excuse for not including him in the party was that, when the Queen was told which ministers to expect, Mr Secretary Brown could not be found. It is not easy to lose a Foreign Secretary. And, since the House was voting that evening on a three-line whip, the missing minister was able to prove that, at the crucial time, he was at Westminster. Notwithstanding the implausibility of the excuse, most people sympathised with Number 10. The meeting was arranged late at night, so it was likely that George was in no state to meet a lady.

When the Foreign Secretary discovered that the Prime Minister had gone to see the Queen without him, he began to roam the corridors of the House of Commons cursing 'the little man', in the voice he usually reserved for public meetings. Embarrassing though that was, worse was to follow. He wandered into the Chamber, sat on one of the benches below the gangway and renewed his complaint against the Prime Minister who had betrayed him. Were such a thing to happen now, graphic accounts of the scene would certainly appear on most front pages of the following day's newspapers and probably on the television news. But, in the kinder climate of the late sixties, George's friends – Gerry Reynolds amongst them – thought that what was left of his reputation could be saved. The formidable Sophie Brown was summoned from the Foreign Secretary's official residence in Carlton House Terrace. I remember the cry of 'Sophie's here!' ringing round the Smoking Room like the sound of the bagpipes which heralded the arrival of the relief column at Lucknow. Gerry left our anxious group, persuaded George that he must desert the Chamber and talk with his wife, and led him down to Speaker's Court where the ministerial Daimler was waiting.

Gerry returned with the glad news that Sophie had taken her husband in hand. 'I saw Sophie put him in the car. He's halfway home by now.' Ten minutes later, the division bell rang and we all trooped off to vote. As we passed the Tea Room we could hear the unmistakeable high-pitched voice. 'The little man has snubbed me once too often.' We all blamed the car. The old-fashioned Daimler was the car pool's choice of vehicle for persons with ceremonial duties to perform, because it was built in a way which allowed passengers to walk in and out without doing very much more than incline their heads. It was particularly favoured by admirals, generals and air-marshals who went to work in elaborate hats. George, having courteously established Sophie on the back seat, walked in the nearside door, narrowly avoided tripping over her feet and walked straight out of the far door. In the Tea Room, he was safe from both his wife and journalists – but not from himself. Before the House rose, he resigned. His friends could not persuade him to withdraw his resignation and Harold Wilson did not even try to make him change his mind. His political career was effectively over.

Glad as I was to become a Minister of State, I would have much preferred time to prosper and progress in a domestic department. For I was, and always have been, an essentially parochial politician. My interests were housing, schools, hospitals and, after a year or two at Sparkbrook, the problems of a multi-racial society.

There were many aspects of defence and diplomacy which irritated me. I had agreed, without any enthusiasm, to see a man from the security services who wanted to brief me about codes. He came into my office, sat down without taking off his raincoat and handed me a sheet of paper on which symbols and names were printed alongside descriptions of what they signified. He said that I must commit them to memory. I promised to oblige at home that night. My visitor was horrified. The list could not be let out of his sight. It had to be learned there and then. I began to oblige, assisting the process by copying out the strange words to impress them on my mind. The pad I had used to help me concentrate was taken from me and the top two sheets – the one on which I had written and the indented page beneath it – were torn up. Writing the secret words was forbidden. I stared at the codes for half an hour and then signed the declaration to confirm that I knew what all the gobbledegook meant. Two years later, when we left office, he came to see me again. He was wearing the same raincoat. I signed a declaration that I had forgotten all the code names. I thought of it as second-time honest.

Working for Denis Healey, however, was a delight. He left me to get on with my job without the constant interference that can ruin a junior minister's life. When I made mistakes, he swore horribly at me in private and defended me in public. He made me laugh and, being an intellectual snob, I took great delight in working for a boss whose grasp of his department – both the complicated concepts of nuclear strategy and the details of logistics and performance – excited the open admiration of even those members of the defence establishment who violently disagreed with much of the policy that he was imposing upon them.

My new job, Denis Healey said, was pay and rations. Then he explained, as an afterthought, that he was going into hospital for a hernia operation and one or two little difficulties might blow up 'whilst he was *hors de combat*'. The only problem that he mentioned specifically was a decision about cratering the roads to prevent unofficial border crossings between Northern Ireland and the Republic. For there was unrest in Belfast and Londonderry. Virtually everybody was afraid that the undoubtedly justified campaign for civil rights would be exploited by the IRA and its armed supporters in the south.

There is a problem about looking back on the time that I spent in Denis's service. He was, and remains, a character, and the anecdotes which are told about characters are often elaborated to the point of invention. However, I suspect that the story about the trauma which followed his hernia operation is true. According to the legend, when Denis came round from the anaesthetic, his bed was surrounded by anxious faces which reminded one observer of Rembrandt's *The Anatomy Lesson*. Edna, his wife, was there. So was the Surgeon General, the Adjutant General, several other generals and various high-ranking civilian administrators. Denis, having survived the beach at Anzio and almost twenty years in the Parliamentary Labour Party, no longer feared death and demanded to be told the truth. Only Edna had the nerve to explain. As the anaesthetic took hold, Denis had fought so hard against unconsciousness that he bit on the apparatus in his mouth with a force that smashed several teeth. The dental operation, the Surgeon General said, would be more painful and more complicated than having the hernia put right. I have never asked Denis if the story is true for reasons that do much credit to my sensitivity. The man who was offered a Fellowship at Balliol to write the definitive work on western aesthetics has always found false teeth immensely amusing. I always feared that, if I had asked him about what he had in his mouth, he would take them out and snap them at me to illustrate his reply.

Whilst Denis was recuperating, Northern Ireland deteriorated fast. Civil rights marches in Londonderry confronted No Surrender Loyalists in a clash which climaxed with the uprooting of paving stones and the smashed pieces of granite and concrete being used as near lethal missiles. The head of the Royal Ulster Constabulary asked the army 'to come to the assistance of the civil power' and General Sir Ian Freeland passed on the request to the Ministry of Defence. On the afternoon of Sunday 24th July 1969, ministry officials crowded into my tiny drawing room to advise on how we should respond. The consensus was that we should wait and that recommendation was passed on to Jim Callaghan – by that time transferred from the Treasury to the Home Office and, in the days before the Northern Ireland Department existed, responsible for the governance of the Six Counties. He accepted my recommendation. That evening, my private secretary telephoned to say that he had formally notified Number 10 of the decision. For although the Home Secretary would have undoubtedly spoken to the Prime Minister, the Ministry of Defence had a special relationship with Downing Street which had to be preserved by constant use. When I arrived at my office next day, I received a message from Harold Wilson himself. We had, he said, been quite right not to rush into the momentous decision to send troops on to the streets of Northern Ireland. 'Once we do that, they may be there for weeks.'

Backed and buoyed up by the Prime Minister's support, I continued to resist the Chief Constable. But a week later the duty clerk at the Ministry telephoned me with a strange request. Bernadette Devlin – not then a Member of Parliament but already famous as the precocious leader of the militant civil rights campaigners – wished to speak to me urgently.

I must have thought of Ireland, which I had never visited, as a highly backward as well as most distressful country. For I was astonished to find how easy it was to make the connection and how clear she sounded at the other end of the line. She said, in the simplest language, that unless troops were out of their barracks, across the Foyle and into Derry city by mid-afternoon, Catholics would be slaughtered. With Bernadette Devlin supporting the Chief Constable, only one decision was possible. I went through the formalities of consultation, sought and obtained Jim Callaghan's approval and became, after I had signed the Army Board Order, 'the man who sent the army on to the streets of Northern Ireland'. For the next couple of years, that description was the accusation that Republicans shouted at me wherever I went. They rarely added that I had responded to the urgent request of Bernadette Devlin.

Ms Devlin herself was notably ungrateful. Six months later, after she had become a twenty-one-year-old Member of Parliament, she attempted to have me impeached. I had founded the

Ulster Defence Regiment, in a vain attempt to replace the B-Specials with non-sectarian reinforcements for the RUC, and was preparing to take the salute at the Inaugural Parade (held prophetically on 1st April) when the Hon. Member for Mid-Ulster produced a photocopy of a memorandum, which she said had come from me. It urged various Northern Ireland institutions not to wait for parliamentary authority before they began to spend money on preparing for the UDR to muster. Dr Horace King, the first Speaker to be elected from the Labour benches, examined the photocopy and, acting on authority which was not always clear, ruled that I had no case to answer. He had noticed, at the very top of the sheet of paper, a mark which he judged to be the left-hand hoof of the stag rampant which stood on the sinister side of the Ulster coat of arms. The letter had, he decided, been written on Stormont notepaper from which the official heading had been incompletely cut off. I have no idea if that was so. I only knew it did not come from me.

Ms Devlin was not at all abashed by the rejection of her plea for my political destruction. During one debate she menaced the Labour front bench with a brown paper bag which she seemed to say contained 'mace' that had been used on Northern Ireland protestors. Suddenly she began to tear the bag open. Ivor Richard, the Parliamentary Under Secretary for the Army, had, like me, been to the Democratic Party Convention in Chicago, where a substance by that name was sprayed, with terrible effect, on Vietnam protestors. We both ducked beneath the table which separated the two sides of the House. Beyond our view, Ms Devlin brandished a piece of wood into which nails had been hammered. We giggled with embarrassment and relief. Reginald Maudling, a couple of rows in front of the Soldier of Destiny, seemed less reassured by the discovery that she was using the word in its medieval sense. During the previous debate she had pulled his hair and only Alec Douglas-Home had come to his protection with an ineffectual attempt to drive the assailant back by flicking his silk handkerchief at her.

By the time that Ms Devlin made her mark on the House of Commons and Reginald Maudling, troops were on the streets of Belfast as well as Londonderry. I was at lunch with almost the whole *Sunday Times* Insight team – who were thinking about writing a Penguin Special on Northern Ireland – when my private secretary telephoned with the news that Jim Callaghan thought the time had come to help the police in the capital. I regarded the message as more of an instruction than a request and said that I would sign the warrant immediately upon my return to the Ministry. I had barely returned to my table when General Sir Victor Fitz-George Balfour, the Vice Chief of the General Staff (happily not in full dress uniform), rushed into the restaurant followed by his ADC. There followed a heated argument in which the General asserted that, 'Young officers are taught that time spent on reconnaissance is never wasted.' I replied that, 'Young Ministers of State learn that Home Secretary's instructions are never ignored.' I thought my riposte wonderfully witty. No doubt Sir Victor thought that my conduct was typically craven.

A couple of weeks later Sir Victor and I were in conflict again. Denis Healey had asked me to work out a formula by which soldiers who were posted to Northern Ireland – billeted in derelict factories and abandoned chapels – received a 'hard living allowance'. The Army Board believed that only active service justified extra pay. But, when it convened to discuss my scheme, the Board chose to attack my application of the Secretary of State's idea rather than the idea itself. The Vice Chief of the General Staff was the chosen instrument of their criticism. Denis Healey dealt courteously with his first dozen amendments – accepting some, rejecting rather more and thanking General Balfour for each of his suggestions. But Denis's nerve snapped when the VCGS asked about the qualifying criteria. 'How long must you serve in the Province before the bonus is paid? I went with the Minister on his day trip. Do I get it?' Denis licked his pencil dramatically. 'I am writing in a new rule, Victor. Anyone with a private income of more than a hundred thousand pounds a year is ruled out.' Everyone except General Sir Victor Fitz-George Balfour laughed. Half rising from the table, he was foolish enough to say, 'With great respect, Secretary of State, my private income is none of your business.' Denis put his head on one side in what he believed to be an affectionate posture. 'Victor,' he replied, 'everything that you do is my business. And if you go on arguing with me, I'm going to crawl under the table and chew your balls off.' No more amendments were proposed to the Northern Ireland Special Payments Regulation.

So much of the summer of 1969 was devoted to Northern Ireland that I was able to escape from taking a formal holiday. But, when the early autumn came, Denis – who assumed that I longed for beach and sea – suggested that I should be compensated for what the Ministry called a sacrifice by making an official visit to Edinburgh at the time of the Festival. I do not recall what plays we saw, but I do remember that I took the salute at the Tattoo, visited the Polaris base at Faslane and a 'boys' regiment' in basic training. In preparation for my day with the boy soldiers, I went to dinner at the headquarters of Scottish Command. I arrived late. That day, Yorkshire won the Benson and Hedges Cup and I had watched the television broadcast in my hotel room, right up to the moment of victory. My host, General Laing – who was waiting for me, magnificent in mess dress and red-lined cloak at the top of the steps which led up to his front door – showed not the slightest sign of impatience. The senior officers who worked with me and for me at the Ministry of Defence were the most polite group of men that I have ever met. Almost without exception they treated formal courtesy as if it were a basic requirement of Queen's regulations – like tweed suits for the weekends, expensive luggage and a brown felt hat to be worn at all times in preparation for being recognised and needing to return a salute. I always believed that deep down inside they writhed with indignation at having to take orders from a thirty-five-year-old vulgarian. But they never showed it. General Laing, having unnerved me with his unreasonable good manners, assured me that I would enjoy my day with the teenage recruits. He was wrong.

I had assumed that the sixteen-year-old lads would be strapping, weather-beaten youths from the Highlands of Scotland, made sturdy on porridge and burly by tossing the caber. They were, without exception, puny, whey-faced and, most disconcerting of all, extensively tattooed. It was the tattoos that did it. The boy soldiers were obviously the undernourished children of the Glasgow poor – reared on chips in fetid tenements and allowed to disfigure themselves because no one really cared about their welfare. Strangely enough, my emotional reaction was not all that far from the truth. Recruits to boys' regiments (as distinct from junior leaders' schemes) almost by definition lacked proper family guidance. For they signed on for seven years with the colours and, once a parent had endorsed that decision, they were in bondage to the Queen until their time was served. I heard from their instructors that, to many of the lads, the army became both father and mother – and I believed it. But I could not imagine why that justified an under-privileged boy of sixteen being allowed (and often encouraged) to sign away ten per cent of his life – especially when their commanding officer confirmed that more than half of the recruits wanted to leave but were refused release. That morning, on a hillside overlooking the Clyde, I determined to end, not the recruitment of boy soldiers, but the practice of legally binding them to the colours.

Denis Healey wisely suggested that we proceed by stealth and set up a committee. The Army Board was strangely co-operative until they realised that the investigation would not be carried out entirely by soldiers. Denis overcame their resistance with his usual combination of brutal humour and humorous brutality. I asked Terry Neill (captain of Arsenal and Northern Ireland) to be a member of the inquiry. He agreed, but his manager sent me an angry letter saying that Neill could not agree to anything without first obtaining his permission – which he withheld. I had forgotten that professional footballers, like boy soldiers, were bondsmen. Jimmy Hill gallantly stepped in and ensured that there was one member of the committee who would mean something to the subjects of the inquiry. The only lay member of whom the military establishment really approved was the chairman, Lord Donaldson – not only a peer but, more importantly, a wartime colonel. Jack Donaldson was a friend of Tony Crosland and turned out to be the most radical member of the committee.

True to the tradition of official inquiries, the Donaldson Committee dragged on and it had still not reported at the time of the general election in June 1970. So its recommendations went not to Denis Healey and me but to the Lords Carrington and Balneil. In the end, the members were unanimous – soldiers no less than civilians. Boy recruits, they wrote, must, after a suitable period of notice, be allowed to leave the army. When I wrote an article calling on the new government to accept the recommendation, the National Council of Civil Liberties denounced me for having done nothing about the problem myself while I was a minister.

I cannot claim that I did much to liberalise or civilise life in the armed forces but I did at least endorse one other reform before my military engagement ended. The request for a revolutionary change of policy was made to me early one spring morning by General Sir Charles Harington, the Chief of Administration, Personnel and Logistics.

Harington was – indeed still is – the glass of fashion and the mould of form. He dressed and behaved with an immaculate elegance which made David Niven look like a New Age traveller, and he always spoke with an fulsome courtesy which obliged him to preface almost everything he said with an exaggerated apology. One morning he came unexpectedly into my office expressing his usual regret that he had to waste my valuable time with one of the items of trivial business which it was his unhappy duty to bring to my justifiably bored and understandably impatient attention. He said that 'The Wren' wanted to see me and added that I would no doubt be relieved to know that, having introduced us, he would no longer burden me with his company.

The Wren was not, as I expected, the head of the Women's Royal Naval Service but one of her deputies or assistants. Apparently Harington could not – or more likely pretended that he could not – tell one senior woman officer from another. The Wren said that she had hoped the day would never come when she needed to make such a request, but that it was her painful duty formally to ask for a change in the instruction given on medical advice to female ratings. It had become necessary, she explained, for ships' surgeons and the like to be allowed – assuming that their conscience allowed – to distribute contraceptives. She added, as if she were compounding a felony, that the doctors should operate exactly in the manner already common amongst civilian general practitioners.

I know now that I should have agreed at once and instantly ushered her out of my room. My only excuse for what followed is that I was motivated by nothing more reprehensible than curiosity. And I put my question in as delicate a form as I could. 'But I thought that the navy always issued . . .'

The Wren, no doubt anxious to reciprocate my tact, leaped in before the question was completed. Her response was part theological, part metaphysical. The issue of condoms – called sheaths in those days – was a traditional precaution issued to jolly tars before they went ashore in foreign ports. But the purpose of that provision was not the prevention of conception but protection against disease. The navy never had been and never would be a party to contraception, but the health of the fleet was the proper concern of their Lords of Admiralty.

I suppose that I must have looked perplexed for she went on to explain why an extension of the old rule was necessary. 'Until now,' she said, 'it has never been necessary with the girls. But now we find that the married ones are lending their devices to single shipmates.' Then she produced the argument which she knew was decisive. 'We can no longer be ruled solely by the principles of morality – it has become a question of hygiene.' I said that I understood completely and would sign the necessary papers as soon as they were prepared for me.

My other naval engagement took place in Singapore, where I stayed during New Year 1969 with Admiral Sir Peter Hill-Norton, Commander in Chief, Far East. I was sent out with specific orders to emphasise the inflexibility of the defence review, which, in effect, brought all British forces home from the Far East. Lee Kuan Yew – Singapore's Prime Minister – was pressing hard to retain a British presence in the area. He had already persuaded the Australians to contribute a squadron of jet fighters towards an air defence system as long as the United Kingdom provided radar and various other forms of technical support. No doubt I passed on Denis Healey's message in a particularly heavy-handed way. But I did not realise that I had caused any offence until, after a day of hard talking, the Commander in Chief took me to the New Year's Eve party in the Straits Hotel. As we went into the dining room, a clutch of beautiful young girls offered us fancy hats. But they were not the sort of cheap rubbish that comes out of crackers. I had just chosen a six-foot-wide sombrero when Admiral Hill-Norton came running towards me carrying an Indian headdress of such size and splendour that Sitting Bull would have been proud to wear it. Shouting in the way that must have made his orders audible above a Force 8 gale, Sir Peter insisted, 'This is the one for you, Minister. You've been proving that you're the big chief all day.'

The party went on most of the night. All I can now remember is a trio of young Singaporeans – dressed in immaculate Mandarin costumes – singing 'If this ain't love, then it don't rain in Minneapolis in the winter time'. Back at Flagstaff House, the

Commander in Chief's quarters, I found in my jacket pocket one of the Chinese crackers that had deafened the diners in the Straits Hotel. I fired it out of the window. As the explosion reverberated around the tropical garden, I remembered the Royal Marines who were patrolling the perimeter wall to guarantee my safety against local insurgents. For several minutes I expected one of them to climb up the wall and swing through the window into my bedroom. Nobody came to my rescue. Perhaps they were used to the behaviour of well-entertained ministers. I dreamed that Admiral Hill-Norton had instructed them to leave me to my fate.

For the next six months, life was all the defence review. Infantry regiments were amalgamated – after angry protests from retired officers and detailed interference from Buckingham Palace by the various Honorary Colonels. Princess Margaret took cap and collar badges particularly seriously and the heraldic drawings which I sent for her approval were often returned with notes scrawled across the delicate art work. 'Indian lion *must* be bigger . . . Paschal Lamb seems to be grinning . . .' I have always wondered if it was my resistance to her aesthetic improvements which prompted her to dress me down at a reception for Queen Alexandra's Royal Nursing Service. She could not have been provoked by anything I said that evening, for she started on me before I had straightened up from my bow.

Her diatribe mostly concerned the quality of accommodation which had been provided for the army in Ireland and the embarrassment which she and her husband had been caused, during their tour of Japan, by questions about the way in which we treated our soldiers. For a second, I could not think of anything except the citizens of Tokyo and Kobe worrying about the level of comfort which we provided for our troops. Then, through the haze of incredulity, I heard Her Royal Highness say, 'They'd be better off in tents.' I suppose that I was still not concentrating. For I replied, 'With respect' – always a dangerous preamble – 'that may seem so now. But when winter comes . . .' Princess Margaret began to shout. 'That was a simile. Don't you know what a simile is?' She shouted so loudly that even the commissioned nurses of QARNS had time to stop and stare. So I thought it best not to say that, at best, she had used a metaphor.

In the early spring of 1970 I visited the doomed V-bomber force in East Anglia and, after a morning's terrifying parachute training, skimmed over Lincolnshire in a simulated low-level raid which ended with my pilot reporting to base that Cleethorpes had been wiped out. Having survived lying flat in a Vulcan, it was decided that I was ready for the Red Arrows – the RAF's Acrobatic Air Display Team.

The night before I took to the skies over Anglesey was spent in the officers' mess at RAF Valley, where the only topic of conversation was the strategic importance of keeping the whole of Strike Command within bathing distance of the Cyprus beaches. I had been warned about the Cyprus syndrome. Michael Carver, long before he had become a Field Marshal and Chief of the Defence Staff, had told me that it was Air Force wives who wanted to be stationed in the Mediterranean – an aberration which he attributed to sociological differences between the services. 'Soldiers marry soldiers' daughters. Airmen marry barmaids.' Next morning I realised that the preoccupation with Akrotiri and Episkopi was probably prompted by compassion. They did not want to talk about the rubber suit.

At first, as I climbed inside, I thought it was intended to keep me warm. For it had tubes leading out of strategic places which I assumed would be attached to a heating system. But a young man connected them to a giant bicycle pump and slowly inflated me. Noting my surprise, the pilot explained. 'To help with G-force. Stops your blood and guts slopping about at high speed.' His explanation did nothing to contribute towards the stability of my intestines. I walked towards the aircraft with all the dignity of which a Michelin man is capable and, to my alarm, was hoisted into my seat in the *front* cockpit.

I heard the hissing noise as soon as my head was jammed into the American Football-style helmet. At first I feared that my suit had burst and that, once air-borne, G-force would tear out my lights and liver. So I spoke as calmly as I could into my microphone. There was a moment's panic, before I switched to 'receive', when I feared that since I had received no reply the pilot was dead. Then I heard his confident question. 'Hissing? Thumping in background?' If it had happened before, there was hope of a cure. 'It's the bloody intercom,' he said. 'Exaggerates the sound of nervous breathing. And rapid heart beats. Nothing to be embarrassed about.'

Despite his reassurance that fear is not a cause for shame, I felt I had to agree when he asked me if we could do a 'gentle roll'. There are no gentle rolls. Upside down, G-force hit me and produced the sensation of red hot cannon balls rolling about in my large intestine. I was still half unconscious when we flew over Beaumaris Castle – the only possible explanation for my agreement that we should 'take a closer look'. As we fell out of the sky like the kamikaze end of the tourist trade, my only fear was that I would still be conscious when we hit the ground. The next thing I heard was the Commanding Officer – broadcasting from the control tower – to congratulate the squadron on a perfect formation landing.

The RAF public relations department had been hard at work. As I climbed out of the cockpit, a visiting Air Marshal stepped forward to present me with a Red Arrows tie – official recognition that I had been with the aerial acrobats in the particularly wild blue yonder. Whilst the television cameras turned and the flash bulbs exploded, I held out my hand and clutched at the memento of my daring. It fell symbolically on to the tarmac. Three or four times, I tried to grasp the cellophane package and three or four times I failed. 'Cramp,' said the Station Commander. 'Fear,' I told him. I had grown out of one of politics most tedious diseases – ministerial machismo.

When I got back to London, the Chief of the General Staff, Sir Geoffrey 'George' Baker, had left me a message. He was worried about the third night of the Earl's Court Royal Tournament, when I was due to take the salute. He believed that a general election was imminent and, were Labour to lose, I could hardly be the army's guest of honour. Would I mind avoiding possible embarrassment by pulling out now and allowing him to invite a member of the Royal Family to take my place? I suspected it was Princess Margaret. It was not the most tactful of messages and my pompous reply was almost justified. I was not prepared to plan for the defeat of my party. In any event, I knew more about politics than he did. The general election was months away. Two days later, the Prime Minister asked the Queen to dissolve Parliament.

I no longer feel ashamed of my miscalculation. For it was nothing like as great as the one which Harold Wilson made. He believed the evidence of the opinion polls, which proved that the fiasco over *In Place of Strife*, like the devaluation of the pound, had been forgotten. Harold himself was far more popular than Edward Heath, the sun was shining and England was going to retain the World Cup which Bobby Moore's team had won in 1966 – the year of Labour's previous victory. England were knocked out in the quarter final after Peter Bonetti, substituting for the injured Gordon Banks, failed to hold a shot which every elderly man watching the match on television was sure that he could have saved. Labour supporters blamed their party's defeat on the disappointment of a football-mad nation. Peter Bonetti thus became the first goalkeeper in history to lose a general election.

But, at the time of the dissolution, few people would have predicted a defeat either for England or for Labour. Certainly the naval officers of the weapons research establishment at Bath – with whom I spent the fateful day – thought a Labour victory unavoidable. They did not welcome it. But they took it for granted.

I stood in the Ward Room at Bath – glass in hand – and watched Harold Wilson speak to the nation, courtesy of the six o'clock television news. It was the most flagrant exploitation of the medium that I had ever seen and, even now, I am astounded by the memory of its effrontery. Harold sat in the garden of 10 Downing Street with the summer breeze ruffling the leaves of the St James's Park trees above his head. At one point – just as he was mentioning the years of peace and prosperity which lay ahead – a bird, which I thought to be a lark, could clearly be heard opening its heart to heaven somewhere over Whitehall. The sailors, who by then were almost choking on their pink gins, had no doubt that the blithe spirit had been bought from a Westminster pet shop and released, at the strategic moment, by some fellow travelling employee of the BBC.

Ministers of State play little part in the national campaign, so I was able to spend most of the campaign in Sparkbrook, although I was required to deputise for Denis Healey, first at the Queen's reception for winners of the Victoria Cross and then at the 'beating of the retreat' on Horse Guards' Parade. I entertained Her Majesty on the balcony of the Admiralty whilst, down below, her husband took the Marines' salute. In compensation I was allowed to occupy the same vantage point for the Trooping the Colour next day. Better still I was offered the opportunity of hosting a party for the French Defence Minister – thus qualifying for the provision of free champagne for any of my friends who cared to join me. The ceremony had already begun, and the bottles were open, when I heard that gunboats had been stolen from Toulon harbour and the Frenchman was not coming. It was Monday before my private secretary broke the news that, in the absence of an official foreign visitor, I would have to pay for the champagne myself.

Sunday morning canvassing remained part of the Birmingham political tradition and we methodically worked the roads of Fox Hollies – our one marginal ward – week after week. Two weeks before polling day, our reception was rapturous. Then, on the last Sunday of the campaign, we were greeted with something between contempt and hostility. I tried to remember that, back in 1964, everybody had seemed hostile, yet I had still won. Indeed, on the eve of that glorious victory, nobody had turned up to my eve of poll meeting.

Nobody turned up either to the factory gate meeting that I held outside Lucas Batteries in Forman's Road on the day before the 1970 election. In 1964 and 1966, the lunch-time whistle had barely stopped blowing before the Transport and General shop stewards had ushered their members across the road and on to the dusty recreation ground. We waited in the loud-speaker van until one o'clock and then drove away, frightened and humiliated. At first, *The World at One* did nothing to lighten our hearts. The *Evening Standard* opinion poll put the Tories in the lead.

Then, immediately after the news headlines, Robert Carvel – the *Standard*'s distinguished political editor – was interviewed about his paper's poll. He advised that its result should be ignored. He had spent the morning at the Conservative press conference where he had seen Ted Heath 'fighting for the soul of the Tory Party in defeat'. That evening, comforted but not convinced, I had supper with John (now Lord) Harris, Roy Jenkins' principal lieutenant. In order to put my neurosis to rest, he telephoned Walter Terry, the Labour-inclined political editor of the *Daily Mail*. Terry had no doubt that Labour were as good as elected. He enlivened our evening with a story of Ted Heath getting out of a private plane on the previous scorching afternoon and being offered a pint of ice-cold lager by an honest British workman who had been disturbed whilst digging a trench at the airport, and persuaded to take part in the publicity stunt. According to the anecdote, Heath looked into the lenses of the assembled television cameras and said, 'No thank you very much. I had a cup of tea in the plane.' We all agreed that old Ted could never win an election. We said the same about Margaret Thatcher eight years later.

Even on election day, I was not sure that we had lost until I got to the Pebble Mill studios of the BBC where, whilst waiting to celebrate my own election by talking to Robin Day in London, I saw George Brown broadcasting from the count in Belper Town Hall. George Brown was telling the world that he had 'lent' the constituency to his Tory opponent and that he would expect it back in two years' time. He spoke with the total absence of conviction which was to be expected of a man who knew that his political career was over. George had caused me nothing but trouble. But I found the sight of him in defeat acutely painful. I knew that I was staring mortality in the face.

The Birmingham Labour Party had arranged a victory social in the Rainbow Room of the Central Co-operative and, having muttered a few meaningless platitudes to Robin Day, I drove off to the celebration without thinking much about how awful it would be. By coincidence, Roy Jenkins and Brian Walden arrived at the double glass doors just as I was about to push them open. They were coming out as I was going in. Brian made a speech about how sorry he was, not for himself but for us. It made me feel much worse. I decided to spend what was left of the night in the Sparkbrook Labour Club.

On the day of the State Opening of Parliament, Roy Jenkins took me to lunch at Brooks's Club. We walked to St James's, but – without needing to consult each other – instinctively veered away from the short cut through Downing Street, in those more tranquil days still a public thoroughfare. Downing Street belonged to us no longer.

'Opposition,' I said, 'is awful.' Jenkins was not the man to let a piece of sloppy thinking pass uncorrected. 'Up to now,' he said, 'you have only experienced deprivation of office. Opposition is far worse.' During twenty-one of the next twenty-six years, I was destined to learn how accurate that judgement is.

CHAPTER
5

Opposition was worse than either I had imagined or Roy Jenkins had predicted. My gloom was intensified by Harold Wilson's insistence that I should become the Party's Deputy Foreign Affairs Spokesman. Working again for Denis Healey was some consolation – but not enough for being forced to devote my life to a subject in which I had little or no interest. What was worse, I knew that I would have to make constant visits to distant countries of which I knew nothing.

Many of my colleagues were openly envious of what they regarded as my chance to tour the world. One of the symptoms of the parliamentary disease is the belief that getting on board an aeroplane is an intrinsically exciting experience – wherever it may be going. I have never been able to share that view. It may be that my judgement on parliamentary travel was prejudiced by two early excursions.

In my first year at Westminster, I had visited Argentina as the guest of Luz y Fuerza – Light and Power – the union of the electricity generation industry. I have no idea why they invited me to their thirty-fifth birthday celebration, or why their thirty-fifth birthday was celebrated in such style. I suspect that they had hoped for Harold Wilson or George Brown and worked their way two hundred and eighty places down the Parliamentary Labour Party to me. Whatever their reasons, they paid for me to fly to Buenos Aires.

Luz y Fuerza was a relic of the Perónista trade union movement. Its members talked incessantly of Juan and Evita, distributed subversive pamphlets and insisted on their guests wearing button-hole badges that displayed the Argentinian flag at the front but which, at the flick of the lapel, revealed the heads of their heroes. According to the Labour attaché at the British embassy – who was my chaperon – they involved me in enough illegal activity to guarantee my deportation and make a long prison sentence at least possible. When we visited the offices of the parliamentary splinter group which they supported and a curtain was suddenly pulled aside to reveal a full-length picture of the deposed dictator, the harassed diplomat stood in front of it holding his jacket as if he was imitating a bat. He had convinced himself that I had been invited to Argentina for the sole purpose of the Perónistas obtaining a picture of a British Member of Parliament paying homage to their lost leader.

I found the intrigue fascinating. But the Perónista tradition did create food problems. The General had called his followers 'the shirtless ones' and, although Luz y Fuerza members were invariably prosperous, they felt an obligation to demonstrate that they were shirtless in spirit. So they always took off their jackets in restaurants. In consequence, we were asked to leave some of the best hotel dining rooms in Buenos Aires. But that was the least of my culinary problems. The real horror was goat. Perón, twenty years before, had tried to improve Argentina's export record by prohibiting the domestic consumption of beef on three days each week. By the time that I got to South America, Argentina had more steak and chops than it knew what to do with. But the shirtless ones still insisted on being beefless on

Mondays, Wednesdays and Fridays. I came home hoping never to
see a goat again.

On my first ministerial visit to New York back in 1968, the food
had been unexceptional but the programme had been highly
eccentric. I had immensely enjoyed standing just one row behind
Vice President Humphrey on the Labor Day saluting base which
had been erected in front of the General Post Office on Fifth
Avenue. It had been a mild shock to discover that my hero was
wearing thick make-up, but my distress was quickly dispelled by
the pleasure I felt at taking part in what, in effect, was the opening
of the Democrats' Presidential campaign. My host – an official of
the public service union – told me that all the visiting dignitaries
had been invited to appear on a special television programme and
whisked me away to Radio City Music Hall.

The programme was the Jerry Lewis Muscular Dystrophy
Labor Day Twenty-four-hour Telethon. I was introduced to
Mr Lewis, asked how things were in England and told to stand
quietly in the corner of the stage whilst Joan Crawford compered a
fashion show. The cards from which Miss Crawford read had,
somehow, got out of order. So what she described never bore any
relationship to the clothes which were paraded across the stage.
When the star realised that she was not synchronised, she threw
all her cribs in the air and then, after some persuasion, joined me
in the corner of the stage whilst a man inflated balloons and
knotted them into the shape of animals. He was followed by a girl
in tights who did a ventriloquial turn that was built around a llama
rather than a dummy. Then Jerry Lewis reappeared with Vice
President Humphrey. Between them was a smiling blond child
who, Mr Lewis whispered to five million viewers, would be dead
by next year's Labor Day. Burt Bacharach came smiling to the
piano and the doomed child led us all in a chorus or two of 'What
the world needs now is love, sweet love'. Nobody else I know has
ever been part of a quartet in which the other three participants
were Joan Crawford, Jerry Lewis and Hubert Humphrey. And –

apart from Marlene Dietrich, whose late night, one-woman shows I had attended at two consecutive Edinburgh Festivals – I have never heard of anyone except me who has been accompanied by Burt Bacharach. But despite the distinction of taking part in what must have been a unique performance, I regard that afternoon in New York as one of the most excruciating experiences of my life.

With the memory of Argentina and New York on Labor Day stored in my mind, I accepted the obligations of Deputy Foreign Affairs Spokesman with deep apprehension and set off on my first official visit with no expectation of anything except blood, sweat, tears and embarrassment. It was to the Middle East. There were one or two glorious moments. In those days, Beirut was a beautiful green and white French colonial city. Its tourist beach, although made famous in 1959 by the American marines who had carefully picked their way ashore between the sun-bathers, was totally unblemished by the visible scars of war. The Palestine refugee camp – fetid and overcrowded – was well out of sight of the casual visitor. Before I moved on to Cairo and Amman (where King Hussein's tanks were driving the PLO out of the city by the simple technique of shelling one of the suburbs) I visited Walid Jumblatt, the leader of the Druze, in his mountain fortress. There I re-enacted one of the old black and white pre-war comedies, with me playing the part of the bewildered Englishman abroad. Jumblatt – in kaftan and keffiyeh – emerged from under one of the mosaic-covered arches and approached me across the fountain-filled courtyard. His bodyguard carried a huge machine gun and a servant, one pace behind, held a huge brass coffee-pot and two tiny china cups. Not sure how to greet a prince of the East, I gave a little bow. 'Before I forget,' said the chief of the Druze, 'do give my regards to Dick Crossman when you get back home. But I'm afraid that he hasn't improved the *New Statesman*. It isn't the magazine it was when I was at Oxford.' Next day I went to Baalbek and saw what is left of the Temple of the Sun – the most spectacular of all the Middle East's antiquities, not excluding

either Petra or the Pyramids. Twenty miles from the river, what is
left of the great Corinthian columns stared out against the desert
skyline. And – back in 1970 – the temple itself still looked like the
Victorian painting which hangs in the Garrick Club. Descendants
of Phoenician traders hid in the shadow of the crumbling walls
offering astrakhan coats and blankets to travellers on their way to
Damascus. Thanks to my experience with Jumblatt, I expected
them to ask me if the Portobello Road had changed much with
the years.

I flew from Amman to Libya, where a meeting with Colonel
Gaddafi was to be the highlight of my whole Middle East tour. In
those days, Gaddafi was regarded as quaint rather than wicked.
He had deposed our friend and ally King Idris. Indeed, he had
done it in a way which had caused me intense personal embarrassment. During my last few months in the Ministry of Defence,
I had signed an angry minute to the Treasury just before I left for
lunch one day. It expressed my impatience at the time it was
taking to obtain approval for a million-pound improvement programme to our base at Tripoli. On the way back to my office I read
in the *Evening Standard* that Gaddafi had expropriated it. But
despite the occasional blemish on his character, he was not, in
most observers' estimation, the monster which he subsequently
became. He was a loony in a black tent, and I looked forward
immensely to meeting him. When I landed in Libya I was handed
a message from the Opposition Chief Whip. I was to return to
London on the next flight.

The House of Commons was debating what came to be called
'Tory Trade Union Laws'. *In Place of Strife* had been forgotten by
the party which had initially supported it, the trade unions which
had so bitterly opposed it and especially by Barbara Castle who
had once regarded it as essential to industrial peace and economic
progress. Barbara, indeed, was leading the fight against the 'penal'
measures which were designed to deny the right of working men
and women to free association. Reinforced by the spirit of the

Tolpuddle Martyrs and the memory of the Combination Acts, she was determined to 'keep the law' out of collective agreements.

There was, of course, no real hope of Labour defeating the government. But in those innocent days – long before Margaret Thatcher had declared real war on the unions – Ted Heath was regarded as the arch reactionary and all the forces of progress had to join together in a show of righteous solidarity. The forces of progress included me. So I was required to abandon my visit to Libya at once and return to London and the debate on the industrial relations bill. A combination of ambition and cowardice made me book a flight on the next plane home. My only consolation was that, because my mother was away at a local authority conference, my father was staying in my house in London. I would spend an extra couple of days with him.

I drove straight from Heathrow to the House of Commons in plenty of time for what I assumed – having been in Araby for more than a week – would be a ten o'clock vote. I was quite wrong. The government had guillotined the bill – that is to say, put a time limit on the discussion. But although the debate was finished, there was no way of preventing the Opposition from voting on the innumerable amendments which had been passed over simply because time had run out. Voting had begun that afternoon at four o'clock. By six o'clock, when I arrived at the Commons, the House had divided seven times. There were still about forty divisions to go and, as each one took about fifteen minutes, it was likely that we would all be walking in and out of the division lobbies until breakfast time on the following day. I stuck it out until about ten. Then, because of a combination of frustration at being brought back to London, impatience with the futility at the whole exercise and jet lag, I went home to bed.

As I walked through Parliament Square, a polite young man asked me why I was not taking part in the Great Protest. I told him, 'Just because the Shadow Cabinet are making bloody fools of themselves, there is no reason why I should do the same.' The polite young man was a recent recruit to *The Times*' parliamentary staff.

My comment on the conduct of my elders and betters appeared on the front page of the first edition. I do not know how William Rees-Mogg – editor of the paper in those days – discovered that my opinion had been obtained by a journalist who had not identified himself. But when he found out he was horrified. In that more gentle age, even when the rules were broken by mistake, *The Times* made amends. The story was taken out of the paper's second edition and Rees-Mogg – who then lived round the corner from me – came to my front door with the offending article and his apologies.

It was well after midnight when he rang the bell and I came slowly downstairs expecting a message from the whips, demanding my return to Parliament. My father – who was asleep in the basement bedroom – took longer to regain consciousness and the door had slammed shut before he had made his anxious way into the hall. He was, I knew, a worrier. So I said, at once, 'Nothing to worry about, Dad. Just the editor of *The Times*. He's brought me a copy of tomorrow's paper.' My father's expression changed from anxiety to awe. 'Does he do that every night?' he asked.

The attenuated tour of the Middle East was my one official foreign visit. But in the second year of my reluctant responsibility for foreign affairs, I crossed the Atlantic ten times. On each flight, I felt more guilty than I had on the previous trip. Westbound, I always knew that I should not be leaving England. Eastward Ho, I was equally certain that I should be staying in the USA.

It was all Roy Jenkins' fault. He had introduced me to Richard Neustadt, Professor of Government at Harvard, adviser to a succession of Presidents and director of the recently created Kennedy

Institute of Politics. One thing led to another. For I became something called an *ad hoc* visitor. Then Adam Yarmolinsky – Assistant Secretary of Defense in the Kennedy Administration – telephoned to offer me a Visiting Fellowship, an honour which was only slightly tarnished by the subsequent discovery that Robert Maxwell had been the previous year's incumbent. Officials of the Institute – who were happy to boast that Eric Roll and Keith Kyle were former Fellows – always insisted that Maxwell had called in Cambridge, Massachusetts during a business trip to America and declared himself associated with the Institute of Politics without the Faculty's authority and that it had then seemed rude to issue a press statement which denied all knowledge of him. I never found the explanation convincing. For the Institute was made up of men who prided themselves on their intellectual and moral rigour. They were, for example, totally unwilling to consider the possibility that appointing a sitting Member of Parliament as a Visiting Fellow could only lead to disaster. But it did.

After two or three months – in which I tried to fit in appearances at Harvard around the Easter, Whitsuntide and summer recesses – I began to suspect that my constant requests for airfares home to crucial votes and essential constituency engagements was making my Fellowship non-viable, speaking moneywise. I tore up the notes I had made on Boston as a contribution to my seminal work on Big City Politics, and locked, for the last time, my set of rooms at Winthrop House. But, before I left, I went for a day's campaigning with Senator Edmund Sextus Muskie as he pursued the Democratic Presidential nomination in the New Hampshire Primary.

Muskie was famous for his lack of tact and excess of temper. When I joined him at a senior citizens' condominium, he was exhibiting the characteristics which were to drive him out of a presidential campaign which he might have won. The elderly resident who had been chosen to greet him was an exile from the Senator's home state of Maine. After the gushing octogenarian had curtsied and presented him with a pair of hand-knitted bed socks, Muskie gave a speech of thanks which mentioned – almost in passing – that anyone who lived in Maine was called a Mainian, whilst anyone who chose to leave was a maniac. The elderly lady took immense exception to the allegation of mental disorder and cried, 'Shame on you, Senator.' Muskie asked her if she could still recognise a joke when she heard one. The 'still' was assumed by everyone present to be a cruel comment on the old dear's age. As the candidate's minders ushered us out of the building, Muskie asked me if it was true that in England there was one, month-long, general election campaign every four or five years. I answered, 'More or less.' He asked me, 'What the hell does that mean?' before he explained that he was under stress because he had been campaigning continuously for seven years – Senate, House, Gubernatorial, Primary and Presidential. 'It's beginning to get to me,' he confessed. I thought it wisest not to tell him that I had already guessed.

Next day in New Winchester (in New Hampshire everything is called New something), I joined Muskie at the working breakfast with which he began each day. His press secretary described the political complexion of the local newspapers – a task never performed in Britain, because they are all known to be Conservative – and his diary secretary set out the twelve-hour schedule. It began with a visit to the local high school.

Muskie leaned – confidently and confidentially – towards me. 'Tell you what will happen. As soon as I've finished my address, a young Black kid will come forward and ask, very politely, why I told the Conference of Democratic Mayors and Governors that it was too early for an Afro-American to run for President. It happens every time. They hope that I'm going to fly into a rage.' I felt reluctant to interrupt him. So I waited until he had finished his denunciation of the Republicans, their slimy tactics and particularly rich Black kids who were prepared to act as racists' stooges. Then I asked him, 'How will you deal with this question?' 'Easy,' said Muskie – rather aggressively, I thought, in the circumstances – 'I shall simply explain that it isn't true. I shan't accuse the kid of anything. Just say he was mistaken. I actually said that I wanted the day to come when an Afro-American could become President.' Thus, psychologically prepared, the Senator joined his cavalcade and we all swept off to the high school.

The students – who rose with military precision when Ed Muskie walked in – were universally clean and tidy. The girls all seemed to have modelled themselves on Pat Nixon and one young lady, groomed and poised far beyond her years, presented Mrs Muskie with a huge bouquet of flowers. It was carefully wrapped in cellophane and I remember thinking that the virgin goddess who carried it had probably been kept in the same pristine condition until a few minutes before the ceremony began. Muskie gave a lucid and informative speech on foreign affairs. The principal called for questions, and a young immaculate Black youth put up a courteous hand. He was handed the microphone. 'Would the Senator please explain why, at the Conference of Democratic Mayors and Senators, he said that the time has not yet come for a member of my race to be President of the United States?' I waited for the carefully prepared response.

Admittedly, I was at the very back of the high school hall and my view was partially obscured by the press photographers. But from where I was sitting, it looked as though Muskie was about to leap from the platform and strike his accuser. His long grey face swelled red with rage. For a few seconds he had to fight to make the words come out. Then he engulfed his questioner in a torrent of fury. He called the guilty man a liar, asked how much he had been paid to ask the question and described him as a disgrace to his community and family. Reporters rushed out to telephone their stories and a couple of men in Brooks Brothers' suits – standing anonymously at the back of the meeting – smiled at each other in quiet satisfaction.

I did not go on with Muskie to New Manchester. So I missed the moment of history when, next day, he announced his retirement from the presidential race. The *New Manchester Leader* had claimed that Mrs Muskie was a drunk and that her conduct on the campaign bus embarrassed journalists and confirmed the diagnosis. In response to that allegation the Senator had wept with rage and shame. In those days politicians were supposed only to cry on advice from their public relations consultants. Muskie was finished.

Back in Britain – a self-proclaimed expert on the politics of the United States – I appeared as one of the principal speakers on a television debate in which Westminster politicians advanced the claims of the presidential candidates to an audience of expatriate Americans. It was a convoluted broadcasting format which was typical of programme planning in the seventies. My opponent was Julian Critchley, who ended his spirited support of the Republican nominee with a phrase which, whilst undeniably memorable, he will almost certainly have chosen to forget: 'There is still honour to be found amongst the American people, and that is why they will vote for Richard Milhous Nixon.'

For the next two years, the focus of the foreign affairs debate shifted from America to Europe – though the discussion was enlivened by politicians who seemed genuinely to believe that Britain should remain an Atlantic rather than a Continental power. I was part of that Labour Party generation which felt a cultural – if not an ideological – affinity with the United States. We were the children of the war, Hollywood movies and current affairs lessons about Roosevelt's New Deal. We felt at home in America. And the election of John F. Kennedy – which we believed to be the victory for youth and reason – removed whatever guilt we felt about our enthusiasm for the home of capitalism and free enterprise. But at least I never thought that I might have to choose between Europe and the New World. I was an enthusiast for the Common Market from the Treaty of Messina onward. By the time that the Six signed the Treaty of Rome, I felt a veteran campaigner for the idea that the British government so foolishly rejected.

Whether we admit it or not, politicians are usually (and rightly) influenced as much by emotion as reason. And I confess to liking Italy and France. That feeling for Italy was enormously increased by three summers in the early seventies that we spent at Aulla – an unprepossessing railway town east of La Spezia. Above the town was a *fortezza* which belonged to the Waterfields – descendants of Victorian explorers, Edwardian painters and British agents who had hidden in the Tuscan hills throughout the war. The Waterfields liked helping lame dogs and good causes. During the 1920s they had more or less kept D.H. Lawrence in one of their other castles. By 1970, however, they had run out of real talent in need of their patronage, so the castle at Aulla was made available – at incredibly low cost – to the likes of me. I sat on the roof garden in the sun, watched the birds which flew a hundred feet below, looked at the hill towns on the horizon, drank, read and wrote. Heaven will be very like the *fortezza* at Aulla.

I now think of the last of those Italian summer holidays not as the end of political innocence but as its last flowering. On our way to Aulla we stayed with Bill Rodgers – where Roy Jenkins called in for a couple of days. Shirley Williams and Brian Walden both stayed at the castle and Tony Crosland came for a day and (after going through a ritual pantomime about the size of his room and the quality of his food) remained for a week. Although we were out of office, we all believed that Labour's idea was too strong to be rejected forever. And if anyone had predicted that, within a decade, Williams, Rodgers and Jenkins would be in a new political party and Walden would be helping Margaret Thatcher with her election broadcasts, we would have assumed that they were making a silly joke.

In the summer of 1972, we picnicked together in what we believed to be a deserted wood. After lunch – no doubt inspired by the wine – we started to sing first 'Banda Rossa', then 'The Internationale' and 'The Red Flag' and finally 'Jerusalem'. We were just pledging not to cease from mental fight when a tractor drove past. The driver – and his wife and children in the trailer – all looked frightened as well as astonished. 'They think we're a fanatical foreign sect,' said Walden. 'We are,' Tony Crosland told him.

The sect was strangely chauvinistic. So it was not just the desire to oppose which turned the Labour Party against the Common Market when Ted Heath succeeded where Harold Wilson had failed and – with General de Gaulle safely back in Colombé les Deux Eglises – negotiated British membership of what the mindless left called 'a rich man's club'. I cannot remember when I decided that I could not vote against the Bill which ratified the Treaty. But I do recall the relief with which I discovered that a very large number of Labour MPs felt exactly the same. Few of the dissidents were natural rebels and most of them hoped to be ministers in a future Labour government. I was impelled towards revolt by pride as well as principle – two compulsions which, in politics, are often closely related. I kept remembering a Saturday in Morecambe during the spring of 1969.

Harold Wilson had made me speak to the Young Socialists' Morecambe Annual Conference. Peter Shore – then Secretary of State for Economic Affairs – had addressed an anti-Common Market meeting on the Thursday and the Prime Minister had decided that the balance had to be redressed. If another Cabinet minister had delivered the rebuke, newspapers would have written that the government was split. But, in the byzantine Wilson mind it seemed that an assault by a mere parliamentary secretary could be presented to the press as either a majestic reassertion of the truth or a disloyal aberration – depending upon which interpretation seemed most desirable after the speech was made. The only suitable weekend engagement for me to attend was at the end of the pier in Morecambe. My audience was fifty Young Socialists from Lancashire.

Thanks to the support of the Downing Street press office, reports of my speech appeared on the front page of most Sunday newspapers. I was particularly pleased with a full-page comparison between Shore's views and mine which appeared in the *Economist*. It was Harold Wilson who had made me come out of the Common Market closet in 1969 and I would not believe that he would expect me to climb back in and close the door three years later. I could not imagine what I would have said to my European-inclined friends who asked me why I had changed my mind. I have always thought of conscience as someone I admire and respect standing at the back of a meeting and asking me, after I have made a particularly craven or corrupt speech, 'How can you possibly believe that?' I was not going to vote against Europe and I hoped that Harold Wilson had enough sense to accept my decision with good grace.

As the day of the great debate drew near, the most enthusiastic Common Marketeers met with increasing frequency and mounting apprehension. Roy Jenkins (who had succeeded George Brown as deputy Labour leader) naturally took command and presided over endless discussions about the possibility of a 'free vote' – in which Labour MPs would vote according to choice rather than on the instruction of the whips – and how we should react if the Shadow Cabinet decided on rigid discipline. Most of the meetings were no more than the search for safety in numbers. For although we huddled together for warmth, the more we discussed our tactics, the more apprehensive we felt. Two days before the vote John Harris insisted that, despite my 'flu, I must attend the final caucus meeting. David Owen, he said, was going to propose that we all abstained rather than 'voted in the Tory lobby'. I coughed my way across to the House where the need for a positive vote was unanimously agreed – with the enthusiastic backing of David Owen.

Sixty-nine of us voted with the government – or, as we would have put it, for entry into the Common Market. Europe won a glorious victory. But none of the glory warmed my heart. I hated breaking ranks with the Labour Party. As I left the House of Commons to take part in one of those historic broadcasts which always turn out to be an anti-climax, I was accosted by a beautiful girl who had worked with me at the European Movement. Normally, she had only to smile in my direction to make me feel faint. That night, she attempted to give me a triumphant embrace. Nothing can better illustrate my mood than my reaction. I told her to go and rejoice somewhere else. I had no doubt that I had been right to vote for Europe. But I felt all the joy of a police informer who had turned Queen's Evidence against his own family.

The plan – collectively agreed by all the rebels who attended the weekly agonies – was to support Europe on the first, and most important, of the votes and then gracefully submit to the will of the whips during the days and nights of detailed debate which followed. I wrote an article for the *Guardian* which was supposed to set out our collective view. It included a sentence which, most of us agreed, represented the need to balance conviction and loyalty. 'Standing on principle is one thing. Remaining rooted to the spot is quite another.' I was extremely proud of the way in which I had made clear that, from then on, we would all follow the Party line. The agreement lasted for a week.

Roy Jenkins accepted the need to end hostilities. And he realised that if peace was to break out within the Party he would have to make a gesture in the general direction of unity. His statement, constructed with immense care and read out rather hesitantly to the weekly meeting of Labour MPs, managed to be conciliatory without sounding penitent:

I make absolutely no apology for my vote last Thursday . . . I draw a distinction, as I said on Friday, between that vote and a subsequent series of votes. That is not, let me say it myself, a particularly logical position. But I have to try to balance two commitments, both to keep alive the European cause in the Labour Party and to build up the strength of the Labour Party which I believe the country needs . . .

Roy always had an acute sense of history – particularly his own. In his room, when the Party meeting was over and stability apparently restored, he saw me eyeing the hand-written text from which he had read his statement. He asked me if I would like to keep it. I accepted it with gratitude and have it still.

When the plan to follow the Labour whip after the first vote broke down, I was to blame for some of the confusion. I was willing, if reluctant, to vote for every amendment that the Labour Party composed – absurd though some of them were. But I was not prepared to follow Enoch Powell into the lobbies. When I complained, at a meeting of the Parliamentary Labour Party, that we were accepting the leadership of the man who saw the Tiber foaming with my constituents' blood, Michael Foot told me that Powell was a great parliamentarian, democrat and Englishman. Foot's speech did nothing to reconcile me to the idea of making common cause with the politician who had made racism seem respectable. But my qualms were nothing to the crisis of conscience through which Roy Jenkins was battling his way. I was witness to the painful scene in his room when he told Douglas Houghton – the chairman of the Parliamentary Labour Party – that he had forsworn his long-held beliefs for the last time. Jenkins' response to the suggestion that he would have to grit his teeth for a couple more weeks was so uncharacteristically violent that anyone who witnessed it could only conclude that the end was near. In my embarrassment, I walked to the far end of the room and, consumed with neurosis, scratched with my fingernails at one of the bookcases until the veneer was worn away. When, ten years later, I became the tenant of the deputy leader's room, I looked – as soon as I moved in – to see if the marks of my anxiety were still there. They were. I thought of them as a permanent memorial to the disintegration of the Labour Party.

On the weekend which followed Roy Jenkins' *cri de coeur*, there was a party at which all of Labour's pro-Europeans seemed to be guests. There was nothing surprising in that, for we were all friends. But I, at least, was startled to discover that George Thomson – who had been the Common Market negotiator during the dying days of the Wilson government – anticipated becoming Britain's second commissioner in Brussels. Half the MPs there said that if Roy Jenkins resigned, they would resign from the front bench with him. That night I knew that the Labour Party was about to fall apart.

For most of the next week, many of Roy Jenkins' most devoted admirers – amongst whom I certainly numbered – did their best to persuade him to remain deputy leader. After a couple of days, I decided that, whatever we said, he would resign when debate on the European Communities Bill was resumed the following Monday afternoon. But early on the Saturday morning, David Owen called unexpectedly at my house and asked me to drive with him to Oxfordshire in a last attempt to change Roy's mind. I declined with thanks.

I had begun to grow ideologically impatient with Roy Jenkins. I agreed, in virtually every detail, with his position on the Common Market and I sympathised with his growing reluctance to vote against his conscience. It was his views on domestic policy which had begun to worry me. Although I did not know it at the time, the drift to the political centre had begun. The new mood was most dramatically illustrated by an argument we had about a book of essays which was being prepared to set out Roy's philosophical stand, called *What Matters Now*. I believed that comprehensive education – freed from the disability of a competing selection system – mattered a great deal more than he was prepared to allow. Our disagreement ended with a sterile dispute about the rival merits of 'more equality' and 'less inequality'. Sterile arguments are normally expressions of deeply held feelings which are too painful to express openly. Roy and I were drifting apart and I, at least, found the parting painful.

It was not, however, general disillusion that stopped me driving to Oxfordshire with Owen. I had become tired of persuasion and I knew that the time for persuasion had passed. The sooner the catastrophe was over, the sooner we could all rest in peace. That too was a misjudgement.

Owen telephoned me early on Saturday evening with the news that his mission had failed. Jennifer Jenkins called about an hour later, and asked me if I would find John Harris – who was touring America as a Harkness Fellow – and ask him to come home at once and help to manage the deluge of press and television coverage which they expected to follow the announcement. I agreed, with all the enthusiasm of a man who has become the reluctant partner to a suicide.

Purely by chance, I met Roy Jenkins in the Members' Lobby on Monday morning as he was making his way to the Whips' Office to deliver his resignation. He was carrying the letter and, incongruously, he reminded me of a child on his way to the corner shop with his mother's grocery list in his hand.

That was not the day on which the Social Democrats were born. It was not even the morning when they were conceived. But it was the moment when the old Labour coalition began to collapse. I did not realise it at the time, but once the envelope landed on the Chief Whip's desk, the creation of a new Centre Party was inevitable. I do not think Roy Jenkins realised that he was acting as a catalyst to a cataclysm. And no doubt he anticipated that there would be a reconciliation before the election – as indeed there was. But our meeting in the Members' Lobby remains in my memory as the turning point in Labour's history. After that day, the Labour Party was never the same again.

CHAPTER
6

Roy Jenkins resigned the deputy leadership of the Labour Party on the morning of 10th April 1972. Before the end of the day, two other members of the Shadow Cabinet – George Thomson and Harold Lever – joined him on the back benches. Shirley Williams did not. Two junior spokesmen – Bill Rodgers at Defence and David Owen at Health – went with Roy, Owen after announcing his decision in some style from the Opposition despatch box. Denis Howell – the once and future Sports Minister – and I decided, after the briefest of discussions, that we would stay at our posts.

For me, the decision was not difficult to make. I had argued publicly and privately against resignation and I felt no obligation to make the mistake which I had urged others to avoid. Next morning, Harold Wilson sent for me. 'Are you going or staying?' he asked as if he had been worrying all day about my intentions. When I told him what I had decided, he spoke for some time about how much he admired David Owen, but the meeting turned into a triumphal demonstration that he knew every detail about the last-minute attempts to persuade Roy Jenkins to change his mind. Did I know that, when Owen arrived at Jenkins'

Oxfordshire house, he had found the deputy leader taking advice from his closest friends – none of whom was a member of the Labour Party? Harold took great pleasure in naming them, one by one. He then asked me to become the Party's principal Defence Spokesman – the job left vacant by George Thomson's resignation. It was promotion of sorts.

I cannot pretend that I was not excited by the idea of having my own 'shadow department'. Opening defence debates in the House of Commons was part of the attraction. I had begun to despise the flummery of Parliament – the formal courtesies, the contrived jokes, the arcane rules and, above all, the bogus arguments that always ended with a vote which was preordained. What I really wanted was to get my hands on policy. But I had my doubts about accepting Harold's offer. My concern was not whether it would be wrong to take George Thomson's place, but whether it would be popular. Harold, who read my mind, told me that 'they would get over it in a couple of weeks'.

It was immensely flattering to be courted by the Party Leader and vanity was reinforced by logic. There was, Harold argued, no sense in staying on the front bench but refusing to change jobs. What was more, it was important for someone to demonstrate that pro-Europeans still had faith (and a future) in the Party. I have always been susceptible to demands that I come to the aid of the Party. But Harold also knew that I had never been susceptible to him. He suggested that I took a couple of hours to think over his offer and also (very reasonably, I thought at the time) that if it would help he would have no objection to my writing him 'a letter that makes clear that you haven't changed your opinions on the Common Market. And you can publish it.'

I spent the rest of the afternoon running about the House of Commons in search of advice. Jim Callaghan seemed surprised by my question. Of course I must accept. It was my duty to the Party. Denis Healey and Tony Crosland said much the same. George

Thomson said that he would rather the job go to a pro-European than to an anti – not a passionate endorsement, but not total rejection of the idea. Somehow, the news of my indecision became more or less public. Virtually unknown back-benchers asked me what I intended and told me what I should do. At four o'clock I told Harold Wilson that I accepted. Then I raced to my office in order to compose the letter that would tell the world how I had 'balanced two commitments, both to keep alive the European cause in the Labour Party and to build up the Labour Party's strength'. I was so anxious to complete the letter and pin it up on the press gallery notice board that I drafted each paragraph on a separate sheet of paper so that the beginning could be typed whilst the end was still being written in my barely intelligible longhand. I was afraid that Harold – or, more likely, one of his satraps – would brief the political correspondents before I had the chance to make my position clear. I did not know whether the briefing would be 'Hattersley deserts Europe' or 'Hattersley turns his back on old friends'. But I took it for granted that he would cheat if I gave him the chance.

Reading the letter at leisure – more than twenty years after it was written in great haste – I feel only embarrassment at the way in which pomposity and effrontery were combined:

> You asked me earlier today if I intended to resign from the Opposition Front Bench . . . You then invited me to become the Party's Defence Spokesman . . . when I eventually accepted that invitation . . . reluctant to assume responsibilities which in normal circumstances . . .

It was bad enough to write '*eventually* accepted'. But worse was to come:

> Of course I accept your assurance that your objections to Community membership at this time are based on your

genuine dissatisfaction with the current terms . . . I must tell
you, however, that I grow increasingly concerned . . .'

I did not mean to patronise the ex-Prime Minister or to reassure
him that I did not think he had lied to me. But it is not surprising
that Harold resented the letter – even though the idea of writing it
had been his.

The parliamentary press gallery hunts in a pack. And at first I was
a hero. At the Television Centre that night, Julian Amery, the
Minister of Housing, stayed behind after his broadcast was finished
to tell me that his father, my predecessor but two in Sparkbrook,
would have been proud of what I had done. But the next day, the
wolves smelt a different sort of blood. The intention of my letter had
been to combine a magisterial statement of continued commitment
to European union with a demonstration of fidelity to the Labour
Party. In almost every newspaper, however, all I became was the
man who had 'cheeked' Harold Wilson. I was the upstart who had
tried to divert attention from his treachery by insulting his leader,
the traitor who had abandoned Europe and the ingrate who had
deserted Roy Jenkins, the architect of his undeserved success.

Roy Jenkins himself told me that 'the important thing' was not
to allow what had happened to cause a permanent breach between old friends. Then he invited me to dinner. His hopes that a
permanent breach could be averted was not, however, fulfilled.
For the next few days, the papers were filled with unattributed
abuse. On the Saturday evening David Owen – anticipating
another blast against me in the Sunday papers – invited us to
lunch. I recall walking along the Thames Embankment, with a
young Owen in a pushchair, listening to David tell me that he
thought my judgement was wrong but my conduct respectable.
During the later seventies, when we all took it in turns to be
infuriated by the Foreign Secretary, I often remembered that
walk and forgave him whatever offence he had committed that
week.

It was during the difficult early days of my erstwhile friends' antagonism that I began to recognise, though not to understand, the Shirley Williams phenomenon. Shirley – as passionate a pro-European as I – had actually talked about resigning from the front bench and then, rightly and wisely in my opinion, decided against it. Certainly, she had stayed in her old job rather than moving to something which was technically senior, but she had not made the gesture of principle for which the Common Marketeers called. There was, however, not a word of complaint about her conduct. For the first time, I realised that Shirley is surrounded by a beatific light that shields her from the harm and criticism which would be heaped on ordinary people. It is an enviable attribute. If I were offered three benefits to bestow on my godchildren, they would be native intelligence, a metabolism that did not produce surplus fat and Shirley Williams' capacity to be loved and admired whether she deserves it or not.

Not being blessed with such a characteristic, I endured a hard couple of weeks. One day, after a newspaper had reported that a tea room wit had called me 'Rattersley', I had to force myself into the House for a ten o'clock vote. Halfway up the steps inside St Stephen's entrance, I met Sir Geoffrey de Freitas (then Member for Kettering) and his secretary, Betty Boothroyd. Knowing them to be enthusiastic pro-Marketeers, I nodded and hurried on. But Betty – still looking for a constituency to send her to Parliament and not even dreaming of becoming the first woman Speaker – called after me. I stopped and waited for the blow to fall. I had, she said, done right to stand by the Party. After much nudging and meaningful looks, Sir Geoffrey reluctantly agreed. I went into the Division Lobby with my confidence improved, if not restored.

Not everyone was so generous. Over a year later, during the autumn of 1973, I was the subject of a *New Statesman* profile. Its title, 'The Climber', does not accurately reflect its tone. It was considerably more unpleasant than those two words suggest. Far worse attacks have been made on my character and conduct during the twenty-odd years since that article was published, but none has caused me so much pain or remained such a cause of abiding resentment. Although anonymous, I knew at once that it was written by my old friend Chris Price. Nobody else knew how I had hated digging the back garden of my Sheffield house – or could have claimed that I put on my braces when I hoped that the local paper would call round to photograph my labours. In fairness to Price, it must be said he had no way of knowing how much trauma his work would cause. It had been advertised in the previous week's *New Statesman* and – guided by no more than the mindless optimism that has caused me so much trouble down the years – I believed that it would say what a fine chap I was. So I talked to my father about it as part of my campaign to distract him from the operation which he was to undergo on the day of publication. The operation confirmed that his condition was terminal, and the profile contained a slighting reference to his lowly rank in the civil service. It is wrong to blame Price for the problems of deflecting my father's attention from what had been written about me and him – wrong but, in my case, irresistible.

I should have felt almost as angry about the part played in publication by Tony Howard, the *New Statesman*'s editor. But I could never work up the same resentment of his conduct – even before he earned my eternal gratitude by launching the second stage of my career as a journalist. And Tony, being the man he is, did not let my reputation stand or fall by one week's article. His behaviour towards me, whilst chairing a Tyne-Tees Television programme called *Meet the Press*, so offended the monks of a northern monastery that they wrote to me with the reassuring news that they were reporting Howard to the Independent Broadcasting Authority. I could not say that my friendship with Howard survived these vicissitudes, for it has only grown stronger since they occurred. About ten years ago we even gave up making jokes about the two controversial incidents.

It is still not easy to look back on the year of Roy Jenkins' resignation with anything except pain. Most of my unhappy memories are personal rather than political. For months, I was accused of all sorts of crimes by people who had been my friends. Principal amongst my alleged faults was ambition. But the sin of which I was undoubtedly guilty was not even mentioned. I grotesquely over-estimated my importance to the Labour Party. My promotion to the post of Defence Spokesman was an event of absolutely no significance. Had I declined the appointment – indeed, if I had resigned from the front bench altogether, applied to the Chiltern Hundreds or announced my conversion to Zen Buddhism – not a decimal place would have changed in the opinion polls. I learned my lesson. When, almost a quarter of a century later, I announced my intention to retire from Parliament at the end of the session, a couple of commentators suggested that I might be missed. I remembered how I felt when offered promotion back in 1972 and gave them a heartfelt, and wholly accurate, reply. 'The Labour Party will get along without me very well.' There is no point in being sixty if you remain as arrogant as you were when you were thirty-five.

My year as Defence Spokesman was entirely uneventful. I spoke in a couple of debates, visited the Army School of Artillery at Larkhill and attempted – unsuccessfully – to influence policy. When the army's role in Northern Ireland was debated, Jim Callaghan, the Shadow Home Secretary, insisted on speaking.

Then, for no reason that I have been able to work out, Harold Wilson sent for me again. Ted Short, who had succeeded Roy Jenkins as deputy leader of the Labour Party, wished to give up the job of Shadow Education Secretary. It was mine if I chose to take it. It was like a dream come true – or at least like a shadow dream come true. The job I had always wanted – and went on wanting until my political career came to its appointed end – was Education. It is Education, more than any other Department of

State, that offers a socialist politician the prospect of changing the nature of society. The campaign for equality begins, or ought to begin, in schools – offering the children of the dispossessed a chance to escape from this year's deprivation and providing the hope that one day, by constantly devoting attention and resources to the least advantageous section of the community, deprivation will be eliminated altogether. The prospect of becoming Secretary of State for Education was the most exciting experience of my political life. Harold Wilson warned me that I should make no assumption about what would happen when Labour was back in government. But I was not depressed by that. I would acquit myself as Shadow with such transcendental brilliance that, when the election was over and Harold was back in Downing Street, he would not be able to deny my destiny.

I became Shadow Secretary of State for Education at two o'clock on a Thursday afternoon. At half past six that evening, I received a note from the Chief Whip. It told me that I was to lead for the Opposition in the Great Education Debate of the century. Great Education Debates of the Century are held about once every two years. The one into which I was precipitated was scheduled to take place two working days after I was warned that it was about to happen. Cometh the moment, I thought, cometh the Shadow Minister.

A week of so before my elevation, the government had published a White Paper, by name, *Education – A Framework for Expansion*. It claimed to set out plans for a massive long-term investment in nursery classes, schools, colleges and universities. I had a working knowledge of its contents – the sort of thing that any interested layman would learn from reading the more serious newspapers. But I was nothing like ready to make a forty-minute speech which analysed the government's proposal and set out, where necessary, Labour's alternative. I turned to friends for help – particularly Maurice Peston, Professor of Economics at Queen Mary College, London and an expert on public finance.

Maurice Peston told me, without a moment's hesitation, that the whole White Paper was a fraud. There would be, in real terms, no extra investment in education and the confidence trick could be exposed by anyone who knew enough to pass the statistics paper in Part I of the BSc (Econ) degree. I had failed Part I statistics. So, for the next two hours, Professor Peston tried to remedy my ignorance. When it became clear that there was not enough time for me to complete the two-year course, he made an alternative suggestion. He would draft a closely reasoned passage for my speech which would expose the fraud beyond dispute. I would then read it out with something approaching confidence and conviction. As I had not learned the folly of making speeches which you do not understand, I agreed.

The Secretary of State opened the debate with an uninhibited account of the personal triumph which had made the White Paper possible. The House was thrilled with accounts of battles with the Treasury which had been fought and won. Members were then enthralled by accounts of the golden future which the improvements in the education system made not possible, but certain. Britain was to become the most numerate and literate – and therefore the most prosperous – country in the world. Tories cheered – despite their traditional opposition to public spending and a long-standing suspicion of education. Behind me, my Honourable Friends sat glum and silent. It seemed to them that there was nothing for me to say. Some were glad that a nonentity was to be sacrificed. Others regretted that a more experienced David was not to do battle with the undoubted Goliath. Sensing that nothing – or even less – was expected of me, I stood as erect as I could behind the despatch box and read out the piece of paper which claimed that the Secretary of State's speech was at best an exaggeration or, at worst, downright lies. I rattled through the statistical justification for my extraordinary allegation and sat down. For several moments the House was absolutely silent with astonishment. Then the feeble cheer from behind me was drowned by the wave of rage that hit me in the face like the noise coming out from under a football stand when the home team has a goal disallowed.

One by one, they all – including the Secretary of State – accused me of malice, ignorance and jealousy. Winding up the debate, Norman St John Stevas was particularly offensive. Throughout the afternoon and evening, Peston – who sat, smiling infuriatingly, in the under gallery – had kept mouthing advice and sending brief written messages. All he had said and written, time after time, was, 'Say it again. We are right and they are wrong.' I did not believe him. Neither did the next day's papers. So I telephoned and asked him what he thought we should do. His advice was instant and unequivocal. 'Say it again. They are wrong and we are right.'

I was still not convinced. Indeed I was sure that he was wrong. But I accepted his advice on the principle that when outnumbered and surrounded, the best strategy is to attack. So I repeated my allegations whenever I could – articles in whichever newspapers would take them, speeches to anyone who would listen and broadcasts on any channel or wavelength which could be persuaded to transmit my views. When the education weeklies were published, they all expressed surprise that I persisted in my folly. The kindest comment came from the *Times Educational Supplement*, which merely concluded its leader with the suggestion that by questioning – indeed challenging – the government's figures, I had 'miscued'. Maurice Peston telephoned me early on the Friday morning to say that they were all wrong and we were right. I still did not believe him.

After another week of trying to sound confident, Stewart McClure – the doyen of education correspondents and editor of the *TES* – wrote to me. I had advanced my case with such persistent passion that he had become fascinated by the psychology of failure. Why did I continue to compound my error by repeating it so often? I replied by telling him that I was right and everybody else was wrong. It may have been pity which made him offer to put me out of my misery. But, whatever his reason, he suggested that he ended the protracted, if one-sided, dispute by obtaining an authoritative judgement from the one man in the whole world who understood public accounting – Professor Maurice Peston, head of the Department of Economics in Queen Mary College, London.

On the following Friday, Stewart McClure ended his editorial with a handsome apology: '. . . having accused Roy Hattersley of miscuing, we must now concede that he potted black'. I knew nothing about snooker – for those were the days before it was regularly featured on television and my youth had been mis-spent in Labour Party committee rooms. But I knew that I had won the match. And, as I anticipated, all the education correspondents of the serious national dailies followed Stuart McClure's lead. Most of them somehow failed to mention that the Secretary of State's error had first been publicly identified by me. But that, I felt, was no more than natural justice. For even after reading the newspapers' explanation of her deliberate mistake, I still understood neither the reasoning nor the statistics on which it was based. But I had won. A blow had been struck for the Labour Party, and the educational establishment – which, then as now, was numerous and influential – would know that I had held the dagger, even though Maurice Peston had sharpened the blade.

I returned to the battle with a letter to the Secretary of State demanding correction, retraction and apology. I did not receive a reply. The minister who believed so devoutly in high levels of public spending, claimed to have increased investment in education, but published figures which proved that claim to be wrong, was Margaret Thatcher.

Having won a victory of sorts, a sensible shadow minister – particularly one who was dependent upon the Prime Minister's patronage – would have coasted along until the general election. But about six months later, I was overcome by one of the sudden attacks of ideological enthusiasm which have afflicted me (with almost invariably disastrous result) from time to time over the last thirty years.

My desire to make an attack on the British class system was provoked by an invitation to speak at the Annual Conference of the Incorporated Society of Preparatory School Headmasters, held that year in Cambridge. The chairman – the head of a college choir school – welcomed me warmly and made genial, if not very original, jokes about Daniel, the lion's den and the advantage of removing thorns which caused unnecessary irritation. At first, I assumed that the confusion between Androcles and Daniel was intentional. But, as the morning wore on, I began to have doubts about the erudition of my audience. There were murmurs of approval when I spoke with my usual admiration about Matthew Arnold, the Victorian apostle of equality, but it later became clear that they had confused him with his dad, Thomas Arnold, headmaster of Rugby during Tom Brown's schooldays. Nevertheless, the headteachers were as courteous as senior army officers. Even my punchline was accepted politely. 'Have no doubt,' my peroration ended, 'that it is the Labour Party's intention initially to reduce, and eventually to abolish, fee-paying education in this country.'

It was not until some time afterwards that I discovered what had happened after I left. It would probably be wrong to say that the mood changed. For they hated me whilst I was there. But – because of their natural courtesy, or some other characteristic which is encouraged by public school education – they chose to be polite in my presence. It was only when the reports of the day's events appeared in the following week's newspapers that I learned that the chairman, my genial host, had sent his colleagues on their way with a stirring battle cry: 'We beat Hitler in the forties, and we can beat Hattersley in the seventies.'

On the way home, it seemed that my speech had not even caused a ripple in the political pond. That, it turned out, was in part because of a big splash in the Scilly Isles. Paddy, Harold Wilson's labrador, had been involved in an assassination attempt. The ex-Prime Minster, walking his dog along the quay, had somehow become entangled with the lead, tripped and fallen into the sea. He was rescued, unharmed. But, as I read the stories in the evening papers, I began to suspect that there was nothing Harold Wilson would not do in order to keep my better speeches out of the papers.

The lull lasted for forty-eight hours. Then the newspapers launched their attack on proposals which they regarded as an intolerable attack on the privilege of the rich. Harold Wilson disowned me publicly. Tony Benn complained about me to the general Secretary of the Labour Party – not, of course, because he disagreed with my opinions but because I had made my speech without the explicit approval of the National Executive. I attempted to defeat my critics by repeating the offence – the strategy which had proved inadvertently successful in the argument over the education White Paper. I took part in three Sunday night television debates which, somehow, managed to link my proposals to the denial of the freedom to worship, and I was the guest on a David Frost 'special' for which the audience was made up of public school boys and their parents. Not surprisingly, the letters which I received were almost universally hostile. Harold Wilson complained to John Cole that I had 'got religion'. He was right, but it was not a sudden conversion. A radical education policy has always been essential to the sort of Socialism in which I believe. And I have still not lost faith. Unfortunately, my evangelism had made me an electoral liability – an unhappy reputation for an ambitious politician.

In the last year of that Parliament, there was a by-election in Birmingham. Victor Yates – the long-serving Member for Lady-wood – died, as he had lived, with absolutely no regard for the convenience of his colleagues. After immense pressure had been put upon me by Denis Howell, my friend and constituency colleague, I agreed to attend the funeral. I travelled up to the Midlands with Brian Walden and Roy Jenkins.

Jenkins announced, before our train reached Watford, that funerals should not be treated with unnecessary solemnity. Walden and I – comparatively young and normally highly impressionable – did not, at first, take him at his word. So we got out of our taxi, at the late Member's front door, wearing our mourning faces. As if to justify our dolorous demeanour, a group of city councillors – acting as mutes and pall-bearers – rushed forward to slot us into the day's careful arrangements.

A cavalcade of limousines stretched along the full length of the road and we were ushered towards the Daimler that was reserved for Members of Parliament who were not Privy Councillors. It was a hierarchical event so, as we moved up to near the front of the cortège, we passed Austin Princesses and Rover saloons which were designated for use by ex-Lord Mayors, honorary aldermen, councillors and Justices of the Peace. At one point an old man, who walked with the aid of two sticks, asked our escorts which car he could travel in. 'Who are you?' they enquired. He replied that he was 'Nobody. Just an old friend of Victor's.' He was sternly told that there was no car for him. In a way, he was lucky. The church was just around the corner. But we made our distinguished way to its gate via just about every road in the constituency. Traffic lights were turned off and saluting policemen held back the buses and lorries as we made our mournful progress.

Victor Yates's funeral is the one occasion in my life when I have known a lych gate to be used for its proper purpose – rather than a shelter from the rain, a refuge for courting couples or a hide-away for teenage smokers. The coffin was laid to rest under the imitation Elizabethan eaves whilst the bearers prepared to carry it into church. To my surprise, one of the bearers was me. Walden and Jenkins, in a similar state of shock, grasped two of the other brass handles and Denis Howell – whom we blamed for the whole day's arrangements – took up his place as the other member of the quartet and gave us instructions in the stentorian manner of a boat-race cox. Unfortunately, we could not obey them. Victor, a small man in life, was too heavy in death for us to lift. I tried to ignore Brian Walden's suggestion that his money was being buried with him.

Much to my relief, it immediately became obvious that we were not the first four hearty males to fail the coffin-lifting test – no doubt a sign of diminished manhood in primitive societies. For an assistant undertaker rushed forward with a stainless steel contraption that looked like a cross between a hospital trolley and an hors d'oeuvre dispenser from a posh restaurant. The remains of the late Member were placed upon it and we, his grieving colleagues, were told that all we had to do was hold on to the handles and walk down the aisle. The bier would take the weight and most of the mourners would not even realise that we had been forced to rely on artificial aids. We tried our best. But we were barely past the font when it became clear that the dear departed was not lying straight in his last resting place. So it was impossible to steer his Viking funeral ship on anything like the right course. One by one, we were crushed against the side of the pews to grunts from us and little suppressed screams from the congregation. We were rescued by the head undertaker, who pushed the coffin from the back like the man who returns a collection of supermarket trolleys to their proper place.

In my own defence, I must point out that my behaviour during the service was far better than Brian Walden's. I did not giggle when the vicar spoke of Yates as a 'man who would not say a bad word about anyone', or pretend to play 'I do like to be beside the sea-side' on a theatre organ when the coffin disappeared for incineration behind its velvet curtains. Nor did I offend Doris Fisher. Councillor Fisher hoped to be (and did become) Victor's successor, losing the seat at the by-election but regaining it six months later. In a proprietary sort of way, she stood at the church door repeating the mantra, 'What shall we ever do to replace

Victor?' Brian's suggestion that he should have been embalmed and renominated was badly received. But it was that sort of day.

The buffet car was open on the southbound train, so we were able to console ourselves with British Rail *vin ordinaire*. Strangely enough, the wine helped to sober us up. I therefore believe that Roy Jenkins was entirely serious when he observed to nobody in particular, 'That was my first all-day funeral since Martin Luther King.'

The defeat of Labour at the Ladywood by-election was only one of the many signs that the Tory government was sustaining its popularity. So it seemed particularly foolish of the miners – who had scored one notable victory over Ted Heath – to take him on a second time when the country was, apparently, whole-heartedly behind his policies. Because of the pit strike, the country was put on a three-day week. I was never quite convinced that the dramatic 'emergency measures' were necessary. But whatever the reason – fuel conservation or political propaganda – most families sat in candlelight after the power stations switched off their generators in the early evening and working men and women brought home sixty per cent of their usual wages. Most of the newspapers said that the miners were to blame and the miners – under the leadership of Joe Gormley – were the Labour Party's kith and kin. So when Ted Heath called an election on the issue 'Who Rules Britain?', most commentators believed that it could only have one result.

For me, it was a dismal campaign. I expected the Party to go down to a crushing defeat and my elders and betters – in an attempt to reduce the size of the catastrophe – regularly repudiated my policy of abolishing the public schools. I was kept, as much as was possible, off television and radio and shielded from the close cross-examination of political journalists. There was one particularly unhappy weekend when several Catholic organisations condemned me as a religious bigot who wanted to prevent the extension of the true faith. Bishop Dwyer of Birmingham came to my defence and later wrote me a note to explain that, although he bitterly disagreed with all that I stood for, he had thought it right to support me in memory of my father. They had been friends at the English College in Rome during the late 1920s. On election day, it began to rain at lunch-time and by six o'clock – the time at which Labour supporters, according to the folklore, are just beginning to turn out – a near typhoon was blowing down Sparkbrook's grey streets. At eight o'clock I made my last tour of the polling stations and found them almost deserted. I began to worry about holding my own seat, as well as Labour losing the election.

I won with an increased majority. The well-organised and invariably loyal Kashmiris had cast their disciplined vote early in the day. The pundits who predicted a Labour defeat were only half right. Labour did not win. But the Conservatives lost and there followed a weekend of horse trading as Ted Heath tried to hang on to office with the help of the Liberals. Television companies made increasingly frenzied attempts to persuade a senior figure from the Opposition to make a statement about Labour's anxiety to take over. But the Shadow Cabinet had decided that it was best to let the Prime Minister swing in an eerily silent wind. Tony Crosland telephoned me after the weekend Shadow Cabinet meeting to warn me not to rush in where members of the Parliamentary Committee feared to tread. To encourage my reticence, he told me that obedience to the instruction was essential 'if we are to achieve what we want to achieve for you'. Ted Short, who sent me a message to 'stand by on Monday', contributed to my naturally irrational optimism. I had been rehabilitated. The letter to Harold Wilson, no less than the assault on private education, had been forgiven if not forgotten. If only Ted Heath would move out of my way, I could get on with building Jerusalem in England's green and pleasant schools.

Ted Heath resigned on the afternoon of Monday 4th March. For the next three days, life for me was a poor imitation of *Yes Minister*'s opening episode. I sat neurotically at home waiting for the telephone to ring, concentrating far too hard on being anxious to allow me to do anything except occasionally pick up the receiver to make sure that there was no fault on the line. Every time a call came, I assumed that it was Harold Wilson. Usually it was somebody calling to ask if I had heard from Harold Wilson and, I feared, occupying the line which he was impatiently waiting to use.

The announcement of the new appointments trickled out of Downing Street – first the Great Offices of State, then the rest of the Cabinet. Shirley Williams, on her way home from Number 10, called at my house to see what I 'had got'. She broke the news that the Department of Education had gone to Reg Prentice. When the list of Ministers of State was published, and there was still no place for me, I gave up hope. In one moment of desperation, I had telephoned Ted Short – justifying the indignity by telling myself that he was the man who had told me to stand by. He was either too busy or too embarrassed to return my call. On the Wednesday morning, I went to the first Parliamentary Party meeting of the new session – ostensibly to cheer the government but, in truth, to show that I did not care. Roy Jenkins pursued me down the Committee Corridor to say that I had been 'within a hair's breadth of the Cabinet'. The intention was humane, but the news of a near miss only increased the pain.

On the Thursday evening, I decided that the time had begun to rebuild my life. So I called, wholly unannounced, on John Cole – then deputy editor of the *Guardian* – and told him that he ought to employ me to write a weekly column. The idea was not the discursive and inconsequential *Endpiece* that I have written for the last fifteen years, but a political commentary in which a semi-detached radical assessed the progress of the new government. Cole liked the idea. But he was not prepared even to discuss the suggestion seriously until after the weekend. I had, he said, given up politics too quickly. The call might yet come.

The call came whilst I was having lunch the following afternoon with James Margach, the elderly and distinguished political editor of the *Sunday Times*. No doubt I was denouncing Harold Wilson as an ingrate and poor judge of men. But the details of the conversation were blocked from my mind by the head waiter's message. 'The Prime Minister wants to see you in Downing Street, straight away.' I had to borrow a pound from Margach to pay for my taxi.

There was a traffic jam in Trafalgar Square and, nervous in my cab, I felt sure that by the time I arrived at Number 10 the Prime Minister would have lost patience and appointed someone else to whatever he had earlier picked out for me. For once, neurosis imitated life. As I walked through the door of the Cabinet Room, the Prime Minister asked with convincing if bogus exasperation, 'Do you want to be a member of this government or not?' Before I had finished mumbling that I wanted to *very much*, he added, 'We've been trying to get hold of you since Tuesday.' I almost believed him and nearly apologised.

He then went on to explain that he had set aside for me the most important job in the whole government. My official title would be Minister of State for Foreign and Commonwealth Affairs. And to the uninitiated that might sound no more than deputy to the Foreign Secretary. But I was to be the linchpin of Labour's European policy and the prime mover in the renegotiation of Britain's membership of the Economic Community. Of course, Jim Callaghan would be *nominally* in charge. I sat there, feeling like the humble air-raid warden in the war-time poster, who stood amidst the rubble of a bombed-out factory thinking, 'It all depends on me.' It was not until I was halfway home that I realised that I had just been appointed to the middle rank of government.

Then I thought of all the new comprehensive schools that I could have built, the nursery classes which I might have created and, above all, the extra resources I would have passed into the inner cities at the expense of the prosperous suburbs. But in Downing Street I was just grateful to be in the government at all. I smiled and said, 'Thank you, Prime Minister. Thank you very much.'

CHAPTER
7

For the next two years, my ministerial home was the Old India Office – in its bizarre way, the most elegant room in Whitehall. It had been designed, back in the high noon of the Raj, in a style which can only be described as Mogul-Gothic. Its walls were mahogany and mirror and its ceiling was concave like the inside of a minaret. The pictures with which it was decorated had been stolen by Clive from various Indian princes. Throughout my occupation I was under continuing pressure to either return them to their rightful owners or have them stored in an atmosphere which prevented their disintegration. I resisted both demands. The Old India Office – with its two identical doors through which a pair of Maharajahs could enter simultaneously without either of them losing face – was a great comfort to me.

I sometimes thought that the Old India Office and I were meant for each other. By 1974, I had twenty thousand constituents whose origins were buried deep in Kashmir and Pakistan. Occasionally one of them would come to tea. The visitors rarely seemed to feel the ironic pleasure that I thought the occasion justified, but I enjoyed immensely sitting at the table which had once felt the elbows of the Secretary of State for India. My predecessor as Minister of State was Julian Amery, whose father had ruled the Raj in Churchill's war-time coalition. Like the faithful son he was, Julian had searched for and found his father's furniture and restored the Old India Office to its 1945 condition. I declined all offers of modernisation. Leo Amery had been Member of Parliament for Sparkbrook until he was swept away in Labour's 1945 landslide. I thought of him as preparing the room for his successor but two.

In that room, during the summer of 1975, I entertained Ronald Reagan. He was, at the time, ex-Governor of California and aspirant to the Republican presidential nomination which he did not secure for another four years. Like all his rivals, he was making 'a swing through the European capitals' as proof of his international standing. In London he had seen Margaret Thatcher and asked to see Harold Wilson. But the best that the government could offer was me.

The Prime Minister had refused to see him for reasons which were aesthetic rather than political. George Wallace – another presidential hopeful – had been granted audience. But, as a result of the terrible injuries which he had sustained during an assassination attempt, the Governor of Alabama had been violently ill in Wilson's study. Apparently fearing that all presidential aspirants behaved in the same way, he had refused to have another inside Downing Street. Ronald Reagan was passed down to the Foreign Secretary. But Jim Callaghan was committed to visiting the Splot Fair, a constituency engagement which he had not missed during his thirty years in the House of Commons. I was all that was left for Reagan to see.

Ex-Governor Reagan arrived surrounded by muscular men in dark glasses – enough to stand guard at each of the Old India Office's imposing twin doors, and the rather less spectacular pair that led to my private lavatory and the drinks cupboard. The governor, having expressed his gratitude at the privilege which he had been afforded, then spoke for several minutes on the continued Soviet threat to the West. Fortunately – for I would have found it difficult to agree that an invasion was imminent – he then moved on, without drawing breath, to a second favourite theme. All unemployment, he believed, is voluntary. The founding immigrants to America had no jobs to go to but they went out into the desert and prairies and made them bloom. The workless Blacks of the cities should do the same – or at least the modern urban equivalent. The usually well-mannered young men from the Foreign Office who sat beside me made choking noises. I asked a question about the cost of American forces in Europe and Governor Reagan said what a pleasure it had been to talk with me.

As he stood up to leave, he elaborated on the pleasure theme. His visit had also been an honour, a revelation and would, in the future, be a source of continued pride. In recognition of his gratitude, he wished to present me with the California Liberty Medal. He felt in the side pocket of his pale blue, ultra-suede jacket. There was a clanking noise – which I took to indicate the presence of several Liberty Medals. The Governor was clearly finding it difficult to identify the one which was intended for me. After some time had passed, he drew the whole collection – eight or ten, in all – out of his pocket. They came, I noticed, in gold, silver and bronze. To my relief I rated silver.

By the time of the Reagan visit I had become hardened, if not reconciled, to life in the Foreign Office. I discovered, during a week, that many of the meetings were held as a matter of courtesy rather than in order to do any serious business and that the conversations held across conference tables were usually prepared before the confrontations began and therefore ended with an agreement which would have been made if the parties had never met. My initiation into the obligation of protocol began with a visit from Dom Mintoff, the Prime Minister of Malta.

Mintoff and I had a brief exchange of views before I took him for a working lunch with the Prime Minister. I had spent much of the previous evening mugging up the facts on the future of the naval dockyards and examining the assistance that Malta received under the aid agreement. My time had been wasted. By the time that the Maltese delegation got to me, their civil servants and ours had negotiated a new agreement. We walked from the Ambassadors' Entrance of the Foreign Office up the steps into the Horse Guards' end of Downing Street. The policemen gave us gratifying salutes.

For some perverse reason, Harold Wilson insisted on introducing me to Dom Mintoff – even though I had brought him to Downing Street. Flicking his thumb in the manner of a referee tossing a coin at the beginning of a football match, he told the Maltese Prime Minister that I was 'as near as that to being in the Cabinet'. I wanted to kill him.

Nothing about Malta was discussed over lunch. Harold was looking forward with immense excitement to that afternoon's Prime Minister's questions. Whilst we had been in opposition, a member of his staff had bought a slag heap and – having sold off the slag – obtained planning permission for the land. By modern standards, it was not much of a scandal. In fact, it was probably not a scandal at all. But the weaker-minded Tory back-benchers had let it be known that they intended to demand an explanation in the House that afternoon. Wilson told Mintoff that he knew exactly the sort of accusations they would make. Indeed, he entertained his opposite number with some specimen questions – and followed each imitation with the assurance that the real thing would not be as good.

Dom Mintoff was suitably impressed. 'How', he asked, 'will you deal with your tormentors?' Harold Wilson went through his full repertoire of body languages – puffing on his pipe, twisting his wedding ring round his finger and producing a six-inch flame from his cigarette lighter. 'I shall', he said, pausing for effect, 'marmalise them.' As we walked out into Downing Street, the Maltese Prime Minister – who was not wholly conversant with the work of Ken Dodd and the exploits of his Diddymen – asked me, 'What is this marmelising? Is it some sort of parliamentary procedure?'

In my two years in the Foreign Office I was regularly employed as the escort and chaperon for distinguished guests. When I greeted Pierre Trudeau at the top of his aircraft's steps, he was adjusting the carnation in his buttonhole, and he kindly offered me the spare one that he happened to keep in reserve. Daringly we went on to the City of London lunch that made Trudeau a Freeman – me wearing the full morning dress bequeathed to me by Gerry Reynolds at the Ministry of Defence. The beagle who introduced the guests got our names right, but he announced one Secretary of State as 'Minister'. My colleague made him shout a correction.

As he walked across the Heathrow tarmac, Archbishop Makarios asked for a clean shirt to replace the one which he had worn since his escape from the Greek Colonels a week earlier.

I welcomed Mário Soares when he became Foreign Minister of Portugal, but not until after I had entertained to lunch the leaders of the Young Officers' Movement which had toppled Salazar.

The bearded veterans of the war in Mozambique openly wept at the sight of the red carnations – the symbol of their revolution – which covered the table. When the speeches were over, the Head of Government Hospitality asked me why they had been so moved by the way the table was decorated. When I explained, he seemed almost hurt. 'You ordered a very expensive lunch and, to keep within budget, I had to buy the cheapest flowers in Covent Garden.'

Bülent Ecevit, the Prime Minister of Turkey, came to London to complain about the aggressive intentions of the new Greek government. The discussion was briefly thrown off course by Jim Callaghan's observation that 'the young Turks have taken over in Athens'. Intelligence reports had suggested that their more mature countrymen were on the point of invading Cyprus. Ecevit was warned of the consequences of such folly, but his assurances

of peaceful intentions were not wholly convincing. I was instructed to accompany him to the airport and perform a piece
of cunning diplomacy. 'Just as he turns to say goodbye, ask him
outright,' one Foreign Office mandarin told me. 'Ask him if he's
going to invade. He'll be caught off-guard.' I did exactly as
instructed and Mr Ecevit seemed genuinely startled by my
question. Then he answered, 'Of course not.' I hurried back to
the Foreign Office to report peace in our time. The first Turkish
troops to land in Cyprus were on the beach by six hundred hours
next morning. I got to the control room below Downing Street
half an hour ahead of the Foreign Secretary. His official car had
not arrived and he had travelled across London in a comman-
deered milk float.

President Nicolae Ceauşescu of Romania came and went in
forty-eight hours. I accompanied him from Heathrow to Chequers
and, two days later, from Chequers to Heathrow. During both
journeys he complained incessantly about the roads not being
cleared of other traffic and the failure of the Queen to upgrade his
trip into a state visit. The take-off for home was delayed whilst the
President and his party raided the duty-free shop. Their extensive
purchase of tartan rugs, silk headscarves and costume jewellery
were – without either invitation or request – charged to Her
Majesty's Government. The Ceauşescu visit did not however
cause me as much embarrassment as the two days spent in
London by Sven Anderson, the veteran Swedish Foreign Minister for whom I felt a positively filial affection.

Sven expressed the desire to visit the theatre – the sort of
request to which the Foreign Office is always happy to agree.
Such occasions always carry risks. In Sven Anderson's case the
problem was choosing what to see. Foolishly, I picked *Rosencratz
and Guildenstern Are Dead*. I had forgotten how difficult a play it
was, even for an audience whose mother tongue is English. Its
Scandinavian flavour did not contribute much to the Swedish
Foreign Minister's pleasure. I hoped that the following evening's

musical – which also had a Nordic association – would make up for the first disappointment. I did not realise that Stephen Sondheim's *A Little Night Music* was based on *Smiles of a Summer Night* and that the plot, as well as being built around a series of adulteries, required a young Lutheran seminarian to lust after and eventually run away with his step-mother. Sven Anderson was an Elder of the Lutheran Church.

The Swedish Foreign Minister had come to Britain as part of the retinue which accompanied King Carl Gustav on a state visit – the accolade that President Ceauşescu had been denied. Almost uniquely – and for reasons I never discovered – it was a state visit to Scotland. The Foreign Secretary was unable to join the Court when it moved north. He was in Uganda persuading Idi Amin not to execute an elderly Englishman. I was nominated Minister in Attendance.

State visits – as I discovered – principally involve drinking and changing clothes. At the state banquet at Balmoral, the Prince of Wales – whom I had not previously met – asked me by way of greeting if Amin was suffering from general paralysis of the insane, a condition he understood to mark the advanced stages of venereal disease. I looked forward to two items in my programme – the free night on the second day of the visit and the Beating of the Retreat by the Pipes and Drums of the Highland Regiments at the foot of Arthur's Seat. Both turned out to be rather different from what I had anticipated.

I had assumed that my free night would be spent talking and drinking with my Scottish friends, John Smith and Donald Dewar. Willie Ross, the pathologically aggressive Secretary of State for Scotland, had other ideas. One of the guests had withdrawn from the dinner which he was to host. I would take his place. I knew Willie Ross well and liked him immensely, but I never remembered that he had no sense of humour. 'I'll come,' I said, 'if I can sit next to Princess Margaretta of Sweden.' Willie did not even pretend to smile. 'We canna' have a junior minister sitting wi'royalty. You'll come and none of your nonsense.' Sure enough, on the *placement* I was at the foot of the table with the civil servants and ADCs. Just before grace, an elderly Scottish nobleman collapsed. The easiest way of filling his space was to move me up into a seat next to the Princess. Willie Ross clearly blamed me for the old man's illness. Despite her constant appearances in the gossip columns of the sixties, Margaretta was not a hypnotic conversationist.

My private secretary – a man of considerable ability and episcopal manner named Roger Westbrook – tried to prevent me from attending the Beating of the Retreat. It was to be followed by the King of Sweden's reciprocal dinner for which I had to dress up in white tie and tails and he did not believe that, if I hung about with the Highland Regiments, I would be ready in time. I assured him that there would be no problem. 'Have you', he asked, rather offensively I thought, 'much experience of changing into full evening dress very quickly?' That settled it. I sat just behind the colonels of the Highland Regiments in the hollow square around the pipes and drums.

When it was over, I was back in my car within half a minute. Before I could change I had to travel the full length of the Royal Mile for – since there was no room for me at Holyrood House – I was quartered in the Caledonian Hotel. I suppose I was anxious about the journey, because I persuaded my driver to pull out of line as we drove away from the parade ground. He then totally lost his nerve and pulled back rather than face several angry policemen. Unfortunately he pulled back between the two Rolls-Royces which carried the Queen of England and the King of Sweden. I became momentarily as humourless as Willie Ross. I was not even tempted to wave to the good citizens of Edinburgh who lined the pavement.

Back at the hotel, changing into my evening dress – still the suit and shirt which I had inherited in 1969 from my predecessor as Minister of Defence – was completed more quickly than even I had anticipated. I was about to leave my room in order to make an entrance into the lobby down the grand staircase when there was an agitated knock at my door. It was Roger Westbrook. He had cut himself whilst shaving and, since he needed to hold a handkerchief to the wound, was unable to knot his tie which, naturally enough, was of the 'loose' rather than the 'made-up' variety. I completed the task with some difficulty – since, by mistake, it had been heavily starched at the laundry – and suggested that he should see if the razor wound continued to bleed. Westbrook removed the handkerchief as I recommended and a large gobbet of almost congealed blood dropped on to his shirt front.

It was not the moment for artistic speculation, but I could not help observing how wonderfully dramatic a bloodstained evening shirt is. Westbrook showed no signs of appreciating the truly Gothic nature of his appearance. I scrubbed him with a nail brush and then gave him a quick blast with the hair dryer. He went to the dinner with a faintly damp and slightly pink shirt front. I thought that it served him right.

When the dinner was over, Sven and I sat and talked. Did I, he asked me, 'know the Queen well?' Senile, I thought. He is getting senile. But I humoured him by asking how well he knew the King. 'This one not well,' he said. 'He is young and a water-skier. His grandfather I knew very well. He came into my wife's bookshop almost every day.' It seemed to me that if we must have a monarchy, that was the sort to choose.

By the time of the visit to Edinburgh I had become Right Honourable. I was made a Privy Councillor in the 1975 New Year's Honours List – a distinction of which Harold Wilson warned me in the usual official letter. It asked me to signify my agreement in the attached envelope – bright yellow so that it could be easily identified in the Downing Street post room. I lost it. For a couple of days, I agonised about whether I should ask for another one or simply use a House of Commons pre-franked cream bond. Then I realised that if I agonised much longer my silence would be taken to signify that I declined. The House of Commons envelope I eventually used must have got through. For my name appeared in the New Year's Day papers and I was summoned to be sworn in at a February Privy Council Meeting at Buckingham Palace.

A rehearsal was arranged for early on the fateful day and the six of us who were to be admitted turned up sharp and eager. The Clerk to the Privy Council explained his agitation. The Queen did not like Privy Council Meetings to last for too long. Yet that morning, there was an Archbishop of York to be sworn in as well as two different Privy Council oaths to be administered – for Mr Wallace Rowling, the Prime Minister of New Zealand, had more or less got his by post and he was simply going through a confirmation ceremony. 'Three,' said Brian O'Malley, Minister of State for Social Security. 'I wish to use the Douay Bible.' Joel Barnett, the Chief Secretary to the Treasury, coughed and said, 'Four. I wish to swear on the Old Testament.' I wished that I had spoken earlier. But conscience demanded that I should be the last straw. 'I cannot swear at all. I must attest.' The Queen completed the prolonged ceremony without showing any sign of irritation. Jim Callaghan – who had been on duty as one of the established Council members – walked out of the Audience Room with an avuncular arm around my shoulder. The Archbishop of York – dressed like a character from *The Six Wives of Henry VIII* – was waiting outside. Jim steered me in his direction. 'This, your Grace, is Roy Hattersley. Her Majesty had to keep you waiting because he wouldn't swear on the Bible.'

It was a week in which I seemed destined to offend religious authority. Two days later I was a guest at the French embassy, where the ambassador was entertaining Michel Ponitawski, the French Interior Minister. I sat next to Sir John Hunt, the Cabinet Secretary, who announced – in a manner not at all mandarin-like – that the good lunch was particularly welcome since he was being neglected by his wife who was fully occupied in preparing her brother for a month away from home. Sensing that I was supposed to enquire about the reason for such a prolonged absence, I asked, 'Business or pleasure?' Sir John said, in an inconsequential sort of way, 'He's electing a Pope.'

I asked – out of both politeness and real curiosity – if Cardinals (Basil Hume in this case) were prepared for momentous meetings with the same sort of briefings that Cabinet ministers receive. Sir John assured me that they were and went on to explain that he had offered his brother-in-law a little advice of his own. There had been talk in the newspapers about the possibility of a Black pontiff. The Cabinet Secretary was strongly against political considerations influencing the College of Cardinals' decision. 'Before we know where we are,' he said, 'people will want to rotate it like the presidency of the European Commission – Asian one year, South American the next.' 'What', I asked him, 'about divine guidance? Don't you believe in any of that sort of thing?' Sir John put down his knife and fork, dabbed his mouth with his napkin and looked me straight in the eyes. 'I don't believe that God plays conjuring tricks. Neither does anybody with any sense.' For the rest of the lunch, I tried to make conversation with the First Secretary of the embassy, who sat on my non-Hunt side.

Throughout the early months of 1976, I continued to hope for promotion – particularly to the Northern Ireland Office. I dreamed of running that Department, partly because every politician with a sense of history is fascinated by that most distressful country, and also as a result of regular newspaper forecasts that I would replace Merlyn Rees when he moved on to something better. The Prime Minister – still sensitive about newspapers anticipating his reshuffles and, I suspect, suspicious that I had been spreading the rumours of my impending promotion – removed me from the Northern Ireland Committee. But on the Maundy Thursday I deputised for my colleague David Ennals (the other Foreign Office Minister of State) at the meeting that considered how to react to the Belfast Workers' Strike. That Easter weekend was a turning point in Ulster's history. 'Power-sharing', like so many other peace initiatives, foundered on the intransigence of the unionists.

The meeting was delayed because another John Hunt, the Chief of the General Staff, had not arrived back from Northern Ireland. We sat around the Cabinet table talking discursively about the prospects for what the Irish call 'the marching season', when the CGS walked in, still dressed for the Belfast streets in khaki jersey, battledress trousers and gleaming boots. Since Harold Wilson was dominating our conversation it was almost inevitable that he was in mid-sentence at the moment of John Hunt's entrance. The Prime Minister was complaining about the increasing militancy of the Orange Lodges, which he attributed to their infiltration by a new, more violent sort of unionist. 'We are very near', he said, 'to a military takeover.'

The Chief of the General Staff, who was about to take his seat, stifled his apology for keeping the Prime Minister waiting and said, with a combination of pride and resentment, 'It could never happen here, PM. I assure you that it could never happen here.' Perhaps it was because I laughed the loudest that I never attended the Northern Ireland Committee again. From then on, when David Ennals was not available, a parliamentary secretary took his place.

Elsewhere, David and I doubled for each other as necessary and without any problem. From time to time, however, there was some confusion about which of us was responsible for what. Even the Foreign Secretary occasionally made mistakes about the subjects and departments which we supervised. When Iceland announced that it was to enforce a fifty-mile exclusion zone around its coastline, David was originally asked to take charge of the negotiations which, it was hoped, would change the Norse mind.

The error was understandable. David had represented Britain at the Law of the Sea Conference in Rio de Janeiro. On the way home he had written a report which concluded, 'This may have been the most important conference of the twentieth century,' and a civil servant had passed his conclusions on to the Foreign Secretary with the comment, 'On the other hand, it may not.' As a result, Ennals was clearly established in Foreign Office mythology as the expert on three quarters of the world's surface. Just in time – or far too early, depending upon how you look at it – somebody remembered that Iceland was in Europe and fishing was 'within the competence' of the EEC. So I was made General Officer Commanding in what came to be called the Cod War.

I set off for Reykjavik at the head of a delegation which included officials from the Ministry of Agriculture, Fisheries and Food and representatives of the fishing industry. It soon became clear that the MAFF civil servants would be far more difficult to satisfy than the fishermen. MAFF was then the one client department of government – a ministry which believed that it existed to represent the views of farmers, food processors and trawler owners. The Minister – Fred Peart – had come to a firm conclusion about the tonnage of fish which the Icelanders must allow British trawlers to catch in their newly acquired waters. His civil servants travelled north with me to make sure that there was no backsliding.

We were met at Reykjavik airport – which the Icelanders shared with the United States Air Force – by Kenneth East. The British ambassador, an able and conscientious man who sacrificed promotion so that he could stay in Reykjavik and heal the wounds of the Cod War, looked even more gloomy than usual. The Icelanders had, in the technical jargon, 'cut the warp' of a British trawler. That is to say a gunboat had sailed between a fishing boat and its nets, severing the cable which connected them. It was a highly dangerous manoeuvre which risked both collision and the steel hawser, once severed, whipping loose across the trawler deck and cutting in half any fishermen who were standing in its path. The conflict was bound to escalate as fishery protection vessels of the Royal Navy tried to head off the Icelandic attacks by interposing themselves between trawler and gunboat. Sooner or later somebody would be killed. Worse still, as one of my diplomatic advisers pointed out, we would have to decide whether or not to negotiate under duress.

The negotiations went on as they began, with Iceland always one step ahead. We had a 'private' meeting with the Icelandic Foreign Minister. Within an hour he had given a very bellicose public account of what I had believed to be a most friendly discussion. Every time we seemed to be getting near to an agreement, the Icelanders made some adjustment in their demands. Back in London, Jim Callaghan asked Henry Kissinger to put pressure on Reykjavik. The American Secretary of State replied with a quotation from Bismarck which was not an answer to the request: 'How great is the tyranny to which small nations can subject great.'

The Icelanders – who claimed to be the most educated people in the world – were masters in the art of disorientation. During the negotiations they behaved with a joyous brutality which forced us to choose between all sorts of humiliations and, as they hoped, taking responsibility for breaking up the peace talks. In the evenings we were fêted, like honoured guests. However, our entertainment was always specially planned to remind us that we were doing business with Vikings – descendants of the men who had sailed so far in their open boats that their tombstones are to be found in the Great Wall of China and who, having discovered that they had mistaken Venice for Constantinople, sacked the city anyway because sacking was their trade. The books with which we were presented were all modern versions of the Norse sagas, written by the innumerable Icelandic Nobel Prize winners whose houses are signposted in Reykjavik in the way that railway stations are signposted in London. The novels were called *Blood on the Snow, Vengeance's Sword* and that sort of thing.

On one of our rest days, a guide was sent to show us the considerable beauties of the island. Naturally enough, our tour began at the world's oldest parliament. Its Members – who first assembled in AD 930 – were clearly remarkable men, for they decided the fate of their country while sitting precariously on the pinnacles of volcanic rock which nature had arranged around a natural amphitheatre. Nearby there was a pool which, my guide told me, had been used for executing adulterous women. The miscreants were sewn into hessian sacks before being drowned in the icy waters. 'Same period?' I asked. 'About AD 930?' I am sure that his reply owed less to historical accuracy than the desire to unnerve me in preparation for the next day's meeting. 'Last one was 1912,' he said.

No doubt reluctant to spend more time in the company of such unworthy adversaries, the Icelanders themselves broke off the meeting and, for a month, ships of the Royal Navy interposed themselves between British trawlers and Icelandic gunboats, the fishing interests of Hull and Grimsby complained that they had been abandoned and John Prescott visited my office almost every day to demand that I behave reasonably. Asked to describe the difference between reasonable behaviour and capitulation, he never provided a convincing answer. Then – with their natural instinct for causing me inconvenience – the Icelanders demanded an instant renewal of the negotiations whilst I was in Los Angeles.

The journey from California to Iceland is long and wearisome and we were not in good spirits even before we landed at Reykjavik airfield and were met with the news that, earlier in the day, an Icelandic gunboat had again cut the warp of a British trawler. I recall that, as I set off from the embassy to the Foreign Office, a MAFF Under Secretary ran along beside me shouting, 'Don't budge! Don't budge!' I budged a little. But the talks still broke down on the following day.

We hung around hoping that the Icelanders would suddenly be converted to the virtues of compromise. Kenneth East took us to the opera – Carmen sung in Old Norse. I assumed that the cigarette factory in which the plot begins was sheltered employment, for none of the 'girls' who worked there was under sixty. But all thoughts about the production were driven from my head by the news that the local police were worried about our safety. They might also have been worried about our personal hygiene. For the hot water which was pumped into the embassy, straight from a steaming geyser in the hills, had been cut off. When, next morning, Kenneth East himself brought tea to my bedroom and told me that the staff had not reported for work, we all agreed that it was time to go home.

The plane which came to fly us back to London managed to land despite the gale, but the pilot was reluctant to risk a take-off. The police convinced him that the risk in the air was less than the dangers on the ground and we rose unsteadily into the grey sky. As soon as we had escaped the storm, the pilot came to our cabin to renew an old acquaintance. I recognised him at once. 'We played football together at university,' I said. It was his turn to reminisce. 'You broke my nose – although we were playing on the same side.' I hope that I only imagined a man from MAFF mutter, 'Now we know why it all went wrong.'

Back in London, I appeared on the *Panorama* programme which, since it discussed where our fish was to come from after we had been driven out of the North Sea, might well have been called the capitulation programme. One possibility was farm-bred trout – an alternative which suffered from the disadvantage of consuming more protein than they produced. A tame trout was brought into the studio and placed in a huge glass tank just over my left shoulder.

During the evening I learned more about the trout than their immense appetite for protein. I discovered that they do not enjoy being on television and – more interesting by far – they are not constrained by the normal laws of science. My co-star thrashed about with such vigour that he did what Isaac Newton would have regarded as impossible. He overturned the tank in which he was immersed, spilling several gallons of water over my legs and feet, and landing on my shoes – where he performed his death throes.

Mercifully the trout's suicide took place whilst the cameras were pointing in a different direction. So the audience, comfortable in front of their television sets, had no idea what had happened. I carried on as if a large fish was not dying under the desk at which I sat. It was then that I discovered another fascinating biological fact. Trouts, like swans, sing when they die – but not very melodiously. After the programme there were many telephone complaints about one of my adversaries ostentatiously coughing in order to disturb my concentration.

The visit to Los Angeles – which was cut short by the Icelander's sudden desire to discuss cod – was one of my several contributions to the maintenance of the special relationship between Britain and the United States. But it was the least memorable. The only memorable incident was created by Roger Westbrook who – thinking that I was staying up too late on my first day – fiddled neurotically with the nobs under the dining table. It collapsed. The most eventful visit to America had taken place a year earlier and had been arranged to enable me to brief Henry Kissinger on Britain's position in the Mutual and Balanced Force Reduction Talks – negotiations intended to enable both East and West to reduce their conventional forces without a perceptible change in the balance of security. The intellectual attraction of the talks was the need to construct formulae by which a tank regiment could be equated – in terms of military capability – with an infantry division or how many artillery pieces might be sacrificed in return for the enemy disbanding a squadron of helicopter gun-ships. Dr Kissinger seemed distracted throughout the conversation. I had no doubt that he was still trying to restore his composure after the confrontation which had delayed our meeting for the best part of an hour. After I had sat patiently in his outside office for about forty-five minutes my old friend (and

Henry's old Harvard colleague) Pat Moynihan, the recently appointed American ambassador to the United Nations, bounded through the Secretary of State's door. Seeing me, he immediately demonstrated the quality that now makes him the most attractive member of the United States Senate. 'Do you realise,' he bellowed, 'that I'm the first presidential nominee in history to be formally censured before Congress endorsed his nomination?'

On my way home from Washington I stopped at Chicago to address the Illinois Foreign Affairs Council – a group of influential international relations enthusiasts. It was a hot, sticky day and I thought that I ought to change into a dry shirt before I gave my address. My suitcase was dragged from the boot of the Consul General's car whilst it was parked on a busy road outside the Foreign Affairs Council's imposing building. I made myself presentable, spoke, answered a couple of questions and rushed off to the airport. As we assembled our bags for inspection, I noticed that the blue Foreign Office travelling ministerial box – double locked and lead lined for security – was missing. It contained my top secret briefing papers in the MBFR talks and, far more important, the manuscript of my first book of essays, *Goodbye to Yorkshire.* There was a moment of panic when I could not decide if I should catch a later plane or kill myself. The Consul-General suggested that he should telephone the Chicago Police Department. After a few minutes he returned, looking shaken but relieved, to the VIP lounge. The police had told him that a strange object – dark blue in colour, surprisingly heavy, with locks which defied the skeleton keys and decorated with initials which they could not identify – had been found on the pavement outside the offices of the Foreign Affairs Council. They were awaiting a judge's permission to blow it up.

It was the year of the United States bicentennial and the two Houses of Parliament presented the two Houses of Congress with a copy of the Magna Carta. The American delegation hung about in London on what was a difficult day for me, because my mother was in town. Then Roger Westbrook – still my private secretary – had a bright idea. The Queen Mother's equerry was a friend of his. He would arrange for Councillor Mrs E. A. Hattersley to be invited to the Clarence House garden party. We were barely through the gate, when the Queen Mother – all flowery tulle and floppy hat – greeted us. She could not have been more charming as she spoke of the pride that all parents feel in their children. Apparently she was particularly pleased with her elder daughter's success. The conversation must have gone on for a good ten minutes before I said, in my unctuous way, 'We must not keep you. You've many guests to look after.' My mother agreed and, as our hostess turned away, she courteously enquired, 'And to whom have I had the pleasure of speaking?' I am still trying to work out why she did it.

CHAPTER
8

Most of my time at the Foreign Office was, as Harold Wilson had promised, spent on the 'renegotiation' – the revision, part real, part cosmetic, of the terms on which Britain remained a member of the European Economic Community. Within a week of the Labour government coming to office in 1974, Jim Callaghan assembled Her Britannic Majesty's eight ambassadors to the Common Market capitals and handed each one of them a copy of the manifesto on which his party had swept to power. He then instructed them to read the passage on the new government's attitude towards the EEC. They later confessed that they were astonished not by the Foreign Secretary's show of devotion to his election promises but by the discovery that he meant to keep them. Jim's requirement that they each pay for their copy of the manifesto was accepted with good grace.

During my first week in government, I was sent off to a routine meeting of the Agriculture Ministers' Council in Luxembourg. What little business there was to be transacted could more easily have been done by Fred Peart, the actual Minister of Agriculture. But I would be there to co-ordinate. That is to say, keep an eye on Fred. I did neither. All I remember of that first meeting was a

dispute between Peart and my first Foreign Office private secretary, M.I.G. (Mig) Goulding – a designated high-flyer and now
Assistant General Secretary of the United Nations. Goulding, a
man who was as courteous as he was clever, offered to help Peart
in some trivial way which I no longer recall. The Minister
believed that the civil servant was telling him what to do. Peart
realised, halfway through the public dressing down, that he had
misunderstood Goulding's intentions and – being an essentially
generous man – demanded the right to make amends. His
suggestion for the reconciliation was a drink and a game of
snooker (which Goulding did not play) after dinner. The Minister
of Agriculture was so anxious to prove that he was sorry, and the
private secretary was so determined to respond with grace, that
they went on playing and drinking until four o' clock in the
morning. Goulding decided that, in future, his deputy would
attend meetings of the Agricultural Council.

Luxembourg was, in those early months of the Labour government, taking its turn in the presidency of the EEC. So most of the
meetings were held there. I played innumerable games of table-
tennis in the basement of the embassy, always beating Fred Peart
twenty-one to less than five and always being the player who
wanted to give up first. In the embassy garden – at a lonely spot
where I knew we could not be overheard – I brought to Jim
Callaghan, 'by word of mouth', a message from MI5.

For some time the Security Services had been keeping a
suspect under close and continuous surveillance. The man
who was being investigated was a junior employee at NATO
headquarters in Brussels. But he was living in a style which was
entirely inconsistent with his lowly status. He had an expensive
car, a house in the Belgian countryside and a boat in a marina near
Ostend. Both the suspect and his wife made frequent weekend
visits to London and Paris. Lavish spending by junior employees
was always taken by MI5 as *prima facie* evidence of subversion.
The money must have come from the Soviet Union.

The investigation was handicapped by Belgium's tedious restrictions on phone tapping and the reluctance of the Brussels police to take the British suspicions seriously. But eventually they agreed to raid his house. The bottom floor was searched and nothing found. But a bedroom door was padlocked. The police were persuaded to break their way in. The raiding party were engulfed in an avalanche of plastic containers. The suspect's wife was Tupperware representative for Brussels. And she had broken all previous sales records. My message to Jim Callaghan was that the investigation had been discontinued.

Luxembourg was, naturally enough, the scene of the Foreign Affairs Council at which Jim Callaghan set out Great Britain's negotiating position. Before the meeting began, we supplicant British were entertained to a small lunch by Gaston Thorn, the Luxembourg Prime Minister. There was a long reception before the lunch began and one of our party, who was unknown to me, enjoyed himself so much that he began to sway. A waiter, fearing that he would fall down, sat him on a gilt chair. 'Who', I asked Goulding, 'is that?' My private secretary answered with obvious reluctance. 'That', he said, 'is the detective. He shoots from the hip if he thinks the Foreign Secretary is in danger.'

Jim Callaghan's speech – setting out the United Kingdom's historic demands – was delayed until the early evening. The first part of the afternoon was taken up by an Italian application to invoke emergency powers provided by the Treaty of Rome. The Italian economy was in such a state that it needed, amongst other desperate remedies, the exclusion of French cattle from its border. We discussed the free movement of cows for some time. The Foreign Secretary then delivered his speech *con brio*, deftly dealt with his critics and – having strongly cultivated potential friends and signalled his determination to putative enemies – left the last half dozen items on the Council of Ministers agenda to me. Naturally, he flew home in the official aeroplane.

That meant that I had to stay in Luxembourg overnight and, because scheduled flights to London were infrequent, I was desperate to catch the early plane. When I came down into the hall of the embassy residence, Goulding was kneeling on the tiled floor, apparently packing his suitcase. I testily asked him what he thought he was doing and, in self-defence, he furtively reopened the case. Inside there was an automatic pistol. He spoke in a barely audible whisper. 'The detective was sent back here yesterday afternoon to sleep it off. He left his revolver hanging on his bed head.'

Jim Callaghan's first speech to his European colleagues had sounded – as I am sure he intended it to sound – deeply antagonistic to Britain's continued Common Market membership. I doubt if, even then, he was as opposed to the EEC as he chose to appear. And certainly, after he had spent a weekend with other Foreign Ministers at a 'political co-operation meeting' held in Germany's Schloss Gymlich, he became an enthusiastic convert to the idea that the nine nations of the EEC should take up common foreign policy positions. But right up to the referendum which confirmed British membership in June 1975, both he and Harold Wilson thought it necessary to prove that they were not infatuated by the European idea. As a result, I was often required to perform tasks which were inappropriate to my humble rank. I never complained about being elevated above my station.

When the tenth anniversary of the Coal and Steel Community was celebrated in Paris, both Prime Minister and Foreign Secretary declined their invitations with formal thanks. In consequence, I was despatched to the embassy residence – an eighteenth-century mansion in the rue Faubourg St Honoré which had been requisitioned by the Duke of Wellington in 1815 and never returned to its previous owner. It is what estate agents call 'in a prestigious location'. The President of France lives next door in a near identical house called the Elysée Palace.

I attended the anniversary reception at the Quai D'Orsay as the official representative of Great Britain and Northern Ireland. Ted Heath was also on the guest list, having been invited in recognition of his role in leading Britain into the Community. He arrived at the residence a few minutes before the cavalcade was about to set off and sat in his car, silently brooding. No doubt he was anxious to avoid Margaret Thatcher, who was staying at the embassy whilst she performed numerous duties as Leader of the Opposition – the office which she had, a few months before, wrested from him. Had the ex-Prime Minister arrived earlier, he would have found his successor's presence everywhere. The public rooms were full of flowers sent to her by well-wishers. Photographers crowded the pavement outside the gate house, hoping to take her picture. And her private hairdresser sat in the foyer waiting to make running repairs. Perhaps it was the ubiquitous signs of Thatcherism that made Ted Heath even more irascible than usual.

The procession in which it was planned we would travel to the Quai D'Orsay was arranged in strict order of precedence. The ambassador, Sir Edward Tomkins (representing the Queen) and the Minister of State (representing her government) were in the Rolls-Royce, immediately behind the first police car. Ted Heath (representing his glorious past) was in the Jaguar behind the police car which protected the Rolls-Royce's rear end. I was a forty-two-year-old Minister of State and he was a sixty-year-old ex-Prime Minister and the arrangement worried me. So I asked Mig Goulding – the Rolls's third passenger – if he would mind exchanging places with Heath. He thought it 'quite the right thing to do' and I went back down the line of cars to propose the change in arrangements. Ted did not look at me as he replied, 'I'm perfectly all right here. I don't wish to be patronised.' Strangely enough, I still like him.

A couple of months later, I went back to Paris for the meeting which set up the European Council – regular and formal meetings of EEC heads of state and government which had not been sanctified by the Treaty of Rome and therefore could only be included in the European constitution after statutory approval by the Council of Foreign Ministers which, although junior to the institution which it created, already legally existed. The governance of Europe is built around such contrivances.

My presence at the Paris preparatory meeting was even more inappropriate than my attendance at the Coal and Steel Community anniversary celebrations. For there was serious work to be done, and I, as well as being the only participant who was not a full Foreign Minister, was also the one member of the group who could not speak fluent French. At the briefing meeting, Eddie Tomkins did not attempt to disguise his fears about the outcome. I assume that his anxiety was conveyed to the two small dogs that sat at his feet. For when we got up to leave his study, it was revealed that they had both defecated on his shoes.

The meeting was concluded without catastrophe and we all flew off to a formal meeting of the Foreign Affairs Council in Brussels. The five real Foreign Ministers sat round a table at the front of the VIP compartment in the presidential jet, whilst I perched on a dicky-seat at the back. I suspected that the seating arrangement had been supervised by Jacques Sauvagnarges, the French Foreign Minister. We did not get on.

Our mutual antagonism came to a head almost a year later during the discussion of the communiqué which was to be issued after a meeting concerned with human rights. Half of the ministers wanted to record their hope of further progress. The rest, more optimistic, wanted to anticipate that progress would be made. After an hour's fruitless argument I suggested that one might compromise around 'hopefully anticipate'. Sauvagnargnes could not have been more offended if I had run away with both his wife and daughter. 'The President of France,' he shouted, 'could never allow his government to be party to such a denial of Cartesian logic. It is shameful that we should ever even consider such a suggestion.' When Tony Crosland succeeded Jim Callaghan as Foreign Secretary, I prepared him for his baptism of EEC fire by telling him the hopefully anticipated story. At his first Council of Ministers he replied to the speeches of welcome with appropriately gracious thanks. He then added, smiling at the French Foreign Minister, 'And let us have no nonsense about Descartes. I know more about him than anyone here.'

There was, and no doubt still is, much about the formal meetings of the European institutions by which reasonable men and women are bound to be irritated. In the days of my regular attendance in Brussels and Luxembourg there were also occasions when Britain's national interest required a robust defence. Usually the moments of spontaneous patriotism were carefully planned and scripted. Occasionally our enemies' knavish tricks were confounded impromptu.

One morning, I was sitting in the cubicle of a Brussels lavatory, correcting errors in the proofs of *Goodbye to Yorkshire*, when I heard Sir Michael Butler, then a senior Foreign Office official and subsequently our Permanent Representative at the Community, shouting, 'Minister! Minister! Come quickly. The Foreign Secretary has gone off his head.' As I collected the proofs and adjusted my clothes before leaving, I wondered what form the madness had taken and what Butler thought I might do to affect a cure.

Decent, but with the pages of my book in disarray, I discovered that the incident which had prompted Sir Michael's diagnosis had occurred during a discussion of the world circle energy crisis brought about by an OPEC price-hike. Jim Callaghan, following his brief, had contributed a number of platitudes. He had then agreed to the EEC sponsoring an international conference. The problem had arisen when the other Foreign Ministers had taken it for granted that the Community as a whole would be represented by the presidency in the form of Gaston Thorn, Prime Minister and Foreign Minister of Luxembourg. At first, Jim Callaghan had seemed unable to understand that Britain would not send its own delegate. Then, when the procedural point had been explained to him several times, he had tried to describe the difficulty of justifying the proposal to the government and people of a major oil-producing nation. It was his concluding remark which led Sir Michael Butler to doubt his sanity. Looking at President, Premier, Foreign Minister Thorn, he had said, 'If there was no Common Market, Britain would certainly be there and nobody would think of inviting Luxembourg.'

The logic of that conclusion was impeccable. But it was the sort of simple truth that nobody spoke at Foreign Affairs Councils and it was alien to the *communitaire* conventions which were supposed to characterise its proceedings. The idea that the British Foreign Secretary had gone mad was one of the more charitable interpretations of his conduct. Most of his colleagues thought that he was declaring war on Europe. European Foreign Ministers expected their colleagues to demand policies which supported their national interest in the language of European unity. A Common Agricultural Policy which made the Bavarian farmers rich and kept Franz-Joseph Strauss's CDU in the government coalition was 'essential to Europe's future'. And target prices for rice and hard wheat, which made Italian farmers almost as happy as the Germans, were the only way to 'build Europe'. I was always astounded by how decisions which seemed exclusively to benefit France were, when properly explained by the French, revealed to be vital to the full implementation of the Treaty of Rome.

Breaking the convention of communitarian hypocrisy was the behaviour of an outsider. It was also the only way for an outsider to impose his will on the Council of Ministers. When the shock waves ceased to vibrate it was agreed that a British minister should accompany Thorn to the international energy conference and I reminded Sir Michael Butler of what Michael Foot had said in the House of Commons on the day when I made my maiden speech: 'The Right Honourable Member for Cardiff South [that is to say Jim Callaghan] always does everything on purpose.'

By the early spring of 1975, the Common Market 'renegotiation' was successfully completed. Jim Callaghan had obtained enough adjustments in the terms of British membership to justify his recommendation that the United Kingdom remained part of the EEC. Unfortunately, not all the Cabinet shared his view. And a special Labour conference decisively supported withdrawal under the slogan – which the pro-Marketeers had cunningly devised as an escape route – 'Labour Recommends – Britain Decides'. The referendum which followed was not an attempt to hide the divisions in the Party's ranks. The gulf was too wide and deep to be hidden by any contrivance of that sort. 'Consulting the people' was the first victory for Bennism. It ought to have taught us how futile such populist gestures always are.

On the day that the campaign opened, no lesser figure than Francis-Xavier Ortoli, the President of the European Commission, asked to see me. Much to their chagrin all Foreign Office officials – apart from my private secretary – were excluded, at his request, from the meeting. He had come to warn me that a British company was believed to be in breach of Community regulations and that, probably a week before referendum day, assorted Frenchmen, Italians and Germans would raid its West End offices. Would this be represented, by anti-Marketeers, as intolerable interference in Britain's internal affairs? I said that on balance I thought that it would and suggested – with I thought a rather good imitation of his speaking style – how Tony Benn would exploit the episode. President Ortoli agreed to postpone the raid. My judgement about Tony Benn's reaction was confirmed, in Cabinet, the following Thursday. An over-zealous clerk in the Foreign Office registry – the sub-department which stored all official papers – had noticed that the Department of Industry figured prominently in the minutes of my meeting with President

Ortoli and sent a copy of the minute to the minister in charge, Tony Benn.

Jim Callaghan defended me with great spirit. He told me so himself when he asked me to perform a delicate task on behalf of the Labour Europeans who – thanks to the Party's opposition – had no money to spend on our campaign. Jim, perhaps with an eye on his personal future, was anxious to commission an opinion poll on the attitudes of Labour supporters. He had telephoned Derek Raynor, the managing director of Marks and Spencer, and told him to expect an important and highly confidential message. I was to be the messenger who relayed the request for £5,000.

When I got to Marks and Spencer's head office, I was immediately shown into the boardroom, where all of the directors – most of them called Sieff – were assembled behind a long mahogany table. They had the air of men who were expecting an historical announcement. Had it not been for their inadequately suppressed excitement, I would have suspected that Marks and Spencer was the company which the European Commission was about to raid. But it was clearly good news that they expected, though I have never discovered what it was. Despite their obvious disappointment, they did not allow the anti-climax to blur their judgement or diminish their generosity. Sir Marcus (not by then Lord) Sieff replied on behalf of the whole board. He said, 'Of course,' in the tones of a jovial philanthropist who had willingly dropped the change from his back pocket into a beggar's tin cup.

The survey, of course, revealed that Labour voters – like everybody else – wanted to remain in the European Community and the referendum was duly won by the pro-Marketeers. I doubt if ten per cent voted on the merits of the issue or even according to their reaction to the question on the ballot paper. They put a cross against their prejudices and – most important of all – supported the position taken up by the politicians they supported. A referendum campaign with Harold Wilson, Ted Heath, Roy Jenkins, David Steel and (rather reluctantly) Margaret

Thatcher on one side and Enoch Powell, Tony Benn, Barbara Castle and Jack Jones of the Transport and General Workers Union on the other can only have one result. If we ever have another referendum in this country, it will be decided on much the same, irrelevant and inadequate, considerations.

With the 'renegotiation' – theoretically my reason for being at the Foreign Office – successfully concluded, I began to hope again for promotion. Other Ministers of State, notably my old friend Fred Mulley, joined the Cabinet, but I did not receive the long-awaited call. My one consolation was an article in *Time* magazine which set out its prediction of the hundred men and women who would be running the world in twenty years' time. Appearing on the list was even more gratifying than being one of the *Young Meteors* about whom Jonathan Aitken wrote a book back in the sixties – especially since the Americans claimed that I had been 'held back for speaking my mind'. Putting aside all memory of how the Aitken hagiology had been treated – the *New Statesman* wrote that anyone who admired Roy Hattersley and Peter Walker must be a moral degenerate – I waited for Harold to read the article in *Time* and respond to popular demand. He remained unmoved. I suspect he realised, sooner than I, that the American magazine was not a very good picker – at least as far as Britain was concerned. One of the English nominees only made it to Minister of State at the Department of Social Security. Another, after a meteoric beginning, became economics correspondent for BBC Television. And then there was me. The New York journalist had better luck with continental Europe. Jan Olszewski became Prime Minister of Poland after one or two problems and a fresh-faced, thin youth called Helmut Kohl went on to become something big in Germany.

The only immediate change in my status was appointment to the Foreign Office panel which advised the Queen on the appointment of ambassadors – I was shocked to discover that, before we made our recommendations, we examined photographs of the potential nominees' wives – and the addition of the Middle East to my spheres of reluctant influence. I was also asked to take a greater interest in Eastern Europe, which I took as a rebuke for my previous detachment. That, much to my regret, required me to visit Soviet satellites.

I spent four days in Hungary and hated every minute. It was an over-vivid imagination which made me think that the people looked and acted as if they were oppressed as well as poor. But there were too many real signs of totalitarianism to enable me to relax and feel at home. Every public building we visited had armed policemen in the corridors. When my meeting with the Foreign Minister dragged on into the early evening, a message was sent to the opera house telling the management that the performance, to which he was to take me, must not begin before we arrived. The once exquisite icons which were exhibited as a sign of the regime's tolerance had been touched up with what seemed to be acrylic paint. When, on the morning of my departure from Budapest, I was told that the airport might be snowbound, I was nearer to crying than at any time since the dental inspection during my first week at grammar school.

I fought, but failed, to reverse the decision to send me to Bulgaria in the spring of 1976. On the night before I left for Sofia, Jim Callaghan sent for me and – much to my surprise – began to chat inconsequentially. Inconsequential gossip was not Jim's way. But when the talk got round to Cabinet changes and back-bench promotions, I guessed that our meeting had a specific purpose. The Prime Minister was about to shuffle his government and the Foreign Secretary had been asked for advice. My brain was being picked. I said that Bryan Gould was too clever to ignore for long – even though he had asked some silly, and damaging, questions about sterling and the exchange rate. Jim Callaghan expressed reluctance to promote anyone who 'speaks to me as if I've just come down from the trees' and, much to my relief, asked what

Cabinet job I wanted. I said Education. With me, it was always Education.

I arrived at Sofia airport late on the following afternoon and was handed a bunch of gladioli which were so big that I had to hold them in both arms. A military band – in tasselled boots, Ruritanian tunics and steel helmets – played a couple of bars of 'God Save the Queen' and moved on to the Bulgarian national anthem. Halfway through the third or fourth chorus, the British ambassador, Eddie Boland, spoke to me out of the corner of his mouth without relaxing from rigid attention. 'The Prime Minister resigned this morning.' Fearful that distaste for the Bulgarian government had made me ignore much of the briefing, I apologised for my ignorance and asked, 'Is he the big noise over here, or is the real boss the chairman of the Central Committee?' Boland remained at attention, even though the anthem was finished, and said, 'Not their Prime Minister, our Prime Minister.'

At first it was impossible to believe the news. I felt like those parish clerks who refused to nail the news of Queen Victoria's death to their vestry notice boards because they could not imagine the world without her. When I came round I telephoned, with some difficulty, the Department of the Environment. Tony Crosland would, I knew, want to stand for the Labour Party leadership. But a derisory vote would ruin both his prospects and his reputation. It was my task, as a friend, to warn him not to do it. When I got through to his private office, a pert young woman told me that, 'The Secretary of State has already left for the Palace.' The reply was eerily reminiscent of Mr Gladstone hurrying to kiss hands at the beginning of one of his great administrations. In fact, Tony was on his way to an athletes' reception, deputising for his junior minister, Denis Howell, who was ill.

Much to my credit, I completed three days of my five-day visit. They are very fond of goat's cheese in Bulgaria – especially when it is wrapped in foil and warmed until it oozes yellow fat. Three days was enough.

I went straight from Heathrow to the Department of the Environment in Marsham Street where a lift was waiting for me. It climbed, without stopping, to the topmost floor where Tony greeted me with the news that he was already a nominated leadership candidate. 'And there's no point in arguing, it's public so don't argue.' I did not argue, but no doubt I looked disapproving. 'The important thing now,' Tony said, 'is to get a decent vote. I take it you'll vote for me.' It was a statement not a question. I said that I would vote for Jim Callaghan on the simple principle that Michael Foot had a real chance of winning and that, for all his virtues, Foot could not become Prime Minister. Tony was incredulous. 'You'll not vote for me? Even on the first ballot?' I said that he had correctly judged my intentions. I thought that I knew him well, but I was not ready for his reaction. 'Then fuck off.'

I did exactly what I was told. The lift in which I had travelled to the top of the building was still, doors open, on the fourteenth floor and I did not take my finger off the 'foyer' button until I was back at ground level. A porter, waiting by the lift shaft, held out an authoritarian hand. 'The Secretary of State would like a word.' I told him that the Secretary of State had already had two, and pushed the swing doors. The man followed me out on to the street. 'Well, he wants another one.' Out of the love I bore for Tony Crosland, I went back. He grinned as he poured me a drink. As always it was whisky and, as usual, I told him that I hated the stuff and then drank it. 'Come to lunch on Sunday,' he said. 'The house will be full of people organising my campaign. But we needn't bother with them.'

Tony Crosland was knocked out of the leadership contest on the first ballot. Jim Callaghan won on the third. I was not at the meeting of the Parliamentary Party which was called to hear the official announcement of the result. The Council of Ministers was discussing Common Fisheries Policy and I was in Brussels, fighting for a fair deal for Scottish fishermen. Willie Ross, the abrasive Secretary of State for Scotland, was sent along with me to make sure that I was not so overcome with the spirit of the Community that I allowed *them* to trawl for *our* fish. Willie could be relied on to keep me honest. He thought that the negotiating brief, which conceded nothing, should have been written in more aggressive language. To my surprise we got almost everything for which we asked. 'What do we do now?' Willie asked. It seemed to me a good moment to proclaim a triumph. 'We go', I told him, 'to the press conference and say how well we've done for Scotland.' Willie Ross, on his last day in government, decided to end his ministerial career as he had spent it – irascibly. 'You'd better go on your own. I couldna' say that we'd done well with any conviction.'

Six weeks later, I was doing not very much in my office when Roger Westbrook came in, radiating excitement. The Prime Minister wished to see me at eleven o'clock. But he could not tell me the reason for my invitation. No doubt I would discover if the news was good or bad when I got there. Jim Callaghan usually treated overseas visits – which he much enjoyed – as if they were an intolerable burden. He once reported after a week in Delhi that the Indian Prime Minister had 'promised four million people at the rally we addressed', and then added, 'I doubt if there were more than three.' That morning he complained about his bad luck in having to stay at home. He should have left at dawn for an official visit to Canada, but a prairie fire had turned into a national emergency and Pierre Trudeau had asked him to postpone his trip until the following spring. So, with time on his hands, he had decided to spend it shuffling his government. Would I like to join the Cabinet as Secretary of State for Prices and Consumer Protection? I told him that I would.

It was, the Prime Minister told me, essential that our conversation remain absolutely secret until the official announcement was made at three o'clock. To encourage my discretion, he added, 'I might change my mind, and then it'll be you who looks silly, not me.' Before I could feel totally depressed by the suggestion that I was still not certain of a place in the Cabinet, Jim Callaghan asked me a question that made me think that I was, after all, secure. 'I want young Kinnock in the government. Would you mind taking him on?' At that moment, I would have taken on anybody the Prime Minister wanted to promote, but the incumbent, Bob MacLennan, was a friend of mine. I argued that he should not be sacked. Naturally my plea for a reprieve was dismissed. As I left the Cabinet Room, the Prime Minister repeated his stern injunction – 'Not a word, to anyone.' I took the vow of silence and hurried home to spread the good news.

There was no mention of a reshuffle on the one or three o'clock bulletins and I did not regard no news as good news. At half past four I left, with debilitating reluctance, for Birmingham, telling myself that, by the time I arrived, the whole world would know that I was a Cabinet minister. It was the era of the transistor and I took mine with me. It reproduced the sound of a two-stroke engine all the way from Euston to New Street.

As the train slowed down at the platform I noticed – first to my surprise and then to my delight – a figure whom I rightly assumed to be the station master. Admittedly, he was not wearing a top hat, but he carried a bowler in his hand and his lapel was decorated with a huge scarlet carnation. When he opened my carriage door and introduced himself I wondered if this was the sort of welcome which Cabinet ministers received at the end of every journey. Then he gave me his message. 'You must telephone Downing Street at once.' As we ran to his office, I had no doubt that Jim Callaghan had found out I had disobeyed him and that, as a result of my indiscretion, promotion had been denied me. Since I could not expect any more good news that day, I began to wonder if I was to be punished with the ultimate penalty. My nerves were not calmed by a private secretary who said that, 'The Prime Minister is very sorry about all this.' Then he explained.

Neil Kinnock had declined to serve in the government – offering instead to look after the miners at the Department of

Energy. Jim was not the man to have his government picked for him and the object of the proposed promotion was to detach Kinnock from the left, not make him Tony Benn's deputy. MacLennan had in consequence been reprieved. As it was thought essential to have the changes reported on the six o'clock news, details of the whole reshuffle had been given to the press at half past five. The Prime Minister wished to offer his apologies for the gross discourtesy of publishing the name of my parliamentary secretary before I had been consulted.

I could not believe that a guilt-ridden Jim Callaghan was fretting in the Cabinet Room about the way in which I had been treated. But, thinking it my duty to take part in the charade, I said that I was grateful for the Prime Minister's concern. It was not a moment to be bothered about civil service conceits. It was not a moment to be bothered about anything. I was forty-three and I had just become a Secretary of State. There was no doubt that I would be in the Cabinet for the next twenty years. And as for Neil Kinnock – I doubted if I would ever hear of him again.

CHAPTER
9

Sir Kenneth Clucas, KCB – Permanent Secretary in the Department of Prices and Consumer Protection – was waiting for me on the front doorstep. I had known, liked and admired him when I was Parliamentary Secretary in the Ministry of Labour back in the mid-sixties and he was as near to a cult figure as it was possible for a civil servant to be. Clucas was an under secretary and, according to folk-lore, being held back because of an incident which his fellow bureaucrats regarded as much to his credit.

Like all rising stars of the civil service, Clucas was required to spend a couple of years in the Minister's private office, and he was appointed private secretary to John Hare. Apparently master and servant got on like a house on fire until image turned into reality. One day, Hare threw a lighted cigar into his waste paper basket and it burst into flames. Private secretaries are notorious for noticing what ministers have missed. But Hare was surprised when Clucas suddenly pointed at the carafe of water on the huge ministerial desk and cried, 'Pour it out,' without even adding please.

Hare, still unaware of the inferno raging at his feet – and thinking that Clucas was thirsty – replied, with a remarkable disregard for his own dignity, 'If you want a drink, you pour it out.' Clucas should clearly have risked a general conflagration rather than argue with his boss. But he was on the far side of a large room and he believed speed to be of the essence. So, in order to stimulate Hare into immediate action, he retorted, 'Don't be so bloody silly, pour the water on the fire.' His shock tactics had the desired effect. But although Clucas had saved the Ministry, he had lost the Minister's confidence. His promotion from assistant to under secretary was delayed. He was still an under secretary when I left the Ministry of Labour in 1969.

I always feared that the story was apocryphal. But I both hoped that it was true and knew why, if it was an invention, the fiction was so widely believed. Clucas was the sort of man who might well have done that sort of thing. It was his independence of spirit which prompted him to tell me, immediately on my arrival, that most of the new department had been recruited from the Board of Trade and were, in consequence, instinctively sceptical about the government intervention in the free market. I decided that it was best to tell him the truth in return. More intervention was what the Prime Minister wanted. And since I was more afraid of Jim Callaghan than I was of the whole administrative civil service, more intervention was what they were going to get.

During my first morning of discussions with DPCP officials, I witnessed again 'the Shirley Williams phenomenon'. Shirley had been my predecessor as Secretary of State and the department's civil servants were in thrall to her peculiar charm. They were openly critical of her record as Minister – particularly her policy of awarding red triangles which were subsequently displayed in the windows of virtuous shops. The officers who served and advised me wanted to end the butter subsidy (which helped the better off far more than it assisted the poor), repeal the legislation that enabled the government to set the minimum price of bread, and stop talking about the National Consumer Council as if it were powerful enough to act as a counterweight to the Trades Union

Congress and the Confederation of British Industry. Yet – despite their impatience with the Minister's ideas – they loved the Minister. Losing her was a bureaucratic bereavement for which there was no consolation. No successor could possibly have filled the gap in their lives. They were particularly suspicious of me.

The civil servants' apprehensions were increased by my appointment of two 'special advisers' – the right of every Cabinet minister. David Hill, who had been my all purpose assistant since 1971, was accepted without any fuss. He was what political advisers are supposed to be – a young and able Oxonian who had abandoned industry for politics. His tasks were easily enough defined. He would keep me in touch with both Labour Party policy and grass roots opinion (by no means certain to be the same thing), remind me of my manifesto commitments and plot with other political advisers in other departments of state. The problem was Maurice Peston – the hero of the statistical victory over Margaret Thatcher. Peston was a professor of economics. So they feared that he would want to interfere with policy. Their fears were absolutely justified.

During my period of exile in the Foreign Office, Maurice Peston had worked at the Department of Education and Science for Reg Prentice – the man who left the Labour Party and, after crossing the floor of the House, became a Tory minister. In 1974, he had been promoted over my head because, unlike me, he could be trusted. Peston had, therefore, already been away from his university department for two years. And he had been warned – both by his colleagues and his wife – that by remaining in the public service he was risking the collapse of his academic career. Nevertheless, Peston agreed to join the Department of Prices. Indeed, he said that, if necessary, he would accept appointment in the rank of under secretary grade, even though he had served as a deputy secretary in the DES. He did, however, have one stipulation. A car-park space, underneath the department's head office in Victoria Street, had to be placed at his permanent disposal.

The Department of Prices lived in cramped conditions. The Victoria Street building was the head office of three ministries – my own DPCP, Industry, and Trade. The idea was that common services would provide the economies of scale. Living cheek by jowl, however, created tensions which more than outweighed the advantages of obtaining central heating from the same system. In the early days of the Wilson government, Tony Benn was Secretary of State for Industry and his uncomradely conduct had so offended the delicate sensibilities of Shirley Williams that she proposed the upgrading of a side door and its designation as the official and separate entrance to her distinct and sovereign department. When that scheme failed, she accepted with relief a plan to move the whole department down the Thames to Millbank Tower. I arrived after the removal (of the department, not Tony Benn) had been agreed but not completed. So the car park was crowded.

The Civil Service Commission was adamant about the terms of Peston's appointment. His academic distinction, professional status and previous rank in the DES made it essential that he joined the DPCP as a deputy secretary. The Head of Services in the triple department was no less obdurate. No parking space could be provided. So, for a week or more, it seemed that Maurice's advice would be denied me. Then a piece of unoccupied concrete was found behind the coke bunkers and Peston submitted the first draft of his job description. Both the permanent secretary and I rejected it, though for different reasons. It read, 'To give spurious intellectual justification to the Secretary of State's political prejudices.'

Peston's strange sense of humour remained a feature of the department's life. During the fraught negotiations which preceded the repeat of the minimum bread price legislation, I was confronted by angry bakers who wanted to keep the price of the standard loaf artificially high. They challenged me to admit how much I paid for my wholewheat, granary or rye. 'The Secretary of

State', Peston replied, 'knows the value of everything and the price of nothing' – an answer which bewildered a group of men who had barely heard of Oscar Wilde.

I should have known what to expect from Maurice Peston. At a Fabian school which we both addressed, during my early weeks at the Foreign Office, a lady had complained about the room in Ruskin College annexe which she shared with her daughter and offered to exchange it, with daughter *in situ*, for one with a washbasin. Peston asked the girl to stand up – which she foolishly did. Maurice said that he would keep his washbasin. Behaviour like that becomes infectious. At least that is my excuse for sending Peston, during the same conference, 'The Attenborough Telegram'.

Richard Attenborough had sat next to me at a Foreign Office lunch arranged in honour of the Canadian Prime Minister. Our conversation had turned to football and he had invited me to a match between Chelsea (the club of which he was then a director) and Sheffield Wednesday. Maurice came with me and was almost instantly annoyed by Attenborough who – when the two men were introduced – said that he had hoped to meet Peston for years. Unabashed by the professor's insistence that, 'Nobody has heard of me,' Mr Attenborough (as he still was then) continued to be the perfect host, even apologising for Sheffield Wednesday's defeat. In the weeks which followed, both Peston and I received so many invitations to Attenborough functions that his enthusiasm for our company became a joke. Whenever his name was mentioned one of us would maliciously cry, 'Honours List.' We composed bogus letters of recommendation, invented titles, composed mottoes and sketched coats of arms. Richard Attenborough's knighthood was announced on New Year's Day 1975.

I cannot imagine what madness prompted me to send the telegram to Maurice. But I can remember what it said. 'Naturally delighted. Thanks for all you did to bring it about. See you soon. Dickie Attenborough.' I did not intend a hoax. I assumed that

Peston would realise at once the telegram's origin and think of it as an extension of our longer running joke. My assumption was wrong.

Maurice, fuming with indignation, brought the telegram to the Fabian weekend school at which he was subsequently to choose the washbasin rather than the daughter. I was giving the first lecture and he arrived just after I had started. Instead of listening to me, he stared hard at the contents of a yellow Post Office envelope. Then he stared at the reply he proposed to send as soon as I had finished. At the coffee break he showed me both the telegram and the response. I confessed. Maurice and I went back to London separately.

I have always suspected that the Silver Jubilee Medal Fiasco was Maurice Peston's revenge for the Attenborough Knighthood Telegram. The Silver Jubilee Medal was awarded to several thousand loyal subjects, amongst whom I was included despite my undisguised reluctance to participate in the celebrations. I had intended to attend the Service of Thanksgiving for no better reason than a desire to enjoy a hour in the splendour of St Paul's Cathedral. But when I discovered that I had to be in my pew a hour before the Queen arrived, I decided to pay homage to Sir Christopher Wren on some other occasion. I was, however, at Buckingham Palace with the rest of the Cabinet when we presented our commemorative gift – a Georgian silver coffee pot which the Queen had actually chosen as something which, since it would be in regular use, would remind her of the Callaghan administration. The decision to ask Her Majesty what she would like to receive from her ministers was Jim Callaghan's own – taken after a desultory discussion in the Cabinet during which Shirley Williams had proposed that our gift should be a saddle and John Morris, the Secretary of State for Wales, had suggested a clock set in a lump of coal. I paid my contribution towards the Cabinet's gift and forgot all about the Jubilee.

Because of the large number of recipients – more, it was said at the time, than even the Victory Medal – the Jubilee Medal was sent through the post. Maurice Peston saw the little box on my private secretary's desk and, believing it to contain wedding cake, stole it to eat with his morning coffee. When he discovered his mistake he amused himself by drafting a statement for me to issue to the press:

> I accept this honour not on my own behalf but as a tribute to those anonymous heroes and heroines on whom I depend.

Somehow the 'draft' fell into the hands of the news department who, believing it to be my work, prepared dozens of copies for distribution. The messenger who was taking them to the press gallery in the House of Commons was intercepted just before he handed them to the waiting journalists.

Every member of the Cabinet received a Jubilee Medal and, by the time that it was presented by our postmen, we all felt that we should have also been awarded wound stripes. For we had lived through what came to be known as the IMF crisis.

During the forty-two days that the IMF crisis lasted, the Cabinet held six special meetings. For most of the time, we were chasing shadows. We now know that the crisis had its origins not in the weakness of the pound, or in the extravagance of the government, but in the minds of whoever it is who provides or withholds 'international confidence'. But that made the crisis no less real. According to official statistics, the Public Sector Borrowing Requirement was £12 billion – a trivial deficit by the standards of modern deficits but one which Denis Healey, quite independently of the International Monetary Fund, determined to cut to £9 billion. His judgement was impeccable. For to have accepted the £12 billion deficit of government spending would have been to provoke an uncontainable run on sterling. But the Chancellor's impeccable judgement was based on a Treasury miscalculation. When the government set out on its agonising assault on public expenditure, borrowing was – in reality – already lower than the target figure which we cut, slashed and carved in order to obtain.

Inevitably the argument about how we should make up the IMF package developed into what newspapers described as an argument between right and left. As is usually the case with such disputes the alignment of forces was far more complicated (and much more fluid) than so simple a description of the situation suggests. The Chancellor's initial proposals were supported by the *soi-disant* realists – Eric Varley (Industry), Roy Mason (Northern Ireland), Bill Rodgers (Transport), Bruce Millan (Scotland) and Edmund Dell (Treasury). The left were led by Tony Benn (Energy), who thought that it was possible to get the economy back on its feet by repeating a series of clichés concerning greed not need, the inherent weakness of capitalism and the innate wisdom of the workers. He was followed, from time to time, by Stanley Orme (Social Security), Albert Booth (Employment) and John Silkin (Agriculture). But occasionally they were seduced by the more sophisticated arguments of Peter Shore (Trade), who proposed an alternative which he was inclined to describe as 'The Alternative'. It involved import controls, tougher limitations on the movement of capital and a planned depreciation of the pound. Tony Crosland (at the Foreign Office) led a small band of optimists who believed it necessary to keep calm, consider all the options, resist the IMF's most draconian demands and do all we could to protect both employment and public services. I was his man from the start. For a time, Shirley Williams (Education), Harold Lever (Paymaster General) and David Ennals (Health) were also at his side. But his campaign was doomed from the start. It was – to corrupt an idea from *1066 and All That* – Right but Reasonable. At desperate moments like the IMF crisis, reason rarely prevails.

These were, by any standards, desperate days. But even the fight against bankruptcy has its lighter moments. At one Cabinet meeting Tony Benn – who has always specialised in improbable metaphors – announced that the trade unions were following the path to freedom which had once been trod by the subject peoples of the colonies. Having thrown off the shackles of imperialism and achieved Dominion status, they were engaged in the battle for full independence. I was rash enough to suggest – not quite *sotto voce* – that the comparison was 'the most stupid idea that I have ever heard'. It was not the sort of comment of which the Prime Minister approved and I was waiting for his rebuke when Denis Healey casually observed that his long-held doubts about my judgement had been confirmed. Tony, he said, had often made more stupid comments than the one which I had misidentified. And he offered examples to prove his point. There followed a general discussion of the subject. Jim Callaghan – who could recognise when the Cabinet needed to relax – let the argument go on for about five minutes. Then he reproved me for interrupting a colleague and invited Tony to continue his analysis of the problem which we faced together.

It was Denis Healey's habit to while away the time that he had to spend listening to his colleagues by cutting articles from the morning's newspapers. What he did with them after they had been filleted from the page was never clear. But the act of dissection had, in itself, an effect on the rest of the Cabinet. For Denis carved away with a razor blade. Admittedly it was contained in the sort of holder which, before the war, could be bought for sixpence from Woolworths. But that gave it the appearance of a home-made flick knife. Denis kept it on a keyring which was attached to his braces by a long chain. The result was that his critics had to advance their arguments against a background of rustling, rattling and slashing.

One day, Denis was slicing happily away when Tony Benn announced that Peter Shore's plan – derisively dismissed by its opponents as a 'siege economy' – could work without a massive reduction in public spending and a substantial increase in unemployment. Denis did not look up from the surgery he was performing on *The Times* as he asked Tony to name one reputable economist who supported the idea of a painless solution to Britain's problems. The answer came back without a moment's hesitation: Wynne Godley. Denis carved on as if he had been confounded. Then, dramatically, he held up a couple of column inches which he had pruned from the letters page. There followed a few minutes of theatrical business of which Donald Wolfit would have been proud – smoothing the paper, focusing on the type and trying to pronounce the words. Eventually he managed to read the brief but authoritative assertion that the Alternative Strategy had to be accompanied by severe deflation. Then, after a titanic struggle with palate, teeth and tonsils, Denis pronounced the signature: 'Wynne Godley, King's College, Cambridge.'

It is obvious now that there was never much chance of Denis Healey's IMF proposals being defeated. Tony Crosland fought a dashing rearguard action and won whenever the battle turned into hand to hand combat. But the Chancellor had reserves. The silent minority – John Morris (Wales), Merlyn Rees (Home Office), Elwyn Jones (Lord Chancellor) and Fred Peart (Leader of the House of Lords) – were waiting to follow the Prime Minister's lead. So was Michael Foot – the Leader of the House and deputy leader of the Party. Though his heart was somewhere between Tony Benn and Peter Shore, he clearly believed that loyalty required him to stand shoulder to shoulder with Jim Callaghan who, rightly and inevitably, came out for the Chancellor.

As the debate ground on, Tony Crosland's supporters fell away one by one. Shirley Williams, true to character, thought it her duty to rally to the besieged Chancellor. Harold Lever was sent off to Washington as the Prime Minister's emissary and, as Jim intended, became so enmeshed in the Treasury's preferred policy that he felt committed to it. David Ennals, having been offered extra resources for the health service, naturally enough declared himself a winner and gave up the fight. I have no idea how long I would have stayed on the burning deck.

Fortunately my resolve was never tested. In the aeroplane, on the way back from a European Summit, the Prime Minister told the Foreign Secretary that the debate had gone on long enough and that he proposed to ask the Cabinet to accept the Chancellor's proposals. Jim also set out what he regarded as the consequences of continued disagreement. If Denis were to be defeated, it would be a repudiation of the Prime Minister's economic judgement – a situation which no government could survive. He assumed that Tony was sensible enough to accept that the time had come to rally round Denis Healey. He was right.

Tony Crosland came from the airport to the House of Commons where, in a splendid reversal of events of the week of Harold Wilson's resignation, he came straight to see me in my room on the Upper Ministerial Corridor. He began to tell me where my duty lay as soon as he walked through the door. The Prime Minister had come to a decision and the rest of us had no choice but to accept it. Tony, who never shrank from patronising a friend, had told the Prime Minister that he would make sure I behaved sensibly, and Jim had replied, 'He'll be all right. I know about him. I appointed him to my Cabinet.' Clearly Tony was still not quite convinced. For he added, 'If I can swallow it, you can. Remember, no heroics.' He need not have worried.

When he was convinced that I would behave sensibly, he invited me downstairs to the grand but inhospitable room which is the Foreign Secretary's House of Commons home. As he poured the drinks, he told me, by way of consolation, 'We never could have won anyway.' He was wrong. Beating the Chancellor of the Exchequer – and by implication the Prime Minister – would have been a catastrophic mistake. Denis Healey would have been forced to resign, the Party in Parliament would have split down the middle, sterling would have collapsed and the government might well have been brought down. But it could have been done.

Halfway through the extended discussion of Denis Healey's proposals, the arithmetic of support and opposition became obvious to anyone who could add up. When the debate began, certainly ten and probably twelve Cabinet ministers were opposed to the cuts in public expenditure which the Chancellor's proposal involved. Even if it had not been possible to cobble together a majority for any alternative, it would certainly – had the critics combined – been possible to make changes to the package that were far more substantial than the limited amendments which were accepted as the price of buying off the individual ministers. Changing Denis's mind required the creation of a credible alliance. And David Hill, my political adviser, assumed that the protection of public services was a cause which would unite Cabinet rebels of every sort. He therefore approached Frances Morrell, his opposite number in Tony Benn's office, and suggested an alliance. The idea was rejected point blank. The Bennites could see no advantage in making common cause with the Croslandites.

At the end of the long debate – with Denis, at least in personal terms, triumphant – the total cuts were still a few million pounds short of the savings for which the Chancellor asked. Jim Callaghan, fighting despair, said that he would take part in no further discussion. A sub-committee was set up with the explicit instruction of finding the necessary savings. I was added to it as an afterthought.

As soon as we convened Tony Benn spoke eloquently about the futility of '*pro-rata*' cuts – each minister bullied and cajoled into making a propositional contribution on the basis of equality of suffering. He then said that he was prepared to fund the outstanding deficit from changes in his department's contribution. The whole amount could easily be met from an increase in fuel prices. It was Joel Barnett, chief secretary to the Treasury, who explained that the increase would make possible the purchase of coal from previously 'uneconomic' pits. Tony was, as always, faithfully following the policy of the National Union of Mineworkers. As a result he became the one member of the Cabinet to volunteer 'IMF cuts'. I offered to sacrifice the butter subsidy as long as the saving was used to hold down the price of school meals, and was sternly told by the Prime Minister that neither he nor the Chancellor was making bargains. For different reasons Tony Benn and I did not boast about our flexible approach to the IMF Review. Though I think we both understood that the autumn of 1976 was the time that the Labour Party changed.

After the 'IMF Crisis', Labour was no longer the party of public expenditure. The impression left by both the debate and the decision was not simply that a sensible government spends no more than it can afford. The whole idea of public expenditure – both its social merits and its economic advantages – was suddenly challenged. Labour began to examine precepts which it had previously taken for granted. And for a political party that is only one step away from acknowledging the possibility that its long-held beliefs are wrong.

The trauma through which the Cabinet went was later revealed in a television 'reconstruction' which claimed to reproduce, in a sixty-minute broadcast, the long hours of debate. When the Prime Minister discovered that the programme was being made he forbade the Cabinet to help with its production. So when Peter Riddell, then political correspondent of the *Financial Times*, and now political columnist on *The Times*, said that he was to play me, I refused to help him write his lines. The result was a broadcast which I hope has not been kept in the archives of Independent Television.

As soon as I switched on the 'reconstruction', I realised how great a mistake I had made. For it was immediately obvious that not all of my Cabinet colleagues had accepted the interdict. Dick Clements of *Tribune* (playing Tony Benn) and the *Guardian*'s Peter Jenkins (as Tony Crosland) seemed particularly well informed. They dominated the programme. Both, to my astonishment, reproduced the speeches of their real-life counterparts in exact detail, only omitting points which had subsequently been proved wrong. The result was fascinating television. It revealed a battle between two ideological giants in which the great principles of socialism were measured against the necessities of economic reality. The two Titans were, undoubtedly, the stars of the show. But other participants – portraying Shirley Williams, Peter Shore and the Chancellor himself – played noble parts. Unfortunately their well-informed and lucid discussion was constantly interrupted by one Cabinet alter ego who kept repeating, like a parrot trying to get itself noticed, the same slogan: 'Socialism is about equality and we cannot have greater equality if we cut public spending.' The man with the one-track mind was played by Peter Riddell. Looking back, I feel proud to have become so firmly associated with the one idea which is both demonstrably correct and the bed-rock of socialist belief.

Perhaps it was my performance on the reconstruction that made the Prime Minister doubt the wisdom of my participation in a *Panorama* profile. It took him almost a month to agree. So the filming began just as we, at the Department of Prices, were beginning our assault on the tea blenders – a group of gentlemen who, in the opinion of the Price Commission which had examined their books, were operating a cartel. I was astonished to discover that the blenders had agreed to our discussion being recorded by the BBC film crew. I prepared for the confrontation with even more care than usual. The civil servants who briefed me all expressed the hope that I would do most of the talking. They were not, said Deputy Secretary John Burgh, natural performers.

There was a brief interval between briefing and meeting, during which David Hill persuaded me to comb my hair and the television people set up lights. Then the civil servant

returned. At first I thought that their numbers had been aug-
mented by a young lady who had never given me advice before
but, when I stepped forward to introduce myself, I realised that an
assistant secretary who visited my office almost every day had
spent the intermission covering herself in extravagant make-up.
The combination of heavy sun-burn, scarlet lips and thick bifocals
was not a complete success. But it certainly captured the tea
blenders' attention. The cameras were captivated not by her
appearance but by what she said. As soon as the pleasantries
were over she launched a clearly premeditated attack on Ty-
Phoo, Brooke-Bond and the Co-operative Wholesale Society in
turn. After about half an hour I ended the meeting, partly because
I could not force my way into the conversation but mostly so as to
avoid unnecessary punishment being inflicted on the tea blenders
who were clearly no match for my heavyweight. The tea blenders
capitulated. The newspapers said that the CWS had broken ranks
and decided to make a voluntary cut in the cost of English
Breakfast rather than accept the humiliation of a statutory price
reduction. But I believe that they were afraid to face a return
match against the virago in the pancake make-up.

In those corporatist days, the four 'economic ministers' in the
Cabinet – Denis Healey, Eric Varley, Albert Booth and I – used to
have regular meetings with the TUC and CBI in the hope of
securing 'agreed policies'. The meetings with the TUC were
often passionate but always genial. The CBI, led by Sir John
Methven, were obstructive and tedious. Denis Healey rushed
into one gathering and, whilst the participants were standing
around waiting for the proceedings to begin, slapped Sir John on
the back and told him, 'I can't stand that miserable bugger,
Methven.' Later that evening Methven – not, I am sure, in
retaliation – complained that he had discussed how to relieve
pressure on the pound so often that he was beginning to feel *déjà
vu*. He then made the mistake of translating the phrase into
English and explaining to Denis that the original was French. For

the next ten minutes, the Chancellor of the Exchequer addressed the director-general of the CBI in fluent Italian. He then moved on to perfect German. Latin followed. Finally he spoke French, acting as his own interpreter, sentence by sentence.

I did not look forward to negotiating a new statutory prices policy with the CBI – not least because the CBI did not believe in statutory prices policy. To my immense annoyance, three of my officials, led by Deputy Secretary John Burgh, expressed the hope that the initial meeting would not go on into the evening, for they had an engagement which they could not miss. I was even more irritated when they turned up at the briefing meeting wearing dinner jackets and bow ties. I did not, at first, realise the significance of the CBI delegation arriving in similarly formal dress. At half past seven – with very little progress made – Sir John Methven announced that the discussions must be adjourned. He and his colleagues then left for Covent Garden, accompanied by his guests – three senior officials from my department.

We drafted a new Prices Bill more or less over the CBI's body and, despite Labour's single figure majority, its Second Reading was agreed without much difficulty. But the Committee Stage – the line-by-line consideration of every clause – had to be taken on the floor of the House. For had we 'sent it upstairs' to be considered by a committee of fifteen Members, Labour would have had no majority at all. It was an ideal opportunity for my 'shadow', Mrs Sally Oppenheim, to shine. Normally she specialised in nothing more difficult to handle than complicated personal attacks on me. But we assumed that when the Prices Bill came up for detailed consideration the Honourable Member for Gloucester would be able to inflict some damage. We were right.

We later discovered that the combination of guerrilla warfare and last ditch rearguard action was planned by her deputy – a young man called Cecil Parkinson. Years later, during the *longueurs* in a television discussion, he talked to me about the work he did with Mrs Oppenheim. Did I, he asked, realise how much she had resented the way in which the director of my *Panorama* profile had filmed her retreating figure – 'not Sally's best view' – and included the shot in the broadcast over her comments about my eating habits? Did I also know that the same director had made the film about the Falklands which, only that day, Mrs Oppenheim had described in the House of Commons as treacherous and treasonable? 'Sally', said Cecil, 'has a long memory.' Two days later, the story appeared in a gossip column. I did not tip them off.

The Oppenheim-Parkinson partnership worked so well that, after an almost complete day of discussion, the Committee Stage had made virtually no progress. Mike Cocks, the government Chief Whip, told me that it was capitulation time. Remembering the complaints which I had received hours earlier from various geriatric back-benchers, I put up only token resistance. At Westminster it is always the midnight of the soul when the House is still sitting at three o'clock in the morning.

My only request – I pretended that it was a requirement – was decent discretion. If I was to lose most of my bill and the Tories were to get home to bed, it was essential that the government appeared to have initiated the retreat on behalf of the sick and wounded MPs who were being kept out of their beds by the all-night sitting. Mike Cocks assured me that Humphrey Atkins, his opposite number, was a gentleman who would not condescend to talk to the newspapers. All he wanted was the completion of the Prices Bill and the release of his reluctant warriors. We would all meet in the Opposition whips' office in half an hour's time.

On my way to the meeting – which I approached with all the pleasure which the German General Staff must have felt on their way to Luneberg Heath – I was stopped by a group of journalists who told me that they had learned (naturally enough 'on lobby terms') that I had agreed to sign Mrs Oppenheim's instrument of unconditional surrender. It seemed too late to reverse the retreat.

But prudence, not the most heroic of political virtues, prompted me to ask, as soon as Humphrey Atkins had poured out the champagne, whether or not the meeting was to be confidential. Mr Atkins put down his glass, clapped his hands and announced that the meeting was over. He went on to say that I was questioning Mrs Oppenheim's integrity (which was true) and that no gentleman could possibly tolerate my conduct, which was silly.

Mike Cocks followed me out into the Members' Lobby. 'You've done it now,' he said. 'It's humiliation stakes.' Back in the Chamber, Mrs Oppenheim moved 'that the committee reports progress and asks leave to sit again' – which amounted to abandoning the debate that night and perhaps for ever. I replied that the government would continue the debate until the Committee Stage was completed. When a point of order forced me to sit down, Mike Cocks, sitting beside me, hissed, 'For God's sake don't make it any worse. Things are bad enough as it is.' The debate rumbled on for the next six hours, but we made very little progress.

Then Mike Noble, my parliamentary private secretary, came into the Chamber, putty-faced and bleary-eyed. He leaned over my shoulder and asked if I knew that, in half an hour's time, we would have completed the longest sitting since the war. It was not true, and I do not know how the rumour began. But it swept through the House and, suddenly, Labour MPs who had been sleeping in the library were on their feet in the Chamber asking rhetorical questions about what the country would think when it discovered that the Tories had kept Parliament in session for longer than any time in the last thirty years – in order to frustrate Labour's plans to keep prices down. After a hurried consultation on the Opposition front bench, Humphrey Atkins sent Mike Cocks a message. He thought that the rest of the bill could be wrapped up in an hour or so.

On the way home I was stopped by Stan Crowther – the Member for Rotherham and part of the Labour Party's solid centre. 'The lads in the tea room', he said, 'feel better than they've felt for months.' We had outsmarted and outlasted the Tories. 'Between you, Mike Cocks and you have done a good job.' It was my job to maintain party morale. So I decided not to explain that it had all been done by mistake.

The Prices Bill was the first test of the Liberal-Labour Party Alliance. In the Cabinet discussion, I had supported the pact because of two mutually compelling reasons. It was the only way of keeping Margaret Thatcher out of office and, almost as important, the government was required to pay only a nominal price for the Liberal's support. We were required to avoid implementing policies which offended our partner's conscience. But we were not obliged to introduce measures which our allies nominated. After the pact had been agreed, I realised that the Prices Bill had been negotiated with the CBI and TUC, agreed by the Cabinet and approved for printing by the House of Commons. It would be published the day after the new alliance was announced without – as far as I could make out – the Liberals ever knowing that it existed. I telephoned David Steel to warn him of the surprise he would receive the following day. As always, he could not have been more reasonable. But he warned, 'I'll keep you in control in future. I'm going to ask Nancy Sear to keep an eye on you.' Lady Sear was my shadow for two years. I was so afraid of her that I asked Professor Peston to take special responsibility for inter-Party relations. They had both been Readers at the London School of Economics. I had no doubt that the help she gave my department was built on her agreement with Maurice that the Secretary of State was intellectually inadequate.

The problem with the Prices Act was that it did not hold down prices – at least not prices in general. It was really an instrument of competition policy which was best used to prevent monopolists from exploiting a market which they controlled. Inflation could only be beaten by the rigorous application of the appropriate fiscal and monetary policy. After a visit to the London Business School I became convinced that the remedy ought to include a revaluation of the pound. I put the idea to Denis Healey, who rejected it with something approaching contempt. Then I asked Jim Callaghan if we could discuss the exchange rate in Cabinet. He was scandalised, and he explained why in some detail. No previous Prime Minister had taken colleagues into his confidence in the way that he had. But to suggest an open discussion of sterling was an absurd attempt to take advantage of his good nature.

It was frustration which made me act so foolishly. But, at the time, it seemed that all I could do was start some sort of public debate. My only immediate opportunity was the Yorkshire Conference of Labour Women. I travelled to Harrogate with a text which advocated nothing new by way of exchange rate policy but speculated about a number of possible alternatives. The Yorkshire ladies – who had originally invited Shirley Williams to talk about putting red triangles in shop windows – did not enjoy my speech. But the newspapers got the message. I travelled back to London overnight so as not to miss that week's Cabinet and read the headlines over breakfast. The journalists had deciphered my coded message. Suddenly the previous night's speech did not seem such a good idea.

At Downing Street I stood outside the Cabinet Room, waiting with my colleagues, for the butler to announce, 'Ministers, the Prime Minister is ready for you,' and half expecting that I would be told that Jim Callaghan wished to see me privately in the upstairs study. Just before ten o'clock, Denis Healey came through the door – all singing and dancing – and, catching sight of me, shouted, 'That was a bloody marvellous speech you made last night. I must congratulate you properly.' He then walked towards me and slapped me on the back – so hard that I staggered across the vestibule and hit the coat rack on the far wall. I went into the wash-room to see if my nose was bleeding or only bruised. Next day I got a note from the Prime Minister. He was content to leave the reaction to my Harrogate Speech in the Chancellor's hands. Six months later I was witness to Denis Healey's second assault of the year.

It took place at Chequers at the end of a long day which the Prince of Wales had spent in Whitehall. After sitting in on the morning's Cabinet, Prince Charles had lunch with the Prime Minister. Denis was there because he was so senior. I owed my invitation to the dubious distinction of being the Cabinet's youngest member. His Royal Highness was modest, interested and receptive. Indeed, when he made a speech on industry a couple of weeks later, he included some of Keynes's more critical views on British businessmen which had been drawn to his attention by Michael Foot during his visit to Downing Street. But I doubt if any of us – including the Prince – wanted to go through the process a second time over dinner. Charles began the evening badly by asking Denis about his undergraduate membership of the Communist Party. He then began to tell a long and complicated story about an Australian air hostess asking him if he was really going to be king one day. The Prince of Wales told us that when he admitted that he was heir to the throne, the young lady asked him, 'Kind of scary, isn't it?' Putting on his boyish look, Prince Charles confessed to her and us that it was. Denis leaned across the table and, smiling maliciously, observed, 'Serve you right, you shouldn't have joined.'

Denis Healey had become the dominant force in the government and Jim Callaghan's obvious successor. Indeed in the winter of 1976–77, there was no other serious candidate. Tony Crosland, successful though not quite at home in the Foreign Office, seemed out of the mainstream of political debate – which then, as now, concerned the economy. Tony liked holding one of the Great Offices of State but longed to be back in the real world of domestic politics. We had been friends for ten years – visiting each other's houses, drinking in each other's House of

Commons rooms and laughing about (and sometimes at) our colleagues' foibles. He had taken me with him when he advised Michael Foot, then deputy leader of the Party, not to visit India during Mrs Gandhi's unjustified 'emergency'. Let us, he had said, see 'how a man of principle reacts when moral obligation and personal inclination conflict'. He had put his argument against the visit in typically Crosland fashion. 'Look here. J. P. Narayan's in prison. You can't go.' Michael did not agree.

Tony continued to damage his prospects of the succession by making superior jokes about back-benchers who annoyed him. Denis Healey's jovial brutality was, in its strange way, part of the Party's egalitarian tradition – the Chancellor of the Exchequer punching it out, man for man, with some unknown troublemaker. But when Tony's aphorisms were repeated in the tea room there was only a mild ripple of laughter for 'In a decent society, people like that are shot without trial', and not even a smile in response to the assertion that 'To be the conscience of the Labour Party you have to be a real shit'.

In all our years of friendship, Tony and I had never eaten together in a restaurant – though I often heard him say how much he despised his colleagues who enjoyed lunching and dining out. Then, much to my surprise, he suggested that we might have lunch together after a Thursday Cabinet. 'Arrange something,' he commanded. 'I don't know the names of any restaurants.' I booked a table at the Gay Hussar – then still a favourite with socialist politicians of modest means. We travelled to Greek Street together. Throughout the journey, Tony claimed not to recognise the streets through which we drove.

As soon as we settled at the table, Tony announced that the lunch which followed his first wedding had been held in the upstairs room. Hugh Dalton – Chancellor in Attlee's government and patron of promising young men – had presided. Nicholas Kaldor, the distinguished Hungarian economist, had sat at the other end of the table for the improbable reason that he, and his wife, were to accompany the Croslands on the tour of France which was to be their honeymoon. Tony described the lunch as 'excruciating'. Dr Dalton's booming voice had drowned all other conversation. He spent most of the lunch leaning across the young bride whilst he discussed Tony's earlier *amours*. After an hour or so, with Hilary Crosland near to tears, Tony suggested that Kaldor fetched the get-away car. He was gone for almost an hour. So, fearing that he was lost somewhere in Soho, the Croslands went to look for him. As they descended the stairs, Tony heard Dr Dalton's exultant cry, 'Well, I think that we got them off to a thoroughly bad start.'

The anecdote over, Tony turned to the real purpose of our lunch. He had, at last – after almost a year at the Foreign Office – decided to spend a weekend at Dorneywood, the Foreign Secretary's 'official country residence'. He regarded the whole idea as faintly ridiculous – particularly since he owned a more attractive house down the road at Adderbury. But it seemed right that he should visit Dorneywood. It was my duty to join him.

Dorneywood is not a beautiful house, but it is big. Indeed everything about it is too vast for comfort. After lunch Tony lined up four armchairs in front of the biggest television set which I had ever seen, poured out huge drinks and announced that he expected complete silence for the next ninety minutes. I assumed that we were to watch football – televised games being one of Tony's many obsessions. But after much ineffectual turning of knobs and pushing of buttons, an old Ealing comedy lit up the screen. 'You are,' Tony announced, 'about to see the love of my life – before this one came along.' Susan Crosland never minded being called 'this one'.

The lady for whom we waited was June Thorburn. Although she went on to greater things, in that afternoon's film she did not have a starring role. In fact, Miss Thorburn had no role at all in the first half hour of our vigil and, no doubt because of impatience, Tony identified several other actresses as the girl of his one-time dreams. Susan – exasperated by a flattering comment he made about an even then not youthful Brenda De Banzi – walked across to the screen and poked a finger in Miss Thorburn's electronic eye. 'Isn't she lovely?' Tony said unabashed. 'I met her at the old theatre on the South Bank. Roy Jenkins and I went there one summer to see a French farce.' In my naive way I asked him how he met – I meant picked up – an actress at the theatre. 'No idea,' Tony told me. 'She wasn't an actress then. She was selling icecream.'

Later that afternoon we walked in the Dorneywood garden and talked, as we always talked, about why we made so little progress in converting our colleagues to what seemed to us the true view of socialism. We both knew that socialism was the gospel of equality and found great difficulty in understanding why anyone believed anything else. In those days, genuine egalitarians like Crosland and me were said to be 'on the right wing of the Party' because we could not pretend that nationalisation would save the world, or that the Soviet Union was a democracy, or that every strike was justified. It was in the Dorneywood greenhouse that what began as jokes about Peter Shore's opposition to compulsory seat belts turned into a general argument about personal freedom. Halfway through the conversation Tony said – as an aside not as an *obiter dictum* – that, until we were truly equal, we could not be truly free. Then we resumed our attacks on politicians who never read anything worthwhile and regard ideological speculation as a waste of time. We moaned on for another ten minutes or so and then went back in the house for another drink. Two weeks later, Tony died. One day it may be resurrected, but British egalitarian socialism died with him.

CHAPTER
10

Tom McNally, the Prime Minister's political adviser, told me that Jim Callaghan was not sure if Tony Crosland should be replaced by 'an old stager' or a 'young Lochinvar'. Certain that I came into neither category, I waited for the announcement with something approaching detachment. My modesty was entirely justified.

At the time of Tony's death, Margaret Jay, Jim's elder daughter, was in Downing Street cooking breakfast for her father. Audrey Callaghan, Margaret's mother, had been hurt in a White-hall road accident and Jim – in Margaret's own words – 'couldn't open a tin of soup'. So her younger sister looked after the injured mother whilst she kept house for the helpless father. Jim – not usually regarded as an emotional man – was deeply moved by Tony's death and, for some time, found it difficult to think about appointing a new Foreign Secretary. Then, after a day or two of doubt, he forced himself to consider the rival candidates. Suddenly, the inspiration came. 'I've got it. Young Lochinvar!'

Margaret, perhaps more out of respect than conviction, endorsed her father's choice. 'Roy will do it very well.' The Prime Minister looked bewildered. Then, he replied with almost equal uncertainty, 'Roy? Roy Hattersley? I never even thought of him.'

Jim, for all his many virtues, is not a literary man. So his quick recovery is a tribute to his speed of thought rather than his erudition. 'It couldn't be him. Young Lochinvar must come out of the west.' David Owen represented Plymouth.

Margaret told me the story over a year later when her husband had become our ambassador to Washington and I was passing through. It was late at night and I sat recovering from social hypothermia. During dinner there had been a fierce argument between Henry Kissinger and the French ambassador about – of all things – the relative size of embassy swimming pools. The ambassador had emphasised one of his points by wagging his fork in Henry's direction and had covered my front in particles of kidney turbigo. Nancy Kissinger, trying to be helpful, had mopped my chest with her damp napkin and my shirt had turned transparent – revealing several spots as well as both nipples. Believing the wet look to be out of fashion in Washington that year, I had clutched my single-breasted dinner jacket around me as if I were fighting to keep warm in a blizzard. The account of Owen's rise to fame did nothing to warm my heart.

Despite his lack of faith in my diplomatic skills, by the time of Tony's death I became the Prime Minister's almost invariable choice to represent the Party and government on television by-election broadcasts. Between 1976 and 1992 I spent night after night affecting modesty in victory or (more often) trying to look indomitable in defeat. Even on the rare days of glory, it was an unrewarding way in which to spend the two hours after midnight. So I looked forward with particular anguish to the Grimsby contest. Tony Crosland's majority was too small to make a Labour victory even remotely possible. It was little consolation to know that, on the same night, we would hold Ashfield – one of our safest seats – with at least a respectable vote.

Labour held Grimsby. And in the studio at the Television Centre we did our best to entertain the handful of viewers who waited for the foregone conclusion at Ashfield. Then, to our astonishment, the reporter announced that there was to be a recount. As I explained to Robin Day, the only possible reason for the delay was doubt about whether or not the Liberals had lost their deposit. Since my theory was plausible and none of us had much else to say, Robin repeated my explanation to what we liked to think of as 'people at home'. His description of how deposits are lost was interrupted by the Ashfield returning officer's formal announcement. After two recounts, it was confirmed that Labour had been defeated.

Despite that night's display of mindless optimism, I was also the Labour Party's nominee to the Manchester Exchange by-election programme. Just as I was about to leave for the studio, I was telephoned by the Prime Minister – an extraordinary event for a Cabinet minister in the bottom half of the pecking order. When the familiar voice enquired 'Roy?', I assumed that I was to be rebuked for some misdemeanour. But Jim Callaghan, in his most avuncular mood, wished to advise me about how I should approach the evening's broadcast. Information just in from Lancashire confirmed that Labour had lost. The best way to minimise the defeat was to anticipate it. He therefore suggested that I announced the bad news as quickly as possible and set out the reasons why victory was always beyond us – old register, unpopular local council, demolition of council houses previously occupied by Labour voters. It was, said the Prime Minister, the time for 'honest dignity'.

Being out of honest dignity practice, I tried to make up in quantity what my concession of defeat lacked in quality. I embraced failure with such a passion that some viewers must have thought Labour would be lucky to get any votes at all. Robin Day, no doubt with the memory of Ashfield still clearly in his mind, urged caution. But my pessimism was infectious. It was generally agreed that the government would be humiliated. Labour won.

Early the following morning, the Prime Minister telephoned me for the second time in twelve hours. 'Look,' said Jim, 'I really did believe what I told you last night.' I told him that I had never even suspected that he had intentionally deceived me. My assurance of confidence in his integrity could not have been entirely convincing. For he thought it necessary to add some collateral evidence to support his protestation of good faith. 'If we'd expected to win I'd have put David Owen on the programme, not you.'

Jim's high opinion of David was, in my view, wholly justified, but the Foreign Secretary did make enemies with a remarkable facility. During his years as Under Secretary for the Navy – back in the days when I was Denis Healey's Minister of State – his relationship with Ivor Richard (now Labour's leader in the House of Lords, but then Under Secretary for the Army) was, at best, frosty. Ivor became Britain's permanent representative at the United Nations and David inherited him with the Foreign Office furniture. When Ivor returned to London to attend Tony Crosland's memorial service, David demanded to know why he had not made a formal request for permission to leave his post in New York. Ivor never forgave him.

A year or so later I flew to America as guest of the Foreign Affairs Council of New York. Because the government had no overall majority in the House of Commons, Maurice Peston and I were obliged to fly out on Concorde on one day, give my lecture in the evening and fly back by Concorde on the next. With a couple of hours on my hands, I suggested to Maurice that we called on 'old Ivor'. We were led to his outside office where a polite young man told me that Mr Richard was very busy. On cross-examination, he admitted that the permanent representative was alone. It was probably jet lag that gave us the nerve to walk past the factotum and into the inner sanctum where Ivor was sitting in his shirt sleeves looking into the middle distance. I recall that he was wearing scarlet braces. 'You're not busy at all,' I said reproachfully. 'Oh yes I am,' he replied. 'I am thinking of ways to damage the Foreign Secretary.'

I never believed that David Owen meant to cause such general offence – or even knew the effect that his behaviour had on those who suffered from it. On one bizarre day towards the end of Jim Callaghan's dying government, he actually protested to me about my inability to 'accept kindness graciously' after he had tempted me to throttle him. The incident took place after one of the very few Cabinet meetings ever to be held on a Friday morning. The agenda was as unusual as the day of the week. The government was at odds with its supporters over membership of the European Community and Jim Callaghan hoped to reconcile his obligations as Labour leader and Prime Minister by sending the general secretary of the Party a letter which set out a 'mutually agreed position'. The Cabinet had been called together to approve the draft but the whole document – including its 'secret' classification – was printed in the *Financial Times* on the day that the Cabinet met.

When the meeting began with the Prime Minister's denunciation of the saboteur who had leaked the letter to the newspaper, I experienced a trauma which I had been spared since my schooldays. I first feared that Jim suspected me and then – as the excoriation of the unknown culprit continued – began to believe that I was guilty, even though I had not even seen the draft letter until after the *FT* went to press. The Prime Minister then announced that he knew the culprit's name. The crime had been committed by one of the older Cabinet members who resented the sudden rise to fame of the juvenile Foreign Secretary. I was younger than anyone there except Owen himself. But I was on the point of joining the ranks of those psychotics who confess to crimes which they have not committed, when the division bell rang. We were a minority government and the twenty-two Cabinet votes were needed in the House of Commons.

'Come down in my car,' said David Owen on the way to the Downing Street door. As we sped out into Whitehall, he tapped me patronisingly on the knee. 'Look,' he said, 'You've nothing to worry about. I said to Jim this morning, "Say what you like about old Hattersley, he stabs you in the front, not the back." So you're in the clear. No need to worry.'

During the couple of minutes which it took us to cross the corner of Parliament Square I lost all feeling of guilt and became, instead, outraged by the thought that I had ever been under suspicion. It was the sort of effect that David Owen had on people. The power to turn friends into enemies, and the ability to offend when only conciliation was intended, was one of the Foreign Secretary's special gifts. They are not qualities which are normally associated with diplomacy.

Although my main departmental concern was inflation, I was drawn more and more into the complicated relationship between the government and the trade unions. In the last desperate year before the general election, I was given the job of 'co-ordinating' policy on public sector pay, or – to describe my obligations more simply – holding down wages despite the TUC's refusal to co-operate in a fourth year of pay restraint. Because of my new responsibilities for pay policy, it was thought necessary for me to know – and if possible to like – all of the senior trade union leaders. My familiarisation programme began with Terry Duffy, the new president of the Amalgamated Engineering Union. I invited him to lunch.

He was more than half an hour late. So, when he arrived at the Gay Hussar, Kenneth Clucas, Maurice Peston and I were staring impatiently at the beaded curtain which covered the door. We all saw him at the moment when the beads parted, magnificent in a white double-breasted jacket of the sort which is normally only associated with dance band leaders on cruise ships. He came towards us with all the confidence of what he had once been – a Royal Marine NCO. Toothbrush moustache twitching, he spoke in the West Midlands accent which I came to know and almost to love. 'Have you heard the one about Johnny Boyd and the geisha girl in the sauna bath?' Sir John Boyd, the general secretary of the AEU, was famous for being careful with money – which no doubt accounted for Terry's story ending with the punchline, 'If it costs as much as that, I'll do it myself.'

Terry was brave, tough, loyal, honest and incapable of sustaining a continual line of thought. He was also irresistibly quaint. Many years later, he told me that the political conduct which he despised most was behaving 'wibbly-wobbly' – by which he meant bending with every political wind that blows. He then went through my Shadow Cabinet colleagues, one by one. 'John Silkin, there's one who's wibbly-wobbly. So is Stan Orme, even though he is a member of my own union.' He then added, 'I hate that Jim Mortimer.' I asked Terry if he hated the general secretary of the Labour Party because he was 'wibbly-wobbly'. The time-served engineer replied, 'No. Because he used to be a draughts-man.'

Being the leader of a craftsmen's union, Terry was not an enthusiast for incomes policy – which he feared would blur the distinction, as well as compress the differentials, between skilled and unskilled workers. In a sense, he typified the dilemma which eventually made the failure of the policy unavoidable.

Neither the government, nor its supporters in the unions could ever make up their minds if pay policy was a sacrifice, made by the workers on behalf of the nation as a whole, or an instrument of social justice designed to protect public services and the purchasing power of the lower paid. Towards the end, we began to emphasise social justice to the point at which low-paid workers were guaranteed an increase far in excess of anything that they could have obtained from free collective bargaining. But by then it was too late. The turning point was the biennial conference of the Transport and General Workers' Union in the Isle of Man where Jack Jones – the old hero of the left – used his last speech as general secretary 'to warn his brothers and sisters that, if they

refused to support another year of pay restraint, the only beneficiaries would be Margaret Thatcher and the Tory Party.' Jack
was booed down.

A couple of months after that conference, Healey, Varley,
Booth and I met the TUC leadership over dinner at 11 Downing
Street. It was our last attempt to persuade them, in the jargon of
the time, 'to accept a five per cent norm' – that is to say, advise
or instruct their members to settle for an increase of no more
than five pence in the pound. Denis Healey suggested to Moss
Evans – Jack Jones' successor – that he should call another
conference and attempt to overturn the Isle of Man decision.
Moss was visibly shaken by the thought of what might happen.
When he managed to reply, he asked, with simple eloquence,
'If they did that to Jack Jones, what do you think they would do
to me?'

It is now generally agreed – even by Denis Healey, the
architect of pay policy – that the government was wrong to ask
the unions to settle for as little as five per cent. With six or seven,
the argument runs, there would have been another year of co-
operation. Perhaps. But Denis should not blame himself. He was
encouraged, at the Downing Street meeting, to press ahead
without the unions' agreement. The leaders of the TUC refused
to give the government its formal backing. But their clear advice
was, in the words of one participant, to 'blind it through'. The
unions' high command believed that rank and file resistance
would collapse in the face of an assault by a determined government. They were wrong. And we were wrong to believe that they
understood their members.

Because the government was unable to impose wage restraint
on the trade unions themselves, the compulsory element in our
counter-inflation policy – 'the penal clauses' as our less literate
critics called them – was directed not against the workers who
demanded an unreasonable pay increase, but employers who
accepted their demands. When the government assaulted the

employers as surrogates for the trade unions, self-interest encouraged the workers to rally to the bosses' cause.

Naturally enough, companies which could afford to finance a wage increase often chose to face the government's wrath rather than provoke what they regarded as an unnecessary strike. The Ford Motor Company, having calculated that a stoppage would be ten times more expensive than the cost of meeting the union's demands, announced that they would not be bound by the government's guidelines. In order to encourage the others – the dozens of companies which were waiting to follow suit – we decided to make an example of the Dagenham free-marketeers by withholding government contracts. The 'sanctions' had to be approved by Parliament. I had to propose the sanctions motion to the House of Commons.

On the morning of the big debate, I woke with a pain in my back which I recognised at once as kidney failure. The doctor thought it nothing worse than pleurisy and told me to go home to bed with the selection of pills which he prescribed. I took the pills but not the advice. Back at my department I sent a message to the private office at Number 10 asking that a replacement speaker be found. The response to my proposal was unsympathetic. I hope that the private secretary lied when he said that he had consulted the Prime Minister, who recalled that on the wartime Arctic convoys pleurisy was the normal state of health, yet the guns and butter still got through to the Soviet Union. Being young and foolish, I went back to the doctor, got more pills to see me through the afternoon, and made the worst speech of my life. It was probably the worst speech made in my lifetime.

The date is carved deep into my memory. If you look up *Hansard* for 13th December 1978, you will find a speech which reads like a calm and lucid exposition of the government's pay policy – except for the replies to interventions. They were gibberish. The secret of my uneven performance is easily explained. I had, on the despatch box in front of me, an 'agreed text' – the arguments in favour of the government's position, to which all ministers who were involved in the policy had contributed. As was my duty, I turned the pages and did my best to read the words. The result was incomprehensible to the naked ear. But, high above in the press gallery, the faithful *Hansard* reporters were following my incoherent ramblings on copies of my speech which had been supplied to them by my department's press office. They wrote down not what I said, but what I was supposed to say – a far easier task than trying to make sense of the words with which I was bewildering the Commons. Only when I was forced to extemporise in reply to interventions did they have to attempt a translation of balderdash into English. Norman St John Stevas boasted for years about the way in which his dashing wit confounded me that day. I am sure that it did. But I cannot remember anything that happened.

Although a number of newspapers prophesied my imminent dismissal, I survived. My driver was, however, returned to the indignity of the car pool. The offence that occasioned his dismissal was failure to meet me at the airport – a misdemeanour which he attempted to excuse with the explanation that he had been losing at cards all day and had just been dealt his first winning hand. But scores of previous offences had to be taken into consideration. The plea in mitigation was compelling but inadequate. He was a character.

In 1976 he expressed his outrage that I did not propose to attend the Armistice Day Service at the Cenotaph – speaking, he claimed, as an old soldier. Realising that his real enthusiasm was for Sunday overtime, I passed off his strictures with the joke that I did not have enough medals to parade without humiliation. Next day he arrived at my front door with a cardboard box in the car. It contained a dozen decorations of one sort or another – many of them engraved with his name. He offered to lend them to me for the Whitehall ceremony. Why, I asked him, after seeing so much service, had he left the army only a private? 'I was corporal once,' he told me. 'But I got busted after stabbing that Iti prisoner on the expedition to Chad.' He knew I would ask him for details. 'He killed my armadillo.' The armadillo was, apparently, essential to my driver's well-being. Tethered to his shoulder, it caught flies before they landed on his face. 'The Iti killed it. So I stabbed him.' He said it as if the sequence of events was obvious. I was sorry when we had to sack him.

Jim Callaghan was very good about my catastrophic speech. When he telephoned to ask how I was, he did not even mention that we had lost the vote. From then on, counter-inflation policy had to be voluntary. We all continued to talk to the TUC and the CBI, but the conversations grew more and more bizarre. The period is typified in my memory by a confrontation, during a Blackpool Party conference, between the economic ministers and the directors of British Oxygen. It was held in the Masonic Room in the basement of the Grand Hotel and Denis Healey sat on the Grand Master's throne surrounded by signs of the zodiac. Prices policy had a mystic quality.

When I toughened the 'price code' – the criteria by which prices could be increased without the complications of a reference to, and an examination by, the Price Commission – I presented my plan to the Neddy Six in the real belief that the new 'tougher stance' would be welcomed. The Neddy Six was the unfortunate name for the half dozen members of the General Council who sat on the National Economic Development Council. Alf Allen, of the Union of Shop, Distributive and Allied Workers, asked me how the new regime would work in practice. It was, he said, his habit to buy his mother-in-law a bunch of flowers each weekend. When, on his way home on the previous Friday night, he had stopped at his usual barrow, a dozen roses had cost seventy-five pence more than he had been charged seven days earlier. What was more they had withered by Sunday afternoon. How would my proposals end such exploitation of the innocent consumer?

Prices policy was, and only could be, an extension of competition policy – with the government and the Price Commission acting as a surrogate for the pressures of the free market. Part of my job, as master of the Monopolies and Mergers Commission and overlord of the Office of Fair Trading, was ensuring that newspaper ownership was not 'concentrated' in the hands of two or three press barons. The Monopolies Act had specific rules about how many papers one tycoon could own. When the Aitken family decided to sell the *Daily* and *Sunday Express* it was my task to make sure that the titles were kept out of the clutches of the Rothermeres and the Berrys.

Neither of the two front runners – James Goldsmith and Victor Matthews – owned a newspaper. So they were free to bid without any reference to me. But both chose to visit my department and explain their motives and intentions. James Goldsmith came along, lay back in his armchair, smoked a large cigar and made his case in great detail and without a single note. Victor Matthews brought a team of lawyers and accountants to set out his case, but kept interrupting them by repeating, 'I must warn you, Secretary of State, the *Express* will still be a Tory paper.' I replied, each time, 'That is none of our concern, Mr Matthews', but he became so embarrassed that I decided to lighten the atmosphere with a little joke. 'I will find it easier to recommend your bid to my colleagues if you assure me that your back pages will call for Geoffrey Boycott's return to the England team.' Unsmiling, Mr Matthews said that he would think about it.

A couple of months later, after the *Express* was his, Victor Matthews was invited to a Downing Street reception for 'Piggy' Muldoon, the Prime Minister of New Zealand. Geoffrey Boycott was there and so was I. Matthews – who had by then got the joke – brought Geoffrey and me together. Turning to the great batsman, he told him, 'You don't realise what a friend you have in the Secretary of State. He said we could only have the *Express* if we said you should be back in the England team.' Geoffrey was magnificently unimpressed. Turning to me, he asked, 'Opening the batting and captain as well? That's what the supporters want. Me as captain.'

Soirées in the Waterloo Room of Downing Street were a rare event for junior Cabinet ministers like me. But from time to time we were dragged off by 'government hospitality' to assist in the entertainment of a foreign visitor. I was required to accompany the Shah of Persia's sister to the theatre, where we saw *The Playboy of the Western World*. Despite her reputation as 'the dragon lady', she was horrified by the play. 'Tell me,' she whispered rather too loudly, 'do young men in Ireland improve their esteem by pretending that they have beaten their fathers to death with a shovel?'

Nothing that happened to me during my three years in the Cabinet caused me more anguish than the sight of David Basnett, secretary of the Municipal and General Workers' Union, in tears at the thought of the way in which some of his members were behaving. David had come into my office for a general talk about how best to end the Winter of Discontent – a name later invented for six months of industrial disruption which, because it was both memorable and descriptive, did the Labour government almost as much damage in the public mind as the rotting piles of uncollected refuse, the pickets outside the hospital gates and the police cars which took the place of strike-hit ambulances. The day before David's visit, newspapers had reported that Merseyside municipal workers had refused to dig graves and that funerals were being indefinitely postponed. David had started his trade union life in the north-west and he felt a wholly unjustified, but entirely honourable, personal responsibility for the anguish which he knew that his members were causing. He kept repeating, 'Who could have believed that Liverpool Parks and Cemeteries Branch would behave like this?' The prosaic – indeed, almost risible – language in which he expressed his distress made his despair all the more moving. His tears reinforced all my emotions

– sympathy for the low paid, contempt for the militants who were exploiting them and sadness that the trade unions, which I had been brought up to admire and respect, were wholly incapable of dealing with the problems of the modern world.

By the time that the government became engulfed in the long cold weeks of strikes and protest marches, the prospects of re-election were already precarious. The ideas on which the government's policies were built – consensus, co-operation, even compassion – had gone out of fashion. Ambition, acquisition and abrasion had become the magic ingredients of success. Voters genuinely believed that economic progress was being held back by a sentimental concern for the sick, the old and the poor. The idea was absurd. But it was the idea of the time and more than a decade was to pass before the intellectual absurdities of Thatcherism were exposed. The Winter of Discontent confirmed all the country's recently acquired prejudices against searching for collective solutions to the nation's problems.

Jim Callaghan was generally regarded as a good Prime Minister. Given another term he might have been a great one. Ironically he denied himself that chance, by postponing the general election beyond the autumn of 1978, and then not doing all in his power to hold it off through the spring and summer of the following year. In the autumn, before the refuse was piled in the streets and the patients were turned away from hospitals, the government might just have survived a general election. Our defeat would certainly have been nothing like so great as the débâcle which followed six months later.

After the autumn of 1977, the government had grown gradually more popular – or at least the unpopularity began to diminish. Labour even started to win by-elections. In the summer of 1978, George Robertson held off the Scottish Nationalist challenge in Hamilton. I have always enjoyed campaigning and I particularly looked forward to going north that sunny June. For I had managed, with some difficulty, to arrange my visit to the constituency on the weekend when England played Scotland at Hampden Park. It was a good year for Scottish football. The Scots had qualified for the World Cup Finals in Argentina. England had not.

On the morning of the match I toured Hamilton shopping centre. Somebody bought me a plastic 'World Cup Tartan Army Football' and I played 'keepsie-uppsie' for the benefit of the accompanying television cameras. I am very good at 'keepsie-uppsie' and the television reporters soon got bored when it was clear that I was not going to fall down or break a shop window. They began to demand that I talked to shoppers about prices. I had learned the hard way that it was important to take some care in choosing whom to cross-examine about inflation for the benefit of news bulletins. Grandmothers, who could remember when gas mantles cost a shilling a dozen, were to be avoided. So were harassed mothers with four baskets, three children and two pushchairs. The ideal candidates were men. But the television companies wanted 'housewives'. So, as I flicked my football from instep to brow, I looked for a serene woman in her early thirties who did not seem to be in a hurry to go anywhere.

After about twenty minutes, David Rose of ITN grew so impatient that he decided to make the selection himself. He approached a middle-aged lady who, had she not been carrying two immense carrier bags, would have been taken as a mourner on her way to a funeral of a close relative. For she was dressed in black and looked immensely unhappy. 'This', said Rose, thrusting a microphone in her face, 'is your chance to speak to the Prices Minister. What have you got to say to him?' She spoke in a firm clear voice. 'With world commodity prices on an upward trend, I think the government is right to restrict itself to selective intervention. Particularly if they intend, as I hope they do, to keep an exchange rate that stimulates exports.' The item was not included in that evening's bulletins.

My visit to the by-election was 'political' rather than 'ministerial'. So I went to Hampden Park as an ordinary ticket-buying fan. But I had bought a couple of good seats, and David Hill and I sat about twenty yards away from the Royal Box. Bruce Millan, the Secretary of State for Scotland, saw us and sent a message to say that a spare car was at our disposal for the journey to the airport. After the match – which Scotland lost – we sat patiently in a giant Daimler waiting for a third passenger to join us. He, I told David Hill bitterly, is drinking at the official reception. The Scottish fans were more bitter still. Pointing at our car, one man shouted, 'These are the bastards who get in free.' Another added, 'That is why we have to pay so much for the fucking tickets.' David, an essentially reasonable man, wound down the window an inch or two and told them, 'You're quite wrong, we bought tickets just like you did.' Unconvinced, the Scotsman expressed his doubts by spitting at the Sassenach free-loaders. Fortunately he was a poor shot. But the gobbet of spittle, running down the glass a couple of inches below his nose, changed David's character. 'I've told you,' he said. 'We paid. And, what is more, we won.' I was surprised by how many Scotsmen heard the softly spoken rebuke. But about twenty of them began to rock the car. We were rescued by a posse of mounted policemen. We arrived at Glasgow airport in a speckled car – black, with spittle spots.

In the summer of 1978, Labour actually crept ahead in the opinion polls and it certainly looked as if the economy was beginning to recover. In comparison with what has since been achieved by fifteen years of almost continuously high unemployment, the reduction of inflation to single figures does not seem much to celebrate. But to us it was proof that Labour was leading Britain towards prosperity. It was therefore particularly galling that the scheduled day of the announcement of the Retail Price Index should be the day after a by-election. Since the statisticians calculated the monthly RPI in the early part of publication week,

I knew by Tuesday that good news was only four days away. So I asked the Prime Minister if I could announce, or at least leak, our success on the eve of poll. Jim could not have been more scandalised if I had confessed to doctoring the figures. When I told him, by way of argument, that all I asked was to change the date not the decision, he reminisced about 1950.

Jim was, at the time, Civil Lord of the Admiralty – that is to say, Under Secretary for the Navy – and his boss, A. V. Alexander, First Lord of the Admiralty and the MP of my youth, sent him to a Cabinet committee over which the austere and upright Stafford Cripps presided. The only item on the agenda was a proposal to reduce the already inadequate cheese ration by a further two ounces. A general election had already been announced and, not surprisingly, another junior minister by the name of Dugdale asked if it was necessary to come to a decision for the next month or so. Stafford Cripps replied that he was not sure of the questioner's identity but, whoever he was, if he allowed political considerations to influence his judgement, he was not fit to be one of Her Majesty's ministers. When Jim told me that story, I should have realised that he was going to be difficult about deciding when to dissolve Parliament.

Jim sent the Cabinet off on its summer holidays with the announcement that he did not wish colleagues to return with advice about when the election should be. We all agreed, privately as well as publicly, that his judgement was certainly better than ours and we should leave him to it. I observed voluntary restraint for almost two months. Then, during the second week in September, I campaigned for seven days in north Lancashire – where many of my friends held marginal seats. I returned to London absolutely convinced that we should hold an autumn election and the temptation to share my view with the Prime Minister was irresistible.

So I wrote him a letter which began, 'I know that you asked us not to give you our opinions on the best election date. Had you not done so, I should have offered you the following advice . . .' The advice was 'go now'. I received in reply a frosty acknowledgment from a private secretary and the *Evening Standard* included me amongst the 'Fearful Five' Cabinet ministers who were begging Jim to postpone the election for as long as possible.

The following Wednesday, Jim made his famous, 'There was I, waiting at the church . . .' speech at the TUC. I had no idea if the message of his address was that the election would come early or late. So I looked forward with unusual excitement to the following day's Cabinet meeting. Before I left for Downing Street I received two telephone calls. The first was from Dick Leonard, an ex-Labour MP who had become an *Economist* journalist when the Boundary Commission abolished his constituency. Leonard had talked to members of the TUC General Council who had entertained the Prime Minister to dinner after his speech. They were convinced that there would not be an autumn election. The second caller was Tom McCaffrey, the press secretary at Number 10. Jim, he told me, was to make a Prime Ministerial broadcast immediately before the six o'clock news. I was the Party's nominee to take part in the discussion which followed. When I asked McCaffrey whether I would be explaining the merits of an autumn or spring election, he told me that the answer was obvious.

The Prime Minister opened the Cabinet meeting with a succinct analysis of the economic and political prospects. He then said that he had written a letter to the Queen which we might be interested to hear and he would be pleased to read to us. It began with a précis of what we had just heard and concluded that it was for the reasons set out above that he did not propose to ask Her Majesty for a dissolution of Parliament that autumn. Jim looked up and, smiling, said that we could discuss his decision if we chose to do so. But he doubted if we would persuade him to send a second message to the Queen, telling her that he had changed his mind.

A ripple of laughter – prompted by several different emotions – echoed round the oval table. The Prime Minister did not join in. 'You're laughing with relief now. But if we have trouble with the unions and get forced out in the winter you'll feel differently.' In all political history there can have been no greater example of prescience and irony combined.

I went to the BBC Television Centre to explain why an immediate election would not be in the national interest – bound by a vow of secrecy to tell no one of the decision until Jim had made his majestic broadcast. The Tory participant in the news bulletin which followed was Lord Hailsham, who stamped about the hospitality room before the programme began, shouting that any fool knew there was going to be an early election and asking why I would not admit it there and then. His first words, in the actual programme, were that he had never doubted that the election would be postponed.

Six months later, after our bit of bother with the unions, we were forced out because the minority parties which had supported us mistakenly believed that it was in their interests to bring us down. Only the Ulster Unionists had the good sense to consider the possibility that they might have something to gain from Labour's survival. Paradoxically, the leader of the Social and Democratic Labour Party, the gregarious Gerry Fitt, had changed from friend to enemy as a result of what he claimed was Roy Mason's sympathy to the Unionists. The anxious meetings which followed the announcement that Margaret Thatcher had put down a vote of confidence always began with a list of what the Chief Whip called 'odds and sods' – members of minority parties who were likely to vote against us. It invariably included Gerry. Every time that we were told of Fitt's willingness to bring the government down, Michael Foot made a long speech about what a great man he was. After Gerry had achieved that objective and Margaret Thatcher had come to power in the subsequent general election, he still retained Michael's devotion. When Fitt

lost his own seat in 1983, he was made a peer in the Dissolution
Honours List – undoubtedly on Michael's nomination.

A couple of Unionist MPs – Harold McCusker and John Carson
– might be convinced to vote with the Labour government. The
rest were perfectly happy to support us as long as they had
something to show for the desertion of their traditional allies.
Their price was the promise of a gas pipeline joining Northern
Ireland to the rest of the United Kingdom.

The Ulster pipeline had been considered by the government
long before any of us imagined that we might need Unionist
support in a vote of confidence. I was a supporter of the idea.
One of the objects of nationalism was the provision of basic
services throughout the United Kingdom. And whilst the Six
Counties of Northern Ireland remained part of the Union, they
were entitled to benefit from the universal supply of natural gas.
Roy Mason – according to Gerry Fitt, the Unionists' friend – was
worried about the political implications of adding another link to
the chain which bound Ulster to Britain. Sooner or later, the
whole question would have been decided by the long process of
ministerial meetings and Cabinet decision. But in March 1979,
the pipeline seemed to me like a gift from the gods. All the
Prime Minister had to do was endorse what I, and several of my
colleagues, honestly believed right and had already suggested.
Then the government's majority would be honourably secured.
But Jim Callaghan would not even consider replacing the usual
weeks of argument with an arbitrary decision. Months afterwards, Enoch Powell – in one of those pseudo-philosophic
reminiscences which were his television trademark – bared
his teeth into the camera and said, 'They could have done it.
They could have had the whole Unionist Party. But they chose
not to.' For once he was right.

So we were left with Harold McCusker and John Carson,
whose demands were moderate. They wanted a special Retail
Price Index which monitored the higher cost of living in

Northern Ireland – an idea which we were already considering along with special calculations of the impact of inflation on other regions. And they asked for Price Commission enquiries into the cost of those commodities which made life particularly expensive in the Six Counties. I was delighted by the suggestion, for we were never quite sure what the Price Commission should do next. We agreed the policy in about ten minutes. Working out the joint communiqué was far more difficult. By lunch I had begun to expect that the negotiations would drag on into the afternoon. The Chief Whip told me not to let them out of my sight. Mercifully they wanted to lunch alone.

The two men presented themselves in my House of Commons room at just after three o'clock and stayed there all afternoon as they argued over and changed the draft text. At eight they agreed to sign and I handed them a pen from a pot on my desk. McCusker wrote his Christian name and then, discovering he was using green biro, tore up the entire document. We stuck it together with sellotape so there could be no arguments about surreptitious changes, as David Hill typed out a new copy. When it was finished we all signed in Waterman's 'writes blue, drys black'. Anne Taylor – acting like a good whip – told me that I must obtain the Prime Minister's approval. On the way to Jim's room I met him in the corridor. He asked, 'What have you been up to?' Instead of replying, 'Trying to save the government,' I handed him the paper. He said that he was 'content'.

By the time that I was ready to witness destiny unfold, the chamber was full, front bench and back. So I sat in the Members' gallery. From there I heard Gerry Fitt say that he would vote against the government and from there I saw Harold McCusker and John Carson uphold their agreement to vote with the government. Back in my eyrie above the government despatch box, I watched the Opposition whips tell Margaret Thatcher how many members had supported the

No Confidence resolution. As she made her mental calculation, she forgot that two of her MPs had acted as 'tellers' and were not therefore included in the total. Fearing she had lost, she hissed, 'I don't believe it.' Her scepticism was justified. The government was defeated by a single vote. When Jim Callaghan announced that 'now the country must now decide', there was a mumble of 'hear, hear' from all sides. The House of Commons likes that sort of historic platitude.

Election campaigns all have distinct characteristics. For Labour, 1983 was ludicrous, and 1987 was desperate. At least 1979 was only dismal. The only moment of hope came on the Tuesday before polling day when the opinion polls suddenly and unaccountably improved. That morning I took part in Labour's last press conference. Somebody asked what inflation level we expected in the following year and Jim invited me to answer, adding, 'You're going to be in charge of these things.' I told him that, 'I had rather hoped for a move,' and he accused me of 'getting cheeky'. The newspapers published smiling photographs of the Prime Minister and me with the caption, 'What a difference a poll makes', and reported 'a new mood of confidence'. They were wrong. We both knew that a Labour era had ended.

On the day after our defeat, I went back to the department to say goodbye. I told Ken Clucas that I hoped we would meet again. Ken told me that he would have retired by the time of my return to government. 'I go in three years. You'll be back in five.' I think that he only said it to comfort me. Then Stuart Hampson – my private secretary in 1979 and now chairman of the John Lewis Partnership – came in with the news that I had to move all my belongings from my room in the House of Commons Upper Ministers' Corridor. Much to Hampson's horror, I took with me the Victorian bell push which had fallen from the wall years before. He hurried me out and, as he slammed the door, the brass Pugin knob came off in his hand. I have that too. Hampson said, as if he feared they were not safe in my hands, 'You'll have to return your seals of office.'

I never saw my seals. The court circular had announced that I had received them when I 'kissed hands on my appointment'. And my career as one of Her Majesty's principal Secretaries of State ended with the news that I had duly handed them in. But, if they existed outside constitutional fiction, they were always kept safely away from me. Shirley Williams and I had lunch together. Then I walked to Buckingham Palace. For I did not want to ask my successor for the use of what I still thought of as my car. The Queen thanked me for the years that I had spent in her service. I bowed, reversed out as was required, and thought, 'One day I'll be back.'

CHAPTER
11

There was no obvious place for me in the list of front bench speakers in the five-day debate which opened the new Parliament. But Eric Varley suggested that I fill the gap left by the defeat of Shirley Williams and follow Mark Carlisle, the Secretary of State for Education. My speech started off well enough but after twenty minutes I began to lose my way. Fortunately, just as it began to flag badly, Margaret Thatcher started to mutter offensive comments about Shirley from what the House, in its pompous way, calls 'a sedentary position'. Having been knocked out at Hitchen, Shirley had become a martyr as well as a saint. So, when I repeated the Prime Minster's not quite *sotto voce* insults, I had to wait for the cries of 'shame' to subside before I could complain about her comments. There were cheers when I sat down. I did not allow myself to wonder if they were for me or for Shirley.

Thanks to Margaret Thatcher's behaviour, I came third in the Shadow Cabinet elections. On the day that the result was announced, I had lunch with Tony Howard – by then editor of the *Listener* – and agreed to write a weekly column for his magazine. We decided to call it *Endpiece*. It was the beginning of my progress, some would say decline, towards the status of full-time journalist. But on that summer's day I had no doubt that writing would be an interesting diversion during my brief periods of enforced opposition. Debbie Owen sat at the next table. She wished me luck. We both expected that David and I would serve side by side in government for years to come.

When Jim Callaghan – the leader of Her Majesty's Opposition – sent for me, I asked to shadow Keith Joseph at Industry. I had almost suggested that I return to Education – the brief which I had held when Labour was last in opposition. But I had decided to stick to the principle, 'Never look back.' To my surprise, Jim asked me who I would recommend to shadow that department. Before I had time to reply, he told me that he had offered the job to Neil Kinnock, who had not been elected to the Shadow Cabinet, but was very popular in the Party. 'When I spoke at the Welsh rally last week,' Jim said, 'they were calling for him to speak, even though he was not on the platform.' He then asked me how I felt about Kinnock being elevated from back-bench agitator to front-bench spokesman. I said, without thinking, that I thought it an excellent idea. I was too concerned with the prospect of making policy to worry about the rivalry of a young man who had not even served the government as a parliamentary secretary. It was a mistake which I was to repeat throughout the next four years.

Jim offered me Environment and responded, absent-mindedly, to my arguments with the promise to think it over and let me know. No doubt he thought it over. He let me know through the nine o'clock news, which announced (without further consultation) that I was to oppose Michael Heseltine at Environment. Although I did not realise it at the time, it was the ideal appointment. Not once in the year during which I shadowed him did I best Heseltine in debate. But thanks to his often reckless pursuit of applause, he exposed more flank than the rest of the Cabinet added together. He also made housing and local government the two bloodiest battlefronts in the first year of the new political war. It was the right place to be.

Part of the joy of shadowing Michael Heseltine was the talent he possessed for causing trouble. Ever since the war, Labour had regarded local government as its personal property. We controlled most of the great town halls. And even in the boroughs where the Tories had a majority, they followed the tradition set by Joseph Chamberlain in Victorian Birmingham and presided over what Margaret Thatcher and her Cabinet undoubtedly regarded as municipal socialism. Heseltine decided to change all that by forcing councils to sell houses and limiting by law both what they could spend and what they could raise by local taxes. Whether he knew it or not, his policy of removing one of the principal checks on the arbitrary power of central government played a crucial part in pushing local Labour parties towards extremism. Denied their democratic right to implement the policies on which they had been elected, councillors all over the country were only briefly satisfied with marching behind red banners and shouting, 'Maggie! Maggie! Maggie! Out! Out! Out!' They decided that if Michael Heseltine could manipulate the law, they could break it. There followed the rent strikes, the setting of illegal rates, the refusal to sell council houses and the attempts to mortgage public buildings. Ted Knight and Ken Livingstone were Michael Heseltine's children.

Fortunately for me, Heseltine was a corner cutter, and more than once he tripped up whilst making that dangerous man-oeuvre. The benefits which I gained from just being about when he fell more than made up for the great mistake of promising to remove the tenants' 'right to buy'.

At the time when I made the promise, I actually believed it wrong to sell council houses. But I knew that it was necessary to express my doubts with caution. However, during the Second Reading of the bill, the junior minister who wound up the debate demanded to know if Labour would repeal the Act, once it became law. Naturally enough, the Tory back-benchers shouted, 'Answer! Answer! Answer!' The proper response was disdainful silence. But, foolishly, I decided to confound my tormentors by getting up and replying, 'Yes'. At the time, it was an immensely satisfying response. But my moment of triumph was held against the Labour Party for the next fifteen years. I was slow to learn that it was better to accept a brief parliamentary embarrassment than to create a long-term electoral liability. My only defence was that William Ewart Gladstone – four time Prime Minister and Member of Parliament for half a century – could never resist reacting to a taunt or challenge.

Michael Heseltine was extremely adept at recognising when it was necessary for him to climb down and regroup. The first retreat of the Parliament was forced upon him shortly before the summer recess. Never believing that a joke is too old to repeat, Heseltine tried one of the oldest tricks in the game – the last-minute announcement of a controversial decision by a written answer which is published just before the House rises. The stratagem would have defeated me, for I have never been an assiduous reader of Order Papers and official reports. But an hour or so before Members were due to leave for their holidays and con- stituencies, a number of *Stakhanovites* brought me the news that Heseltine had 'slipped in' an announcement of his decision to extend compulsory sales to pensioners' flats and disabled people's bungalows. I went to see George Thomas, the Speaker, and told him that I proposed to raise a point of order at ten o'clock. He was horrified.

At ten o'clock, Black Rod – the Sovereign's officer in the House of Lords – was due to bring the Commons a message from the Queen. It could not be delayed. My response was a tactic that was almost as old as Heseltine's written answer trick. Nobody, I assured the Speaker, could be more anxious to preserve the proprieties than I. But I feared that less reasonable elements in my party were determined to expose the Secretary of State's sleight of hand. A point of order raised by me was the best way to ensure that they let off steam rather than exploded. 'Very well,' said Mr Speaker Thomas, 'one point of order and then the ceremony.'

It was the word 'ceremony' which made me understand what should have been clear to me all along. Suddenly, I recalled what every school party is taught during the tours of Parliament. When Black Rod arrives at the Commons Chamber, the door is slammed in his face as a demonstration that the monarch's messenger can only enter the Lower House at Honourable Members' pleasure. I told the Speaker, 'To keep the lid on things, we'll have to keep him out a bit longer than usual.' The Speaker's horror turned to outrage. 'Do you not realise that Black Rod represents Her Majesty? We can't keep him hanging about.'

I decided to explain, as politely as I could, the absurdity of his attitude. 'Are you', I asked, 'telling me that we can't keep Black Rod out of the Chamber because it would be rude to delay pretending to keep him out of the Chamber?' The Speaker seemed relieved that I had at last grasped the point.

The back-benchers who had spotted Heseltine's manoeuvre would not accept that what was right in art was wrong in life. They decided to demonstrate their lack of sympathy for the niceties of Westminster etiquette by doing in practice what we assembled to perform in theory. So they gave reality to another parliamentary fiction by literally 'barring the door'.

Whilst they stood shoulder to shoulder at the bar of the House, I complained about the Secretary of State's conduct, he said that he meant no offence, Tory back-benchers sat glumly like guilty things found out and my honourable friends hooted mock disgust and genuine derision. To make the most of the moment, I said that he had taken advantage of a new Member by persuading him to be party to such devious behaviour. To emphasise the point, I confessed that the naive dupe was so recent an addition to the House that he was unknown to me. The member for Huntingdon rose and waved to me like an evacuee leaving London for the country. It was, to the best of my knowledge, the first time that I saw John Major. More rewardingly still, a week later, I came top in the Shadow Cabinet elections.

Inevitably, Michael Heseltine's Housing Bill ran into trouble. The newspapers began to speculate about it running out of parliamentary time. A bill which has not completed 'all its stages' and become law by the end of one legislative year has to start all over again after the Queen's Speech has opened a new Parliament. And there was a remote chance – much exaggerated by the media – of the 'right to buy' meeting that humiliating fate. The government's problem was less the result of the Opposition's resolute defiance than Michael Heseltine's carelessness. For months he had added new clauses to his original bill – prolonging the debate, making a guillotine impossible and providing almost endless opportunities for Labour to propose new amendments. A couple of days before the House rose I went off to lunch with Ray Horrocks, the managing director of British Leyland, feeling distinctly ambivalent about what lay ahead. There was just the possibility of achieving one of the transient parliamentary victories which seem so much more important in Westminster than in the real world outside. But I would have to stay up all night in order to play a very long shot indeed.

Horrocks, a couple of his colleagues and I were having a drink in a private room at the Dorchester Hotel when a waiter came in with the news that there was a man outside asking to speak to me. 'What does he want?' I asked testily. The waiter said that the visitor had described his business as confidential and added that he had given the name of Heseltine. I went out into the corridor where the Secretary of State for the Environment, together with the junior minister who had tempted me into promising to repeal the Housing Bill, were leaning on the wall. 'We are here to talk about time,' Heseltine said.

I insisted that they wait until Gerald Kaufman – then the housing spokesman in my team – was found and brought to the

Dorchester. Finding him was easier than persuading him to come to the hotel. I suspect that he was hoping to see an early afternoon performance of a film. But when he arrived, he took brilliant command. Horrocks generously abandoned lunch and private room and the four of us sat around the food-littered table. Gerald set out our negotiating position.

'We have a chance of beating you outright. Roy wants us to try.' I tried not to look surprised at the news of my bellicosity as Gerald explained that he, on the other hand, was prepared to compromise. 'But to come to an arrangement we have to have something worth having. It has to be a victory. A real victory. A visible victory. Even then, Roy . . . ' I did not know whether to look intransigent or pretend not to be there. Heseltine asked what it would take to buy me off. Gerald replied that I would settle for nothing less than the removal of special housing from the bill. When the Secretary of State seemed reluctant to agree, he was told that I might not even agree to that unless capitulation came quickly. The surrender was unconditional. 'One other thing,' said Gerald. 'We need your car to get us back to the House of Commons.'

We reported our discussions to Michael Foot who was acting leader in Jim's absence abroad. He said that he needed to confirm what we had agreed with Margaret Thatcher. His obvious pleasure at the thought of a quite unnecessary confrontation with the Prime Minister convinced me that, when the time came, he would certainly be a candidate to succeed Jim Callaghan. Michael enjoyed being in charge far too much for him ever to consider a self-denying ordinance.

There had been talk of Callaghan resigning the Party leadership ever since the day when the 1979 election was lost. I hoped that he would stay on and fight again. Wiser counsels – perhaps thinking of Jim's own best interests – thought that he should go at once and let Denis Healey step almost automatically into his

shoes. Jim stayed a year. The politician who 'always does everything on purpose' wanted to put the Party back together before he
passed it on to his successor. There was never any hope of him
fulfilling that honourable ambition.

In the spring of 1979, the Party was disillusioned and demor-
alised. The complaint against the leadership was not that Labour
had been defeated. We had all grown used to defeat. The bitter
indictment was that a government, which the rank and file had
worked so hard to create, had never even tried to implement the
policies in which the rank and file believed. Public expenditure
cuts, incomes policy and the assault on the unions during the
Winter of Discontent all seemed to confirm that once again the
leaders had betrayed the led. It did not come as a surprise. Ever
since Ramsay MacDonald formed the national government in
1931, Party members had suspected that power had an invariably
corrupting effect on Labour Cabinet ministers. For true believers
there was a special emotional comfort in the pretence that the play
was a work of genius but the actors' lack of conviction had turned
it into a flop. It was an idea that Tony Benn cultivated with a zest
which made it hard to remember that he was in the Cabinet which
he regularly excoriated.

At the 1980 Labour Party conference, Tony Benn's speech was
a long indictment of the defeated government's treachery. His list
of broken promises was made up of policy commitments which
had, in truth, either been kept or never made. The high point of
his speech – and one of its rare, historically accurate passages –
was his denunciation of Jim Callaghan's refusal to include the
abolition of the House of Lords in Labour's election manifesto.
The decision – Jim Callaghan's veto, as Tony Benn described it –
was elevated into a symbol of betrayal, the endemic disease of
Labour leadership. The campaign to change the constitution, and
thus make treachery impossible, was irresistible. Power must be
passed from the invariably perfidious parliamentary leadership to
the ideologically reliable local membership. The process was

described as constitutional reform. But it was intended to shift the Party's point of balance to the left – as David Owen had warned me a year earlier on the evening before the 1979 conference opened.

In the bar of Brighton's Grand Hotel, he had spoken with the abrasive frankness which could, on rare occasions, be attractive. A decision that the whole Party would elect its leader was certain, he said, 'to rule out you and me'. It was, in his view, 'tailor-made for Kinnock'. I knew that he was right. So I took refuge, as always, in a joke. At lunch together, earlier that year, Owen had said that my star was 'temporarily' in the ascendant. I hoped he remembered when I assured him, 'I've seen off other young pretenders. I can do the same with him.' David Owen gave the smile of a man who could recognise whistling in the dark when he heard it.

Benn's speech at the 1980 conference was reinforced by Ron Hayward, the Party's General Secretary. In one of the most wretched speeches which I have ever heard, he confirmed that the Party was in a desperate mood. 'I wish our ministers and our Prime Minister would sometimes act in our interests like a Tory Prime Minister acts in their interests.' When it was over Jim Callaghan asked me for my opinion of what I had heard. I told him that I was undecided between 'deplorable' and 'despicable'. He chose 'despicable'.

Jim Callaghan had tried to make sense of the demand for change by meeting with a handful of influential trade union leaders. He hoped that they could agree a programme of reform which reflected the honourable hopes of greater party democracy but excluded the bitterness which was being unscrupulously exploited by the Bennite left. The proposals which came out of his meetings satisfied no one. He was attacked in the Shadow Cabinet for compromising with extremism and disowned at the 1980 conference by the Benn-led ultras who wanted the whole package – MPs to face reselection each Parliament, leader elected by the whole Party, manifesto decided by Party conference.

The mood at Blackpool was best represented by the delegate
from St Pancras North:

> What we need and what we have a right to demand is a
> guarantee that the next Labour government will implement
> the policies that the Labour Party has decided upon and not
> the policies of a handful of ministers and a handful of civil
> servants . . . That is what these constitutional issues are
> about. They are about getting rid of the divide between
> the policies that we as the Party decide on, the policies on
> which we fight the general election and the policies which a
> Labour government implements in office.

That delegate was Patricia Hewitt. Her ideological progress is a
paradigm of Labour's evolution. Three years later she wrote
identical letters to Neil Kinnock and me – the two front runners
in the 1983 leadership election – offering her services as press
officer, 'when you win'. Neil appointed her, and by 1992 she had
become one of the left's hate figures – the leadership's hatchet
person who rewrote the manifesto to reflect the fears of the
Shadow Cabinet rather than the hopes of the rank and file. She
was also responsible for an injunction that is reproduced verbatim
in David Hare's generally incredible 'political' play, *The Absence of
War*. 'Please do not use the word equality. The preferred term is
fairness.' The line was delivered to me. As I received her reproof I
decided that, in the interests of campaign unity, I would not
remind her of the speech that she had made back in 1980.

The 1980 conference was part tragedy, but mostly farce. After
agreement, by a small majority, on the principle of 'widening the
franchise' for the election of a leader, various attempts were made
to decide what 'widening the franchise' meant. After four days of
chaos – punctuated by emergency meetings of the National
Executive and angry interventions from Eric Heffer – three
different schemes were cobbled together and read out with the

announcement that a choice had to be made between them before the end of the week. Terry Duffy – late and irritated – passed me on his way to the delegation meeting at which the AEU would decide how to cast its block vote. He called back over his shoulder, 'Which of these bloody things is best?' Believing that time improves everything, I shouted after him, 'Vote against them all. You're against them aren't you?' Terry, no doubt anxious not to behave wibbly-wobbly, told his delegates that integrity left them no other choice but total opposition. Each proposal was rejected in turn. So the conference broke up without deciding how a new leader should be chosen. Jim Callaghan made an impromptu speech that made it clear, at least to me, that the Parliamentary Party would have to elect a new leader by the old method, long before a special conference cleared up the mess that the constitutional revolutionaries had left behind.

At first we all assumed that the last of the old style elections would be an almost straight fight between Denis Healey and Peter Shore, with Tony Benn complicating the issue and livening up the contest without having the slightest chance of becoming leader. Then Michael Foot, who had been one of Peter's most enthusiastic backers, announced that he had been persuaded to stand. John Silkin's nomination was, in itself, unexpected. But it was not as surprising as his initial campaign statement: 'Michael, I've got you beaten.' He was knocked out – as was the cruelly abandoned Peter Shore – on the first ballot.

Denis Healey was a self-destructive candidate who seemed to be driven by an irresistible desire to offend potential supporters. Since he was competing for the votes of an electorate which was deranged by fear, participation in the contest was rarely an elevating experience. For a couple of weeks, otherwise sensible people behaved like idiots. Denis, despite my entreaties, refused to contribute to the *Guardian* series in which each contestant set out a personal testament. Phillip Whitehead – a distinguished television producer, then a Labour MP, now a Member of the

European Parliament and normally a man of judgement – would not vote for Denis because Denis would not write in the *Guardian*. Denis, totally unmoved, continued in his brilliant, entertaining but perverse way.

He and I were amongst a party of distinguished citizens who were invited to the residence of the American ambassador in order to lunch with, and listen to, Vice President George Bush. We each shook hands upon arrival and the photographs which were taken of the glorious moment were developed and printed whilst we ate. A complicated podium was then constructed and the Vice President, having mounted it, spoke about nothing very much for ten minutes, concluding with the concession that he had time for three questions. 'Good,' shouted Denis. 'Because I've got three questions to ask.' The third involved the difference between authoritarian and totalitarian regimes – a distinction which Denis claimed the Reagan Administration was unable to make. His point was confirmed by the Vice President, who clearly had no idea what he was talking about. Denis, in exasperation, got down to basics. 'When some regime fastens electric terminals to a man's genitals he isn't consoled by the thought that they have an election every ten years.' Peter Shore drove me back to the House of Commons. 'Denis,' he said, 'really is too bad. If the Archbishop of Canterbury hadn't been there, he would have said balls, not genitals.'

Often, when Denis came into my office, he announced his arrival by performing, round the edge of the door, what he believed to be an impression of a man being strangled. He went through the unconvincing performance shortly after I had torn the wrapping paper from the ceramic phallus that someone had sent me through the post. I assumed that both the gift and the accompanying message – 'Because you are one' – had come from a Tory, for left-wing Labour Party members usually chose to associate me with female genitalia. But – at the moment of Denis's arrival – I was less concerned about where my gift had come from than how I could get rid of it. Denis tore it from my grasp and left, saying that, at last, he had the door stopper of his dreams. David Hill chased him down the corridor, demanded the object's return, and bore it off to the rubbish chute. When he returned, breathless and embarrassed, he apologised for over-reacting with the explanation, 'I thought he might mean it.' I assured him that he had done quite the right thing. With Denis it was always best to assume the worst.

Had Denis Healey been elected Labour leader, the political history of Britain would have been different. He might not have carried the Party to victory in 1983. But we would have been beaten, not annihilated, and during the following five years he would have led a convincing recovery. At the time when Michael Foot defeated him, Denis was comfortably the most popular politician in the country and Michael's name did not even appear in the tables of public affection and esteem. It is, however, easy enough to explain the Party's choice. Michael Foot was the candidate of the quiet life.

Denis's chances were crucially undermined by the half dozen or so potential SDP defectors who voted for Michael Foot in the knowledge that his election would help justify their apostasy – a disgrace to which Tom Ellis, who was one of them, has now admitted on television. But the crucial fact of Michael Foot's victory was the belief that, if he became leader, the constituency parties would calm down. Members of Parliament, about to take part in a secret ballot, were instructed under pain of deselection to show their ballot papers to constituency activists – just to ensure their cross had not been put against the name of the man who capitulated to the IMF. Even many of those who resisted that pressure feared that Denis's election would set off another ex-plosion of hatred against the despised and detested Parliamentary Party. Worse still, they knew that Tony Benn would declare Denis's election illegitimate and challenge him as soon as the rules were changed. Then all sorts of dangerous passions would again be unleashed in constituency managements throughout the country. With Michael, Labour would certainly lose the election, but craven Members of Parliament would have their candidatures renewed and would hold their seats. The Parliamentary Labour Party consciously chose to take refuge in the wilderness. It was a wilful act of political abdication which has few parallels in the history of party politics. By electing Michael, the PLP sacrificed its claim to being the best judge of who was most likely to lead Labour into government. It also inaugurated three years of opposition which were so bizarre that, even at the time, most of us knew that the Party was coming perilously close to extinction.

When Michael's election was announced, Neil Kinnock – his campaign manager – let out the sort of whoop that devotees of cowboy films associate with homicidal Sioux or Pawnee war parties. I was sitting next to Jim Callaghan on the platform of Committee Room Ten at the moment of Michael's triumph whilst the victor himself was modestly hidden somewhere in the body of the meeting. Although Jim congratulated his successor with real warmth, he made no effort to offer him his seat. I thought courtesy required me to vacate mine. *The Sunday Times* subsequently complained that, having managed the unsuccessful campaign, I then tried to ingratiate myself with the winner by leading the standing ovation.

I saw a great deal of Michael during the next three years. He made me Shadow Home Secretary – again a job which I did not want but which turned out to be one of the great pleasures of my political life – and he always treated me with immense courtesy and kindness. But I always felt like a passenger in an aeroplane which was being flown by an unqualified pilot. The problem was not so much the individual catastrophes – the promise that Peter Tatchell would never be a Labour candidate followed by support for his nomination in Bermondsey, the 'donkey jacket' at the

Cenotaph and the habit of speaking most often on subjects which did Labour most harm. What really unnerved me was the feeling that he had no enthusiasm for leadership.

Only once, during the entire three years, did I feel that he was enjoying himself, and that single episode was enough to convince me that he was a good man in the wrong job. Inevitably it involved writing, not politics. I arrived at the House one Monday morning to find a thick envelope on my desk. It was marked 'Private and Confidential. To be opened personally by Roy Hattersley.' It contained another envelope similarly inscribed. The letter inside was headed 'Personal' in Michael's distinctive longhand. I read the first paragraph in disbelief.

Some offences may sometimes be overlooked, and on the point of timing I merely note that you made the choice to deliver the attack at a moment of international crisis on the cowardly assumption, I suppose, that it might not even be noticed. I add also that all previous offences, a long list extending over a long period, will now be taken into account. I expected to find your resignation awaiting me when I arrived in the office this morning. Since I am not even offered an apology, how are we to proceed?

I could not imagine how I had caused such offence. For I had not even made a speech that weekend. No doubt I had made a critical aside to a friend. That was one of my bad habits. But nothing I had done could justify the ferocity of Michael's language. I read on.

Dorothy Parker was not only a poet, a short story writer, a wit, the best exponent if not the creator of that American institution, the wisecrack. She also gave a display of casual courage surpassing that of any of her New York contemporaries. Not being primarily a politician, although she justly counted herself in the Socialist camp, she would have had some excuse if she had momentarily wilted beneath the McCarthyite hysteria which subdued so many. When she was pilloried as a card-carrying Communist, she answered with a contemptuous silence which the Red-baiting press seized upon to incriminate her further. Actually she had the distinction of being a premature anti-fascist with impeccable credentials. One of her best short stories was written from Spain at the height of the Civil War, but when a few years later the United States was involved in the same anti-fascist world-wide war, she was denied the right to leave her country as a news correspondent – thanks to the dossier compiled against her in the Spanish war days by some fascist in the FBI, of course. Even six or seven years later, that same dossier helped to rob her of her livelihood and a husband who did not share her political tastes. But she never whined, never ratted and never informed, although incredibly, in those days informers were regarded as respectable.

This note started as a genial rebuke. It has turned into a legitimate tirade. I write as an enthusiastic addict of *Endpiece* who, however, would not wish to see your various talents directed exclusively to such work.

Endpiece had, by then, moved to the *Guardian* (where it has remained ever since) and I was delighted to discover that Michael read it. What is more, the letter was a good joke. And I was particularly impressed by the leader's knowledge of Dorothy Parker's life and work. But I was not prepared for the telephone calls from his office saying that Michael expected a reply. They went on throughout the day when I was busy trying to be the Shadow Home Secretary and had other things to do. Michael's interest in writing – like his personal generosity – made him a sad as well as unsympathetic figure. I have no doubt that he preferred literature to leadership.

When, in January 1981, the special Labour Party conference met at Wembley to make a final decision about the way in which the leader should be chosen, Michael – elected a few months earlier under the old system – chose not to speak until after the votes were cast. That day I addressed the Fabian Society's lunchtime rally and used the occasion to urge disillusioned members to stay and fight. I now feel embarrassed about my affirmation of 'love and loyalty', but it is not my most painful recollection of the occasion. Halfway through my speech I noticed Shirley Williams and Bob MacLennan standing in the doorway. Marcel Marceau could not have conveyed the impression of cynical detachment more clearly.

Later that day, the conference decided to set up an electoral college with the largest share of the leadership votes going to the trade unions. The fight for one member one vote was temporarily over. Shirley Williams, Tom Bradley (of the Transport Salaried Staff) and I had put the idea to a joint meeting of the Shadow Cabinet and National Executive. And we had been slaughtered by a co-ordinated assault on both the principle and the practice – led by Neil Kinnock. So the result was not a total surprise. The enthusiastic endorsement for a form of election which was so obviously absurd filled me with unaccustomed depression. On the way out of the conference centre, both friends and enemies predicted that the likes of me would soon be driven out of the Party. I could not find my car in the car park. And as I wandered about in the rain, I thought about the future. I was forty-six. I had been a Cabinet minister for almost four years and I was a senior member of the Opposition front bench. My seat was safe and I should have been full of hope for the future. But I had only one clear idea about what lay ahead. If the ship sank, I would go down with it.

We were heading for the rocks again within a couple of weeks. As soon as the electoral college was established, Tony Benn announced his intention of challenging Denis Healey. Michael's reaction was – like so much of his leadership – a baffling combination of the admirable and the absurd. He told Tony, in a vitriolic open letter, that if the confrontation was intended to change the Party's political direction the challenge should be to the leader not his deputy. He never missed an opportunity in public or private to demonstrate his distaste for Tony's behaviour. And he made it clear that he was perfectly content to be the front half of the pantomime horse that Denis completed. But he would not announce that, when the electoral college met, he intended to support Healey. Nor did he vote for him on that fateful night in Brighton when Denis scraped home.

Throughout the period of the deputy leadership campaign, the Party held open-air rallies in the great cities. Denis spoke at them all as incumbent rather than candidate and was normally shouted down by Benn supporters. Tony, who could have stopped all the booing and heckling with a one-sentence appeal, contented himself with pieties about never making personal attacks himself, and Denis did not help his cause by identifying the Benn lieutenant who had co-ordinated the near riot when he spoke in Bristol, but getting the name wrong. I went on *The World At One* to defend the Healey impetuosity and told them that, 'Denis bites y'legs.' The candidate himself – although a Leeds MP – had never heard of Norman Hunter, left-half for United and England, and was deeply impressed by my linguistic ingenuity.

That year, my mother was Lord Mayor of Sheffield and, for some reason which neither she nor I remember, Michael Foot stayed with her in the official residence on his way to the Birmingham rally. We travelled south together and as Michael thumbed through *Punch* he noticed the announcement that I was to join the magazine. It contained the weak, though obvious, joke that I was not leaving the Labour Party. My credentials as a humorous journalist had been confirmed by a life-time membership of the Labour Party – in which I intended to remain. Michael was furious. He knew for a fact that I had never contemplated leaving. He urged me to write an angry letter.

Michael's explanation for the not quite total commitment to Denis Healey was the encouragement which it gave to the nomination of a third candidate who would split Benn's vote. As the result was determined by an exhaustive ballot, the stratagem's attraction was less the help it gave to Denis than the relief that it provided for MPs who wanted Tony to be defeated but were afraid to say so. By supporting a no-hoper in the first round and abstaining in the second, a handful of embarrassed left-wingers made a covert contribution to Denis's victory. But it was a wretched way to decide the future of a great party. And Neil Kinnock – who was said, at the time, to have invented the idea of the Third Man – came to accept that the 1981 deputy leadership election was not his finest hour. He told me so in 1988 when I was challenged in almost identical circumstances and he, unlike Michael seven years earlier, immediately announced his support for his deputy.

Denis won with a majority of 0.01 per cent. Thanks to me, it was very nearly a majority of only 0.009 per cent. Naturally the meeting of the electoral college – in reality the Labour Party conference with a more complicated voting system – was broadcast live on BBC2. The long periods of inactivity were inadequately filled by discussion between nominees of the three candidates. I represented Denis and watched with fascination as Neil Kinnock (on behalf of John Silkin) and Arthur Scargill (speaking up for Tony Benn) demonstrated, both off screen and on, the bitter animosity which was to do so much harm to the Labour Party throughout the eighties. A couple of years earlier they had been allies in the assault on the Labour government – united by their commitment to the mining industry, their criticism of economic policy and their hairstyles. That night they had nothing in common except mutual loathing. After the result of the first vote was declared, I so enjoyed watching the display of their reciprocal dislike, that I forgot where I had left my ballot paper. David Hill found it just in time for me to add my 0.001 per cent to Denis's winning margin.

So I played my full part in making the decision which turned the tide. If Denis had lost, thousands of moderates would have deserted Labour and the Bennite alliance – Trotskyites, one subject campaigners, Marxists who had never read Marx, Maoists, pathological dissidents, utopians and, most dangerous of all, sentimentalists – would have turned the Party into an unhealthy hybrid of pressure group and protest movement. As it was, they merely played a major part in keeping the Conservatives in power for almost twenty years. It is difficult to say who helped Margaret Thatcher and the Tories most – the Social Democrats who claimed that Labour was lost to extremism or the Bennite left who tried to prove them right.

I first heard about the Social Democratic Party from Eric Heffer, the 'rough-hewn' left-winger about whom Michael Foot once said to me, 'I used to think of him as a noble savage, but I was only half right.' On the way into a Shadow Cabinet meeting, Heffer accused me of helping to write a *Guardian* article which was to be published at the end of the week. It was, he said, the manifesto for a new party. He would not believe that I had no idea what he was talking about.

On the way out of the meeting, David Owen mentioned – with what he no doubt thought of as casual courtesy – 'a thing that two or three of us have put together'. It was, he told me, a declaration of support for the European Community and he had no doubt that I 'would agree with every word except the last paragraph'. The article ended with the warning that unless Labour reaffirmed its support for the EEC, the authors – Bill Rodgers, Shirley Williams and Owen himself – would find it impossible to remain in the Party. 'I guess you wouldn't have gone along with that,' he said. I confirmed his judgement.

None of the principal apostates ever mentioned the subject to me again.

Each member of the so-called Gang of Four had a different reason for leaving Labour and creating the new and doomed SDP. Roy Jenkins, on the evidence of his rightly acclaimed Dimbleby Lecture, had come to believe in both the politics of the centre and the intrinsic advantage of coalition. I have never believed that his old friends could complain about his decision to create a vehicle to carry his new beliefs to power – wrong though I believed them to be. David Owen would not condescend to continued membership of a party which so lacked judgement and sense of history that it sacrificed its opportunity of making him leader. Bill Rodgers was always likely to follow where Roy Jenkins led and both Europe and NATO (which he thought to be under threat from the unthinking left) had become the crucial tests of Labour integrity. The Party was temporarily wrong on both issues. Bill – to my surprise – chose not to stay and put it right. Shirley Williams shared Bill's passion for Europe. She also resented being ridiculed and abused at National Executive meetings by Dennis Skinner. She decided that life would be more civilised outside the Labour Party. Although, in Roy Jenkins' famous metaphor, there was always a high probability that the SDP plane would crash before it left the runway, all four of its originators undoubtedly believed that the new party offered them the prospect of power. It is easy to laugh at them now that the mould of the two-party system remains intact. But, at the time, their ambitions seemed at least plausible. During the weeks which followed the SDP's creation, those of us who stayed with Labour were constantly told that a fresh start was 'the only way to beat Margaret Thatcher'. We always denied it in the hope that we sounded more confident than we felt.

It took months for the new party to take shape and most of the Labour MPs who joined – some out of fear that they were already marked down for rejection by their constituency parties, others in the hope of re-creating what they imagined Labour had once been – agonised about whether they should go or stay. Bob MacLennan, the parliamentary secretary who had survived when Neil Kinnock refused to join the government in 1976, was particularly fraught about what he should do. Then, just before the conference that finally determined the new method of electing Labour's leader, he told me that he had almost made up his mind. He took me to lunch to explain that he would either stay in the Labour Party or give up politics altogether and join a New York law firm.

A couple of days later, the Limehouse Declaration – which launched the SDP – was published. I was out at dinner that evening and the meal was delayed by the late arrival of Ian Aitken, who had written the story of the new party's birth for the *Guardian*. He read us the list of defectors which had been added to his article by a colleague who had reported the parade of supporters outside David Owen's house. MacLennan's name was included. When I told Ian about my lunch conversation, the food was again postponed whilst, cursing the incompetence of his associate, he telephoned his paper to correct the error. He was still on the phone when our host switched on the television news and we saw MacLennan smiling in the line-up between Roy Jenkins and Shirley Williams.

Tom McNally – once upon a time Jim Callaghan's political adviser – behaved differently. He was a late convert to the SDP and I was on my way to Austria when I read in *The Sunday Times* that he had defected with the comment, 'I'm not sure what I'm going to say to my dad.' I sent him a telegram from Innsbruck which read, 'Tell him you owe everything to the Labour Party.' Years later, in a television programme, he had the grace to admit, 'I thought that he was about right.'

My attitude towards the SDP was never civilised or sophisticated. In a meeting of the Campaign for Labour Victory – just before the split occurred – David Owen told me, 'There's no point in being nasty to each other. One day we'll have to work together again.' And it took a high level of aggression to bring out the emollient aspect of David's character. But I remain unrepentant about my attitude. A few of the MPs who joined the new party did so out of a combination of conviction and despair. But most left Labour because they believed that they would do better in the new party and then dressed up self-interest to look like principle. By protecting themselves, they exposed Britain to a full decade of Thatcherism. On Saturday mornings, when my constituents bring me their problems, it is difficult to forget that the oppressive immigration regulations, the shortage of rented property, the overcrowded schools and the hospital waiting lists are, at least in part, the responsibility of that nice Mrs Williams and that clever Dr Owen. It is the poor who paid to keep their consciences clear. I was delighted when, in 1990, Lord 'Dickie' Attenborough came back to Labour. But I was astonished when Neil Kinnock apologised on behalf of the Party that had driven him away. True to the lessons that I learned in Socialist Sunday School, I believed in celebrating the return of a lost sheep. But it seemed to me then that the apology should have been the other way round.

In the spring and summer of 1981, I thought less about the remote possibility of a reunion with the SDP than about the urgent necessity of hanging on to those moderate Labour supporters who, true to the spirit of 1961, were prepared to stay and fight for the party we love. They had to be convinced that the cause of sensible socialism was not lost forever. And it was to demonstrate that reason remained, as well as to fight the internal battles against mindless extremism, that Labour Solidarity was created. It was a ramshackle organisation with a silly name, little money, few active members and no great confidence that it would succeed in demonstrating that the Party was not afflicted by collective lunacy. At best we were the Taxis of the Marne – unsuitable and unprepared for active service but ready to rush up to the front rather than timidly accept defeat. When we were dissolved in 1983 there was only one claim which we could plausibly make. Without Labour Solidarity, the Party would have disintegrated. If I reach the Pearly Gates, I know what I shall claim is my qualification for crossing St Peter's picket line. Back in 1981, I was one of the people who stood their ground, argued against absurdity, organised (no matter how incompetently) on behalf of reason and, in consequence, saved the Labour Party.

CHAPTER
12

Margaret Thatcher dissolved her first Parliament after only four years. Before the election campaign had officially started, I was sent off to Lincolnshire with a message for the employees in Scunthorpe's three great steelworks. If Labour won the election, the closure programme which had already been announced by the government would be cancelled. I learned by heart the figures on which the Party's promise was based and arrived at a packed shop stewards' meeting, bursting with information about types, tonnage and potential markets. In my introduction to the Party's plan for steel, I proudly told its potential beneficiaries that I had once been a steel worker myself. Had I, one gnarled foreman asked me, ever been a soldier? Before I could answer he told me that since Labour would leave Britain defenceless and at the mercy of the Soviet Union, future steel production would be decided in Moscow not Whitehall. His colleagues reacted as if his complaint had been the signal for an uprising. There was a general waving of the paybooks which they had kept since they had served the Queen. Nobody said a word about steel. On my way to the local BBC studio, John Ellis, Labour's candidate, assured me that he would win. The branch of the Campaign for Nuclear Disarmament, which he had founded in the town, had doubled its membership in a year. Of course, he lost the seat. More surprisingly, Robin Day lost his temper with me during the lunch-time broadcast. Or, at least, he now claims that he did.

I had agreed to talk about the Labour manifesto – the document described by Gerald Kaufman as the longest suicide note in history, although, at barely thirty-seven pages, it only seemed interminable. It had been agreed – though not composed – the previous week. The act of creation had taken four years. *The New Hope For Britain* was made up of every policy statement which the Party had produced since the previous election. When I heard that Tony Benn was opposed to omitting a single commitment, I tried to mobilise support for selection and editing. To my surprise the hard right – as represented by John Goulding of the Post Office Engineering Union – was an enthusiast for Tony's idea. We were, he told me, certain to lose the election. 'So why not lose it on Benn's terms and teach him a lesson.' It was that heroic view of Labour strategy that made me feel that I would be wise to plan my response to Robin Day's most obvious question – 'How can you support a party which advocates unilateral nuclear disarmament?'

David Hill had no doubt that I should offer one courteous answer, explaining that all political parties were federations of diverse opinion and that, whilst I did not pretend to agree with Labour's defence policy, I supported all of the economic, industrial and social programme. 'If he won't leave it alone,' David added, 'go spare and finish it once and for all. We can't be pursued by this thing day after day.'

Of course, Robin did not leave it alone. So I went spare in the way which I had decided and rehearsed. Why, I asked, was a BBC interviewer acting as the agent of the Conservative Party by asking about the one point of policy with which I disagreed instead of the great volume of proposals that I supported with enthusiasm? Robin has since described his response – 'Chuck it, Mr Hattersley' – as one of the few occasions when he had been rude to one of his guests. I cannot recall if he correctly remembers what he said. If he was right about the words, he was wrong about where the admonition appears on his personal Richter scale. He was often more rude to me than that.

The best example of what he would call forceful interviews (and normal people would describe as verbal abuse) occurred during one *Question Time* when we discussed the morality of abortion. Believing it to be a complex subject, I gave a complicated reply – and, naturally enough, he pressed me for a straight answer. Being a clever man, Robin knows perfectly well that the most interesting political questions cannot be dismissed with a yes or no. But 'the audience at home' likes the simplistic approach and Day popularity was based on populism – which he always pretended to despise even whilst he practised it. Usually I was prepared to play the part of Abbott to his Costello. But I feel strongly about abortion and, having been metaphorically chased around the studio for longer than my patience allowed, I struck what I knew was a low blow by referring to a conversation which had taken place before the programme began. Henry Kissinger was in London and, to Robin's fury, the one BBC interview was to be conducted by Michael Parkinson – 'a chat show host'. So with no other purpose other than to annoy him I said, absolutely gratuitously, that I was not surprised that he had been passed over for the current affairs event of the year. What he replied – cut out of the broadcast – was far worse than 'Chuck it, Mr Hattersley.' And it served me right. Sir Robin disputes my interpretation of the incident and assures me that nothing was cut between recording and broadcast. The transcript – which he kindly sent to me – shows that he asked me more or less the same question four times.

My most vivid memory of *Question Time* is sitting next to the unfortunate Francis Pym as he announced – quite unexceptionally, as it seemed when he said it – that democracy was not best served by the government of the day dominating the House of Commons with a massive majority. Margaret Thatcher did not agree and dropped him from the Cabinet. No doubt she had erased from her mind the broadcasting blotches on her political escutcheon. I was on *Any Questions* with her in Southampton during the 1974 general election when she said that Britain was not ready for a woman Prime Minister.

I enjoyed my Scunthorpe joust with Robin (who by then had become the Henry Irving of radio and television interviews) and, unaware of the impact it would make in the next day's papers, I went on to Edinburgh accompanied by my minder for the campaign – Mary Goudie, the secretary of Labour Solidarity and wife of a distinguished Queen's Counsel. I had been asleep for about half an hour when there was an urgent knock on my door. Outside in the corridor was Mrs Goudie – apparently prepared for bed. Having little experience of such visitations, I was not sure if it was best to slam the door or ask her in before her agitated presence was noticed by other guests on the corridor. When Mary spoke, what she said was so incomprehensible that it might, for all I knew, have been a coded message. 'Have you', she asked, 'heard what young Blair's done?'

Not only had I not heard what he had done, I barely knew who he was. I had vague memories of speaking in a by-election for a polite young man of that name. And, as I recalled, he had sent me a note of thanks – which should, in itself, have distinguished him from other candidates. Assuming that he was fighting a marginal seat and had been caught in a compromising situation by a Sunday newspaper, I invited Mary to step inside and tell me the worst.

Tony Blair, she explained, was a junior member of her husband's Chambers. He had been nominated for Sedgefield – the one safe seat yet to select a candidate – but had not been short-listed by the executive of the Party. Instead of meekly accepting his rejection, he had spent the morning canvassing members of the constituency management committee and, because of his powers of persuasion, the afternoon meeting had begun with his name being added to the panel of hopefuls who faced the selection conference. He had then been chosen to fight, and certainly win, the seat. 'Have you ever known anything like it?' Mary asked. I told her, quite truthfully, that I had not. I decided there and then that this Tony Blair would do well in politics.

New ground was broken on almost every day of the campaign. In my absence, the campaign committee raised doubts about Michael's capacity to lead the Party by passing a resolution confirming its confidence in his leadership qualities – thus giving a whole new meaning to the phrase 'shooting yourself in the Foot'. Leader and deputy leader confirmed allegations that they disagreed about defence policy by issuing a joint statement which set out the compromise between their two conflicting positions. I was prepared for public disputes about doctrine. But the small inefficiencies were too much to bear. One day, when I spoke at a Transport House press conference about crime, the visual aids were left in the Labour Party's Walworth Road headquarters. On the following morning, I chaired a press conference on education. The visual aids arrived, but all the lettering slid off the pictures just as the television cameras focused on the graphs of Tory failure. I telephoned Michael and told him that there was no reason why our sign writing should be as incompetent as our policy formulation and suggested that he set up a small sub-committee to oversee the conduct of what was left of the campaign. He agreed at once and invited me to dinner as soon as I could get down to London. Ten minutes later he phoned back, confirming the invitation but explaining that his agreement to forming the committee was dependent on Neil Kinnock being able and willing to serve as a member.

The dinner was a delight. Michael told stories about Wells, Bennett and Priestley, reminisced about Lord Beaverbrook in a way which was only just on the right side of idolatry and tried to convince me that Byron, Keats, Shelley and Disraeli were all socialists in their hearts. By the end of the evening I had no doubt that Michael assumed that anyone he liked or admired shared his own political beliefs – which left an interesting question in my mind about where he put me on his personal political spectrum. Before I left he took me to his library in preparation for marking the occasion with the gift of a book. Michael possesses the real thing – not the few books along a sitting-room wall which sometimes enjoys that pretentious description in the southern suburbs. The Foot collection is immense, classified, catalogued and carefully arranged in subject order. A quick check in the card file confirmed that it contained two early copies of Robert Blatchford's *Merrie England*. 'Ha!' cried Michael. 'Here's a book, a real book.' He had to be persuaded to sign the title page before he gave it to me. Then he reached down an obscure work by a forgotten nineteenth-century academic and, after a quick flip through the pages, read me the opening passage of an essay on William Blake. It was evidence to support the view – which had been fiercely contested by me over dinner – that *Jerusalem* was not an assault on the inhumanities of the industrial revolution but a defence of free love. 'Don't use that in an article for a month or two,' said Michael. 'I want Jill [his wife] to have it first for her book on feminism.' I drove home not even regretting that we had failed to discuss the general election campaign. I fell happily asleep whilst adapting the question which Ravel had asked George Gershwin. The mystery had intrigued me all evening. Why should a first-rate Michael Foot want to be a second-rate Aneurin Bevan?

The sub-committee which I had proposed was set up and met every morning. But the course of the incompetent campaign was not altered by an inch. I prepared for the Birmingham election meeting rally – held, since we no longer trusted the public to behave properly, on the Sunday before polling day with the carefully controlled security of the town hall from which Lloyd George escaped disguised as a policeman – in the knowledge that all we could do was reduce the size of our defeat. Denis Howell, who chaired the packed gathering, was clearly made of sterner stuff. After Michael had made his speech and sunk back exhausted in his chair, Denis told a story of a girl in his constituency who was celebrating her sixth birthday that afternoon. She had been offered a variety of extravagant presents – dress, bicycle, trip to London, television set for her bedroom. But she had told her parents, 'All I want is to meet Michael Foot.' Denis had arranged to make her dream come true.

A diminutive child, dressed from head to toe in Labour Party red and yellow and carrying a mammoth bunch of red roses, was then led, rather reluctantly I thought, to the platform. I was sitting next to Michael and had recognised the supreme effort of will which was needed to force him to his feet, make him smile and persuade him to perform the hugs and kisses which are the stock in trade of the sort of politician which Michael rightly did not wish to be. Six months later, when Neil Kinnock had been elected to succeed him, I asked the new Party leader (who was essentially his predecessor's protégé) how his patron felt about abandoning the glory trail. 'Relieved,' said Neil. 'Just relieved.'

I was again on the platform for the final press conference of the campaign. But, unlike 1979, Shirley Williams – rather than sitting on the other side of the leader – was half a mile away speaking on behalf of another party. When it was over, half the Labour leadership sat about in an ante-room drinking coffee and trying to think of something to say to each other. I suppose it was nerves which made me ask Michael to promise that he would telephone me as soon as he had seen the Queen. 'I get nervous waiting,' I told him. Nobody laughed.

For most Labour Party members, the most vibrant memory of the last two days of that campaign is the televised broadcast of Neil Kinnock's speech to the electors of Islwyn. 'If the Tories win tomorrow, I warn you not to be old . . .' Its brilliance was beyond question. But it did not have the historical importance that some commentators have claimed. That speech did not win him the leadership election in the week before the contest had started for the simple reason that he had won it months earlier. From the moment that Michael Foot defeated Denis Healey, Neil – whether he admits it or not – worked to succeed his patron and hero. He ought not to pretend otherwise. For the single-minded determination with which he approached that task – drinking with journalists in the House of Commons press gallery bar, entertaining trade union leaders to dinner and becoming what Simon Hoggart in the *Guardian* called 'the most popular boy in the school' – was immensely to his credit. Anyone who aspires to lead a great political party has an obligation to take winning the leadership seriously. I wanted to be leader. But I did not want it enough to devote a whole year of my life to its pursuit. Perhaps, although I did not even admit it to myself, I knew that the Labour Party of the early eighties was never going to elect a pro-Market, anti-unilateralist, survivor of the Callaghan Cabinet. But, what-ever the reason, I aspired to the leadership without accepting the disciplines which might at least have made me a threat to the ultimate and certain winner. Neil is entitled to look back at the 1983 campaign with great professional pride. Even what was, at the time, described as a gaffe – the reference to Mrs Thatcher proving she had guts by making British soldiers leave theirs at Goose Green – was a bonus in the leadership contest. He can only have happy memories of the 1983 general election. What I recall with greatest pleasure is a constituent giving me a four-leaf clover which she had found amongst the weeds in her back garden. There is not a lot of foliage in Sparkbrook. So it was an extraordinary discovery. It brought me luck but not the leadership.

We were on our way home from Birmingham on the Sunday which followed the general election campaign when I heard a news flash on my car radio. Clive Jenkins – the General Secretary of ASTMS, the old foremen's union which had transmogrified itself into the executives' association – had announced at his annual conference that they had hoped to renominate Michael Foot as leader of the Labour Party. But Michael had declined. In consequence, they had nominated Neil Kinnock and Neil had accepted. The race for the leadership was on.

I had no doubt that it had all been arranged weeks before. Neil was undoubtedly Michael's appointed successor – described by his detractors as the son that Foot had never had and the reincarnation of Aneurin Bevan. But I had no cause for complaint. I flattered myself that, if Denis Healey had become leader back in 1980, he would have done his best to secure the succession for me. Indeed, one summer's day in 1978, I happened to be in the same Lake District hotel as Len Murray, the general secretary of the TUC, and he introduced me to his wife with the explanation that Denis would be 'next and then it looks likely to be Roy'. But the chain was broken and the Kinnock machine was towed into the front of the race by Michael Foot. My principal emotion was bewilderment not resentment. I had never doubted that within weeks of the election defeat Michael would retire to the back benches. And I was equally sure that I would want to compete for the succession. But when the moment of decision came – admittedly a week or two earlier than I anticipated – I had no idea what I should do to launch my campaign. Neil's high-powered and well-oiled election machine moved smoothly into top gear whilst I began to think about building a do-it-yourself engine. On that first day, it seemed that everybody was ready but me. I stopped at one of Birmingham's airport hotels and hired a room in which I could watch television. Peter Shore – invited onto the BBC's lunchtime discussion programme to analyse Labour's election defeat – announced that he was a candidate for the leadership. Eating my beef sandwiches, I feared that he had been planning his tactics for weeks.

When I telephoned David Hill, he told me that the press had

taken it for granted that I would be a candidate and assumed that I would use the evening's *Meet the Press* programme (on which I had been booked to appear for weeks) to announce that I would run. Ken Cure – the West Midlands member of the AEU's national committee – had telephoned to promise his best endeavour to secure his union's support. Mary Goudie, the ever faithful secretary of Labour Solidarity, had also spoken to him. She wanted me to speak to her at the first opportunity. For some reason, I feared that she wanted to tell me not to stand. Her number was engaged for what seemed like hours. When I got through she told me of a conversation with John Smith. Typically, John had said that it was up to me to decide if I should stand and he did not intend to persuade me. But, if I did, he 'would vote for Hattersley whether anybody else did or not'. It was not John's support that made up my mind. I was a candidate from the moment when I heard Michael was standing down. John's support just gave me confidence.

The last telephone call was to Tony Howard – host of *Meet the Press* as well as my friend. He told me that unless I stood I would lose all credibility as a serious politician. He added his hope that, during the programme, I would look straight into the camera and announce, 'I am a candidate for the leadership of the Labour Party' – thus enabling a clip from his show to be included in later news bulletins.

Fearing that there would be photographers outside my front door, I went straight to my room in the House of Commons where I washed my hair in the ladies' lavatory and discovered how hard it is to dry more than your hands on a roller towel. Unable to prevaricate any longer, I telephoned the Press Association. My brief statement sounded more heroic than I felt. 'I am a candidate for the leadership of the Labour Party.' At the studio, half an hour later, I did exactly what Tony Howard had instructed. As he had predicted, my announcement led the late evening news. When I got home there was a message from Denis Howell, telling me that

Ladbrokes had made me favourite to win the race and quoted some mysterious figures which he described as odds. I returned the call and told him that, as I knew nothing of betting, I would be grateful for an explanation of what the numbers meant. He replied that I was totally unqualified to lead the people's party, but he would support me nevertheless.

It would have been sensible to go to bed. But I needed to pretend that I was launching my campaign. So, late though it was, I began telephoning the people who I hoped would make up my election team. The obvious candidates were the whips who had helped me in government and opposition. Ted Graham declined my invitation with the explanation that he was too traumatised by his defeat in Edmonton to take any part in political activity for at least a year. Anne Taylor was willing but pregnant. Shadow Cabinet colleagues – though almost unanimous in their support – showed an almost equally universal reluctance to devote three months of their lives to the chores of lobbying union delegates and persuading constituency parties. Long after midnight, John Smith phoned. If I was in need of a campaign manager he was available. I went to sleep happy.

Despite my early lead at Ladbrokes, most commentators assumed that Neil Kinnock would win easily. It was therefore something of a surprise when he accepted nomination as deputy leader and announced that, if the Party so decided, he would gladly serve under me. John Smith had no doubt that I had to react by making exactly the same announcement and, when I told him that I had no wish to be deputy, he reacted with dismissive impatience. 'That's not the point. You can't afford for him to be more reasonable than you are.' I signed the nomination papers for deputy leader with a heavy heart. It was easy enough for Kinnock. He was going to be elected leader.

I had known five deputy leaders. Denis Healey and Roy Jenkins – the two whom I had known best and admired most – had hated the job and George Brown, who had been the first deputy leader in my life, had regarded it as a constant trauma. Whilst I was agonising about whether or not to bow to John Smith's will, I was unlucky enough to meet George by chance in the Central Lobby. We had not seen each other since a year earlier, when we had both taken part in an *Any Questions* programme in Bognor Regis. We had said very little to each other, for George was too busy being outraged by Esther Rantzen breastfeeding her baby between dinner and broadcast. But that evening in the Central Lobby he was in one of his affable moods. He did not have to mention the horrors of the deputy leadership. But the sight of him reminded me of his humiliations.

George tripped towards me on his tiny feet and, noticing that I was wearing a dinner jacket, made one of the oldest jokes in the world. 'I know MPs are badly paid. But I didn't realise you had to work as a waiter in the evenings.' I countered with the second most venerable dinner jacket witticism. 'I'm just off to my Lodge meeting.' George became suddenly serious. 'You don't have to go outside,' he said. 'There is a special parliamentary Lodge. Shall I get you transferred?' We did not meet again.

A week after the leadership campaign officially began, the National Committee of the AEU announced that it would cast its million votes for me. My delight at having secured the endorsement of at least one big union was only slightly reduced by the embarrassing way in which the decision had been taken. The AEU National Committee had twelve members. Eight of them voted for me – though Terry Duffy, as he honourably telephoned to tell me, had initially favoured Peter Shore on the principle that he was the older man and 'my time would come'. I had already urged trade union leaders to ballot their members before deciding which candidate to back, so I had to choose between disowning my most influential supporters and making it seem that my demand for greater democracy was just a way of trying to improve my vote. Terry Duffy, in his inimitable way, solved the dilemma for me.

For no particular reason except it was the traditional way in which to behave, the AEU organised a meeting for me at the Llandudno conference of the Confederation of Engineering and Shipbuilding Unions. My speech was delayed whilst Terry tried to dispose of a pigeon which had flown in through an open window and settled on the table behind which we both sat. Its homing instinct was highly developed and every time he put it to flight, it made a quick circuit of the room and returned to the exact spot from which it had been driven a minute earlier. There was one Kinnock supporter in the room. When his amusement at the pigeon's persistence became too much to bear, I persuaded Terry to stop waving his arms about and shouting 'Boo!' by making a joke about being used to getting the bird. The pigeon remained on the table throughout my speech, rocking gently from side to side, cooing and daintily defecating on my notes. When I sat down, the Kinnock supporter – who had mumbled throughout about the National Committee nominating me – asked how I could justify owing so much to so few, and the pigeon, recognising the aeronautical allusion, flew away.

I decided that there was no escape from the truth. So I answered that, grateful though I was for the AEU's support, I did believe that the union should have consulted its members. Naturally enough I sweetened the pill with several references to the unions well-known belief in democracy, the cost of organising a postal ballot and the National Committee's undoubted capacity for judging the mood and opinion of the rank and file. The Kinnock supporter offered his sincere congratulations on the honesty of my answer and turned, with a fiendish grin, on Terry Duffy. He had heard what his candidate had said. What was he going to do about it?

Terry Duffy rose to his full height and administered a magisterial rebuke. Roy Hattersley was not just the candidate of the AEU. He was the next leader of the Labour Party and would soon be Prime Minister of the United Kingdom. As general secretary of a great union, Terry needed no advice about how he should respond to the suggestion of the man in whom he had placed so much confidence. 'If Roy Hattersley wants a membership ballot, we shall have to give the most serious consideration to a membership ballot. I shall ask the general secretary to examine the proposal at once.' There was a long pause before he confirmed his commitment to democracy. 'Of course, whatever they want, we'll vote for Hattersley. That's what the Executive decided and there's no more to be said!'

Unfortunately, there was. John Smith believed that if the card-carrying members of the Party were given the chance to choose their next leader, they would choose me. Unfortunately, he was wrong. Only one of the constituencies which balloted its members supported me. And that was Sparkbrook. But we did not know that when the Shadow Cabinet – operating at the very margin of its responsibilities – insisted on discussing electoral procedures and carried, by a large majority, a resolution which called on local parties to test the opinion of their rank and file. Two thirds of the Shadow Cabinet were campaigning for me, with the rest divided between Neil, Peter Shore and Eric Heffer. So it was easy enough to insist – despite Michael Foot's protests – that the whole Parliamentary Party be invited to discuss how the election should be conducted.

The PLP meeting was packed. Jack Dormand – the chairman – was about to put the resolution to the meeting when Max Madden, a Bradford MP and press officer to Neil Kinnock's campaign, moved a procedural motion of the sort which I have always made a point of not understanding – Next Business, Previous Business, That the Motion Be Not Put, something of that sort. He produced, almost word for word, Michael's argument in the Shadow Cabinet. Indeed, had Michael not been famous for his probity, I would have suspected some sort of collusion. 'This', he said, 'is none of our business.' Before Jack Dormand had the chance to advance the contrary argument, Michael leaped to his feet with an agility which I had not previously noticed and accepted Madden's motion. The meeting was over.

Despite what the newspapers wrote next day, I insist that I did not lose my temper. I did not bang the desk, kick my chair, wave my hands about or shout. I simply mentioned to Michael, as I passed him on my way out of the meeting, that he had 'betrayed' us. Michael then banged the desk, kicked his chair, waved his hands about and shouted. His exact words were, 'I'll have the skin off your back.' My reply was neither original nor sophisticated. I said what I would have said in the schoolyard forty years earlier. 'You couldn't knock the skin off a rice pudding.' Michael showed no sign of being either mollified or amused by my childlike response. John Smith ushered me out of the meeting.

The story was public property within five minutes. On *Newsnight*, John Tusa said that I had 'blown it'. Newspapers, which had spent three years abusing Michael Foot, described him as a 'much-loved veteran' and predicted that by insulting him I had lost myself the election. When it was all over, Neil – rather gratuitously, I thought – told me that, whoever had run off to the press gallery and briefed all the journalists, it was not him. I told him that it was a matter of no consequence. I had already lost the election when it happened.

It was not only the mood of the Party which was against me. So was the Transport and General Workers' Union and, in those days, the T and G were more important than the *zeitgeist*. When they met for their biennial conference in the Isle of Man – an occasion to which I had learned to look forward with only apprehension – they decided that their members were obviously Kinnockites and that it was a waste of time and money to ask them to confirm what everybody already knew. Seventeen per cent of the electoral college was thus delivered up to Neil on a single morning. And seventeen per cent was enough to set the bandwagon in motion. I was coming out of the Dorchester Hotel – where the BBC had hired a room to film the leadership interview

– when a young radio reporter told me the news from the Isle of Man. Julia Somerville – before her days of glory on ITN – thrust her microphone in my face and asked, 'It's all over, isn't it? Do you intend to withdraw from the race?'

The night before, I had been to see *Mr Cinders*, the revival of a 1920s musical, and for some manic reason which I can neither excuse nor explain, I suddenly found myself playing the part of the juvenile lead. 'I've got a little secret that sees me through the blackest days. Listen and I'll tell you all about it.

> Even when the darkest clouds are in the sky,
> You mustn't cry and you mustn't sigh . . .'

It was not until I had finished my poor imitation of a tap dancer that I noticed the television camera pointing at me with the little red light glowing to signify that my musical interlude was being recorded for posterity.

It took some time to convince Ms Somerville that she had caught me unawares and that it would be unethical to show pictures of my posing as a song and dance man. But eventually, assisted by the camera crew who admitted to being Labour sympathisers, I persuaded her to ask the question again. Another rush of blood to the head almost caused me to reply, 'The contest isn't over until the fat gentleman sings.' Fortunately, given a second chance, sanity prevailed and I answered, 'The Transport and General Workers' Union are only a small part of the electoral college. The campaign has only just begun. I expect to be elected in October.' My comments were adjudged too boring to merit inclusion in the nine o'clock news.

Next day my campaign team met to consider the new situation. In a fit of chivalry, I thought it right to tell them that, since we already knew the result of the contest, I would understand if they – individually or severally – chose to fade into the background. I intended to fight on. And I hoped that they would still all vote for me. But there were penalties to be paid for actively working against the man who would undoubtedly become the next leader of the Labour Party and I would not complain if politicians, with twenty years in Parliament stretching out before them, chose not to pay them. I had just completed my moving little speech when Denis Howell arrived and I felt an obligation to repeat the homily to him. Denis first apologised for being late. Then he told me, 'Don't be bloody silly.' He added that I was also being 'bloody insulting' and suggested that we get on with the serious business.

Not everyone lashed themselves to the mast of the sinking ship. As Neil Kinnock's snowball grew in size and increased in speed, it rolled over more and more of my supporters. Some thought that late conversion might ensure a job in future governments. Others just felt an emotional need to be on the winning side. But more remained than I expected. In the early summer, Barry Jones and Donald Anderson both told me that they would make up their minds in the autumn and then let me know whether or not I could expect their support. As union after union came out for Neil, I took it for granted that I would hear no more from either of them until after the votes were cast and counted. I assumed that we would meet in a House of Commons corridor and I would end their embarrassment by saying that *of course* two Welsh MPs *had* to support a Welsh leader. Both of them wrote to me during the week before the electoral college met. Their messages were virtually identical. I could not win. Their constituencies were voting for Kinnock. But they would vote for me.

On a Saturday before what was regarded as Neil's coronation, Mrs Campbell-Savours – wife of the irrepressible Dale – telephoned me from Cumberland. Her husband needed urgent surgery, but refused to leave for hospital until a proxy vote had been arranged. Could I confirm that one, more or less, would not make any difference? I told her that one hundred more or less would not alter the result and that only a lunatic would delay calling the ambulance in order to put a cross against my name. Campbell-Savours nevertheless persisted in his lunacy and waited at home until David Clarke – who represented South Shields but lived in Cumberland – arrived with the proxy voting form before he made his painful way to the operating theatre. The surgery was completely successful and he was able to return, reinvigorated, to his life's work – being difficult with anyone in authority. There were times when both Neil and I were totally exasperated by a question that he had asked in a Parliamentary Party meeting or a procedural motion that he was pursuing in the House. But I always forgave him everything.

Politics is an essentially sentimental trade. So I was particularly pleased when Jim announced that he supported me and savagely depressed when one morning he told me he was having second thoughts. *The Sunday Times* had written profiles of the two leadership 'front runners' and, recalling Denis Healey's error of 1983, I had gladly agreed to answer a series of questions. Asked my opinion of the Prime Minister who had put me in the Cabinet, I replied, 'Very clever. Very honest. Very brave. But not quite ideological enough for me.' I then added – to make clear that a fulsome compliment was intended – 'That's a better score than I give to any other Prime Minister I've known.' Unfortunately it was not a good enough score to satisfy Jim – which is why he told me that he was 'enquiring of the returning officer if he could cast threequarters of his vote' for me, otherwise, he said, 'I may have to abstain.' Relieved that he relented, I swore to make no more public judgements about my colleagues. And I kept the vow until the day on which I announced my retirement from politics. Then, in a radio interview, I said and meant, 'Harold Wilson was a far better Prime Minister than I realised at the time and Jim Callaghan was even better than I believed him to be in 1979.'

The three newspapers which Labour thinks of as its own – *Observer*, *Guardian* and *Mirror* – came out for me. The *Guardian*, as is often the case, was infuriatingly balanced. Its editorial announced that it preferred Hattersley-Kinnock but could see some merit in Kinnock-Hattersley. The *Mirror* probably did me more harm than good by being pointlessly offensive and describing Neil as 'Michael Foot with less hair and more freckles.' It was not the only damage done by friendly fire. By 1983, I was writing two weekly columns – one for *Punch* and one for the *Guardian*. For emotional rather than financial reasons, I wrote on during the campaign, but I was worried about the suggestion – found most frequently in the *Daily Telegraph* – that I was becoming more and more of a writer and less and less of a politician. An item about me on the *Today* programme was going very well when Alan Coren – rightly described as 'friend and editor of *Punch*' – was asked if I could become a professional journalist. His reply (meant to be kind and complimentary) was, 'He's a professional journalist already.'

The press were so much on my side that I was wholly unprepared for the young man who leaped out from a neighbour's doorway one night and announced that he was from the *Daily Mail*. Flash bulbs exploded whilst he asked me where I had spent the day. I assumed that my answer would be a disappointment. For although I had just returned from Brighton, my visit to that sinful city had been devoted to the annual meeting of the British Association for the Advancement of Science. Just to dry his appetite, I told him the title of my lecture – 'Is it Possible to Construct a Plausible Index of Deprivation?' He gave a triumphant laugh and moved in for the kill. 'When asked if you thought it dangerous to classify families according to their racial origin, did you or did you not reply, "I believe in calling a spade a spade"?' I told him, perfectly truthfully, that to the best of my knowledge I had not used the expression but that, in any case, the words were less important than the idea. Next day my admission that I had made a ghastly mistake – together with a profuse apology for my gross bad taste – appeared on the paper's front page.

I was back in Brighton a fortnight later, for the big event. The election itself took place on a Sunday evening and I went down on the previous day for no better reason than that I would not have been happy to be anywhere else. Halfway through the afternoon a messenger from the Crown Hotel told me that David Basnett, general secretary of the General and Municipal Workers, Union, wanted to see me. I hurried along the promenade in joyful anticipation of the news that waited me. I already knew that the G and M – the second largest union in Britain and the only one to organise anything like a proper consultation of its membership – was for me. Friends in the north-east had discovered that their region had supported me by three to one against all comers and that, on the admittedly crude final calculation, sixty per cent of the union wanted Basnett to cast his vote for me. Their votes were the difference between defeat and disaster, and I could not wait to be told officially that they were mine.

The general secretary did indeed confirm that his membership had chosen me. But he had a suggestion to make. Since I was certain to lose, unity within the Party – not to mention my own reputation – would be best served if I made a concession statement that night and released my supporters to vote for the undoubted winner. Would I have any objection to withdrawing from the contest there and then? I told him that I had very strong objections indeed and elaborated on them in some detail. I had obligations both to the men and women who had worked for me all summer and to the idea on which we had fought our campaign. The title of my election address was 'Duty to Win' and we had spent three months telling the Party that political posturing and emotional self-indulgence were a betrayal of the millions of families who lived in desperate need of a Labour government. I wanted to secure as big a vote as possible for power rather than protest. What was more, I did not want to be humiliated. I think that David Basnett, who was a kindly man, found my last argument the most persuasive. Whatever his reasons, he agreed that, as I would not concede, he would follow his mandate and vote for me.

As I walked back from the hotel, I knew that I ought to be

depressed and disillusioned – or at least bitterly disappointed. But I felt none of those emotions. Perhaps I had been helped to accommodate defeat by my gradual progress from first-day favourite to certain loser. The unions and constituencies had lined up behind Neil singly, not in battalions. So there had been no sudden descent from euphoria to dejection. Every small item of bad news made it easier for me to accept the eventual inevitability of massive defeat and the long adjustment was helped by my pathological inclination to make the best of what I knew to be inevitable. On that Saturday afternoon, I felt that there were worse fates than becoming Deputy Prime Minister and holding one of the Great Offices of State. And I was determined not to spend ten years of my life hoping that a miracle would give me a second chance. I had seen too many deputies ruin the last years of their political lives by festering on the belief that the Party had chosen the wrong man. Above all else I was determined not to join the ranks of the New Adullamites, disenchanted because they had been dispossessed.

Perhaps I celebrate the quality of my vote because its quantity was nothing to boast about. As well as the heroic Campbell-Savours and the resolute Anderson and Jones, I captured the votes of Jim Callaghan, Denis Healey, John Smith, Donald Dewar, Gerald Kaufman, Eric Varley, Merlyn Rees and two thirds of the Shadow Cabinet over which Neil eventually presided.

Neil beat me by a ratio of more than three to one, leaving Peter Shore and Eric Heffer with a handful of votes between them. When I was elected deputy – by a barely smaller majority – my old tormentor, Sam McCluskie, who was that year's Party chairman, invited me on to the platform with the slightly grudging welcome, 'Roy, you had better come up here.' As I rose to walk through the ranks of delegates, Gerald Kaufman, who sat beside me in the body of the hall, advised me about my demeanor. 'When you get there,' he said, 'hold his hand in the air.' The

suggestion was based on his experience as political adviser to
Harold Wilson. 'George Brown did it in 1963 and Harold was
furious. It gave the impression of joint leadership.' Of course I got
it wrong. Instead of grasping Neil's hand in a gesture of equality, I
held his wrist as if he was the champion and I was the challenger
acknowledging defeat. At the young leader's suggestion, the
picture of that moment became the first poster of the new era,
and he often spoke of the grace with which I accepted his victory.

CHAPTER
13

Neil and I got on. We were never soul mates. Perhaps we were not even 'pals' – Neil's definition of the proper relationship between leader and deputy. But we only grumbled about each other in private and went to extraordinary lengths to demonstrate mutual respect. I even read the poems of Idris Davies, a Welsh socialist whose collected works became the standard Kinnock gift to visiting celebrities. The partnership worked because we both wanted to do our best for the Party and because Neil knew that I did not wish and could not hope to replace him. The best deputies are not a threat to the leader. But they are a great deal more assertive than I ever chose to be.

Candid friends – normally called John Smith – constantly told me, 'You must stop him . . .' or, 'You must make him . . .' But bursting into the leader's office with demands and complaints was not my way. Now, I think that it should have been. For although he consulted me on most crucial issues, he often did not even tell me about the decisions with which I was likely to disagree. In the eight years of our partnership, I intruded and insisted on about half a dozen occasions. There should have been more.

I certainly should have nagged him into making more public speeches. A radical party needs to set out the agenda with an authority that only the leader can provide. Neil seemed superbly equipped to perform that task, for he was the best platform speaker of his generation. Yet he was the orator who hated oratory. Tom Sawyer – his close friend who became general secretary of the Labour Party – had an explanation of the strange reluctance. Neil was driven by the fear of failure not the hope of success.

Sawyer insisted that Neil knew how good a speaker he could be and was determined – as 'the heir to Aneurin Bevan' – only to speak when he was sure that he could do himself justice. Great speeches need more than careful preparation. They need the excitement that comes with uncertainty. Kinnock, like Bevan and Foot before him, built his appeal on spontaneity. But the leader of the Opposition cannot afford to extemporise. Neil saw no advantage in entrancing an audience but – because of an infelicitous aside – producing headlines which damaged the Party's prospects. His caution was to his credit. But he should have made the speeches and I should have argued with him until he did.

I did argue – albeit briefly – when he asked me to become Shadow Chancellor. But the real disagreement about front-bench duties concerned not me but Eric Varley – one of the successes of the Callaghan Cabinet whose quiet competence was not the sort of virtue which appealed to Neil. I was sure that Eric was ideally suited to shadow the Department of Employment, and deal with the new 'Tory trade union laws' which would once again force Labour to choose between sentimentality and common sense. Neil, as was often his way, neither agreed nor disagreed but applied a technique which I thought of as 'retreating into Russia and waiting for winter'. He talked round the subject for almost an hour – discussing what the job required, how it should be done, who could not be even considered to do it and why doing it well was essential. But he did not tell me why he was reluctant to appoint Eric Varley or which candidate he preferred. For once, instead of leaving with the feeble farewell, 'Okay, you know my view. Think about it,' I sat out the filibuster. For I knew that, having thought about it, he would appoint someone whose name he did not want to reveal. Neil – having to make the unhappy choice between agreeing with me and rejecting my request – agreed to give Varley the job. I went triumphantly back to my room, where I found an envelope on my desk. It contained a letter from Eric. He was leaving Parliament to become managing director and chief executive of the Coalite Company.

Perhaps I should have argued more strongly to remain Shadow Home Secretary rather than accept what Neil described as my duty to 'drag our economic policy towards reality'. It was a bad time to take on the job. For Nigel Lawson was cunningly contriving the appearance of an economic miracle and floating voters did not want to hear that the spending boom and relaxation of credit control were certain to end in disaster. What was more, I was temperamentally unsuited to the job.

I was able to recruit a remarkably talented group of advisers – professors of economics, merchant bankers, company accountants and businessmen. And, true to the folklore, they could be relied on to agree about virtually nothing. But on one subject they were unanimous. Geoffrey Howe had been a brilliant Shadow Chancellor during the dying days of the Labour government. The secret of his success had been a total absence of alternative policy. All he had ever said was that Labour taxed too much and spent too much – though he said it in a variety of different ways. Labour, I was advised, must find a similar simple formula. Unfortunately, none of my advisers had any idea about what it might be.

Even if they had provided a magnificent sound bite, I doubt if I would have been content to repeat it for five years. Sharing Denis Healey's view that flank is intended for exposure and the head's proper place is above the parapet, I worked away on ideas which ranged from a national investment bank to a penal tax imposed on companies which invested abroad rather than at home. And, of course, I wanted to increase the top tax rates in order to finance improved public services. I still do. It may well be that, one day in government, some of those ideas rise from the grave. By advocating them in opposition, I ensured that life as Shadow Chancellor was never dull.

It was about this time that *Spitting Image* came into my life. Years later, David Steel told me that his standing had been severely damaged by the Sunday night satire in which he appeared as a glove puppet peeping out of David Owen's breast pocket. He was sure that my later persona – tie and lapels covered in spilt food and spluttering through a mist of spittle – must have done my reputation irreparable harm. I now suspect that he was right. But I actually enjoyed the programme and was, I suspect, flattered to be the eponymous hero – the only character who spat.

I always thought of my characterisation as benign – the bumbling old uncle who came round at Christmas to fix the fairy lights and fuses the entire electric system. If I had been Kenneth Baker, a slug sliming my way through the world, I might have thought differently about the programme. But losing patience with the pranks of young Neil – although far from the truth of our relationship – was not an accusation that caused me much grief. I opened the Christmas exhibition of *Spitting Image* puppets in the West End, visited them and put my picture, lovingly embracing my other self, on the front of a book of my essays. I suppose it was another example of my inability to see the whole world as a reflection of politics. *Spitting Image* did not create the impression that I would be the ideal Chancellor. Yet, because I enjoyed it, I worked away at promoting my own destruction.

I was in my room one morning, discussing the ever interesting topic of exchange rates, when a person from the Leader's Office put her head round my door and asked, ever so politely, if I would take Neil's place at Prime Minister's Questions that afternoon. I was immediately filled with joyous apprehension – a common emotion in politicians. I was genuinely frightened by the prospect of taking on Margaret Thatcher. But if Neil had changed his mind or his engagements, and done the job himself, I would have been inconsolable. My team of advisers – highly intelligent, immensely qualified, hugely experienced and (apart from the academics) excessively paid men – became hysterical with excitement at the prospect of playing a vicarious part in the confrontation. I had intended to think about my question over lunch. But it soon became clear that there was no hope of concentrating my colleagues' minds on anything so prosaic as sterling. They wanted to talk about Hattersley versus Thatcher.

For more than an hour, nothing they said helped me with my preparation. Then Charles Williams said, 'At least we know that you've got to avoid British Telecom shares.' The shares were being sold in what, at least commercially, was regarded as a total vindication of the privatisation programme. Americans were 'selling forward' – marketing, at a profit, shares for which they had applied but had not yet received. The practice, although illegal in Britain, was generally regarded as proof that a company flotation was a brilliant success. For it proved that demand exceeded supply to the point at which a black market was created. Another of my advisers wondered if I should ask Margaret Thatcher to condemn the way in which Wall Street was behaving. I could, he thought, make a point about the corporate investors buying out the small shareholders who were supposed to create a property-owning democracy. 'If you do that,' warned Williams, 'she will destroy you.' He offered a prediction of what she would say: 'Angry about success . . . Politics of envy . . . Jealous of government's triumph . . . Don't want ordinary families to be prosperous.' I knew that he was right, but a dangerous thought came into my head.

I would not have had the idea if the warning had come from anyone except Charles Williams. But Charles – merchant banker, sometime chairman of the Price Commission and Labour Peer –

had been a county cricketer. M. C. Cowdrey himself had asked me if the Lord Williams who spoke for the Opposition in the House of Lords was really C. C. P. Williams of Oxford and Essex. Both Bill Edrich (Middlesex and England) and Keith Miller (New South Wales and Australia) had remembered playing against him. And when, in my Cabinet days, I had forbidden him to make an official visit to Hungary, he had sent me a cutting from *Wisden's* describing how he had scored fifty-six off Fred Trueman (Yorkshire and England). His anxiety about my possible annihilation made me think about not speed but spin. What if I bowled the Prime Minister a slow full toss and then, when she had hit me out of the ground, tempted her with a googly? There were two dangers with the plan. I had to survive the howls of derision which would greet Mrs Thatcher's first six. That only required an act of will, but the chance she would 'read my hand' and see the googly coming was a risk that I would have to take. I decided to gamble.

Fortune favours the desperate. I asked the Prime Minister to condemn the 'American speculators who were making a profit by selling Telecom shares before they had even bought them'. The reply followed the pattern of Charles Williams' prediction, but was a great deal more unpleasant in both tone and content than anything that he had been prepared to say. It was some time before the Speaker was able to restore order. Then, pronouncing each word slowly and distinctly in the hope that I would sound calm, I invited Margaret Thatcher to tell me why she rejoiced in a practice which was so disreputable that it had been made illegal in England. There was a pause whilst she thought about her answer. After that it was impossible for her to recover.

I felt jubilant for almost a full minute. Then I began to feel ashamed that so much expensive talent and so much valuable time had been spent in devising a way by which one grown-up could publicly outsmart another. But I did not feel so ashamed that I changed my ways. And the Prime Minister never changed her technique. Whenever I bowled her a loose ball, it went over my head into the pavilion. And she always tried to score a second boundary. When I suggested that the state (as distinct from the parent) might be the best judge of a child's welfare, the idea was dismissed as totalitarian nonsense – allowing me to ask why, if the parents' will was paramount, the government intended to abolish the ILEA, when ninety per cent of London families supported its retention. My allegation that the official calculation of poll tax rates was based on a statistical error was attributed by Mrs Thatcher to either ignorance or malice – interesting alternatives because, as I was pleased to point out, the idea had originated from that morning's Tory press conference. When, after some confusion about nurses' pay, the Prime Minister accused me of 'trying to cause trouble', one parliamentary sketch writer thought that it must be the nicest thing that anyone had said about me for years.

The googly did not take a wicket with every ball. Sometimes Mrs Thatcher hit my first delivery so hard that the match was over before my second delivery left my hand. On one unhappy Tuesday I asked why the government had refused to impose a trade embargo on the then still racist South Africa, expecting the Prime Minister to repeat the general opposition to sanctions which she had declared earlier in the week. My intention was to follow her assault with an enquiry about why she had advocated the economic ostracism of the Soviet Union after the invasion of Afghanistan. But she replied that she was against sanctions for exactly the reasons which I had set out in 1978. She then read out a written answer to which I had put my name when I was a young Foreign Office minister. My resentment was genuine. I was supposed to play the clever tricks, not her. Trying to look unconcerned as the Conservatives erupted in delight, I recalled a Prussian general's reaction to the sight of the cheering crowd at Victorian Ascot: 'What a target for grapeshot!'

I enjoyed a freedom to be flippant which was denied to Neil, and I took Mrs Thatcher on once a month not twice a week. So I was able to catch her out from time to time in a way which was denied to the Party leader. He had to use Prime Minister's Questions as an opportunity to publicise the Party's policies. I could enjoy myself. And so long as I kept my nerve and gave the ball some air, with Margaret Thatcher batting, there was always a hope of occasionally taking a wicket. My success, as every spin bowler will confirm, depended as much on my opponent's thoughtless aggression as on my own careful attention to line and length.

C. C. P. Williams – who had put the slow bowling idea into my head – was managing director of a merchant bank which Robert Maxwell employed from time to time. One morning, Charles telephoned me with the news that Maxwell wished to speak to me. It is, as I was later to discover, the habit of tycoons to make sure that anyone to whom they wish to speak is sitting by the telephone waiting to receive their call. But, at the time of Maxwell's approach, I was unaware of the habit. So I asked Charles Williams what his client wanted. He explained, with some reluctance, that Maxwell had bought the Mirror Group and insisted that I be told at once. The new proprietor suspected – in other words had been tipped off – that the Labour leadership intended to denounce his bid and thought that we ought to know that it was too late to stop him.

Reed, the paper's owners until that morning, had promised to sell it to a consortium of employees. Asked what had happened to those assurances, Charles said that the Maxwell bid was £30 million higher than the workers could raise. He then quickly added that Reed had a legal obligation to do its best for the company's shareholders. 'I would be grateful if you would sound surprised when Bob telephones you with the news.' Affecting surprise was not difficult, and Neil, when I told him ten minutes after Maxwell's call, was genuinely astonished. We both agreed that it would be foolish to denounce the proprietor of the one daily newspaper which unequivocally supported Labour and the saga of Maxwell's new relationship with the Party began.

That relationship was always entirely bizarre. One day he telephoned to say that, 'We would split the Labour Party between us.' If I would 'get Kinnock right' over economic policy he would 'straighten him out' over foreign affairs. When he told me that he proposed to reconcile Neil to the nuclear deterrent by 'first converting Glenys', I decided that his strategy was badly flawed. Nevertheless, I agreed to join him for lunch in order to discuss the Middle East. When David Hill and I were led into the dining room on the tenth floor of the Mirror building, Maxwell already sat at the head of his huge table drinking from a silver goblet. He did not get up. Before he greeted us, offered us a drink or even asked us to sit down, he began to attack Labour for not supporting the Americans' punitive air strike against Colonel Gaddafi.

When David Hill expressed doubt about the wisdom, as well as the morality, of the raid, he was silenced with a wave of the proprietor's huge hand. Then the butler was told to leave and close the door behind him. 'I feared', our host explained, 'that you were going to discuss intelligence reports. And that man is a spy planted by Rupert Murdoch.' Not unreasonably, David asked Maxwell why, if that were the case, he employed him. The response was a mixture of contempt and incredulity. 'That just shows how little you know about business. I don't waste my time worrying about who is appointed as my butler.'

It was a year before we met again. Then, after the usual ritual of making sure I was 'available to speak to Mr Maxwell', he issued a personal invitation to tea the following day. I asked him if he had anything specific to tell me and he asked me to anticipate some good news for both me and the Party. Neil and I agreed that if it was an offer of money I would decline with thanks.

Maxwell's guests were always expected to take part in some sort of ceremony. I was required to perform in a ritual of congratulation. Sam Silkin, Attorney General in the last Labour government and one of Maxwell's legal advisers, had been 'elevated to the peerage'. Charles Williams, already ennobled, was there to join in the fun. Bernard Donoghue – sometime head of Callaghan's Central Policy Review staff, boss of a Maxwell investment company and another new Lord – wisely sent his apologies. We drank champagne and I was also brought tea in a giant cup. As soon as we were alone, Maxwell asked me if I would like to work for the *Daily Mirror*. I told him that, in principle, I would like it very much but that my final decision depended on what the editor – Mike Molloy, another *Punch* contributor – wanted me to do. 'He doesn't know about it yet,' said the proprietor. 'You decide and I'll tell him.' Then, waving his hand towards the giant cup, he ordered, 'Drink.'

I had no wish to prolong my visit and, believing that he wanted to get rid of me, I swallowed the tea as fast as my tender palate allowed. As I gulped it down, Maxwell first stared at me and then the cup. It was not until he began to clap his hands and roar with delight that I noticed that, as the tea receded, it revealed a message which was embossed in gold on the fine bone china. A VERY IMPORTANT PERSON IS DRINKING FROM THIS CUP. Maxwell did not mean it. I heard nothing more from him for a year.

Then, one Sunday night, we went back into the old routine. Would I be available to take a call from Mr Maxwell? When it came, it seemed that he wanted to reminisce. Did I recall the jolly tea we had had together? He was just telling some friends of how we had laughed at the comic cup. I had, he thought, been on particularly good form. What was it I had said about the House of Lords? 'You employ half of them at the *Mirror*. You'll be wanting one yourself soon.' I agreed that I was inclined to make that sort of silly remark but, before I had time to finish my sentence, he reminded me of his reply. 'No, not me.' The conversation ended without any of the usual courtesies. Three days later a reporter telephoned me from the Royal Courts of Justice. Maxwell, who was suing *Private Eye* for suggesting that he had tried to buy a peerage, had claimed that he had received two offers and turned them both down – one from Lord Goronwy-Roberts (conveniently deceased) and the other from me.

My first instinct was to issue an immediate denial. But David Hill persuaded me to telephone Alexander Irvine – yet another Labour Peer and a Queen's Counsel. It was good advice. A public denial of evidence given in court was, Irvine warned me, a contempt. If I wanted to correct or deny what Maxwell had said I could either approach the judge or offer myself as a witness to the other party in the case. Both alternatives were so unattractive that I decided to speak directly to Maxwell. He took my call and offered a grovelling, if unconvincing, apology. He had given evidence under severe emotional stress as a result of a previous witness mentioning Eichmann – the war criminal who had butchered his family. He accepted that what he said was at best misleading and promised a correction the following day.

A young American intern who was working for me at the time was sent to listen to the new day's proceedings. The court rose without Maxwell having made his statement. I telephoned his office and, although I could hear his boom in the background, was told that he was not there. Joe Haines, the political editor of the *Mirror* and a Maxwell confidant, spoke to David Hill. Nothing had appeared in a national paper. What was all the fuss about? David – in his Birmingham rather than his Oxford persona – told him. Maxwell phoned with another unlikely apology. One of his helicopters had crashed in the North Sea and he had been too distraught about the missing crew to think of anything else. He would make his statement before the court rose. The case concluded in Maxwell's favour, during the following afternoon. The correction was never made.

On the day that the 1987 general election was declared, Robert
Maxwell telephoned me in something that sounded like distress.
It was absurd for the deputy leader of the Labour Party and the
proprietor of Labour's only true Fleet Street friend to be at
loggerheads. He wanted to apologise in person. Could he visit
me at home that night as a sign of grace and penitence? I agreed
and cancelled a meeting with my front bench team. Maxwell did
not turn up.

Robert Maxwell provided the moments of black farce during the
first two years of the Kinnock-Hattersley leadership. The miners,
on strike for a year, were the tragedy that haunted us day after
day. Nobody – certainly not Neil – doubted the justice of their
cause. Margaret Thatcher was determined to emasculate the
union and then go on to destroy the industry. And the closure
of Cortonwood Colliery was a declaration of war – issued at a time
when the government was almost, but not quite, certain to win. I
am emotionally and intellectually opposed to strikes which never
do much good for the men and women whose interests they are
supposed to protect. In 1984, it was obvious enough that, with
coal stocks at a peak and private hauliers ready to run the pickets
blockade, the NUM were outnumbered and outgunned. But I
was sure that a strike was right and necessary. It was the miners'
only chance.

For a strike to succeed, the union had to retain the sympathy of
the public and maintain the solidarity of its members. Largely
because of the behaviour of Arthur Scargill they sacrificed both.
His crucial error was the refusal to ballot his members.

I understood – and sympathised with – one of Scargill's reasons
for refusing to consult his members. He said, and no doubt
believed, that men whose jobs were secure had no right to vote
against the union supporting men whose jobs were in jeopardy.
But whatever the feelings in the prosperous coalfields, a majority
of the union would have voted to strike. The risk of vice defeating

virtue is one of democracy's perils and it was Arthur Scargill's duty to either convert or outvote those of his members who thought only of themselves. More importantly he had an obligation not to encourage the outcome which every intelligent observer antici- pated and all the miners' friends feared – a full year of hardship for the striking miners ending with the accelerated decline of their industry.

In the end it was arrogance that made Scargill persist in his folly. He must have known – indeed, it was part of his argument against the ballot – that miners in the prosperous coalfields were looking for a pretext to go on working. By refusing a vote, he gave them the excuse that they wanted. In the desperate, and often secret, discussions, two facts were always agreed by both sym- pathisers with the breakaway 'democratic' union and supporters of the NUM. If a ballot had been held, Nottinghamshire would have voted against a strike. But then, when the majority in the whole union was in favour, they would have felt obliged to take part.

For the new Labour leadership – particularly Neil Kinnock, who saw himself as a miners' MP – the association with Arthur Scargill's intransigence was a desperate trauma. It was also a liability which postponed for a full year the drive towards political rehabilitation. The Shadow Cabinet was faced, week after week, with the need to support the miners' ends without endorsing their means, and Scargill did all he could to compound the difficulties by making constant demands and presenting constant challenges – including a request for a Shadow Minister to speak at each of his regional rallies. After much agony I decided that I could not invent reasons for declining the invitation and simply said that I would not attend.

Throughout the dispute, we all knew what the Party's position should be. There was no difficulty in condemning the occasional outbreak of picket-line violence, and that we did. Criticising the heavy-handed behaviour of some policemen – usually officers brought in from outside the mining areas – was more dangerous but occasionally both right and necessary. The problem was the ballot. From the start, we should have supported the strike but told Arthur Scargill – first privately and then, assuming he remained obdurate, in public – that expediency and principle for once coincided. He must ballot his members.

It was not cowardice which prevented us. Even then, Arthur Scargill's influence was fading, Neil was spoiling for a fight and he knew that he would only improve his opinion poll rating by taking Scargill on. But Labour leaders do not attack a union which is in mortal combat with an unscrupulous employer. It could easily have been argued that our assault was on one man who, whatever his illusion, was not the union. We might have insisted that forcing them to face reality was essential to the hope of victory. But the ghost of the General Strike sat with us in the Shadow Cabinet Room. The miners had been deserted in 1926 and we could not 'break ranks' or 'let them down' again. So whilst we did not attempt to defend the indefensible on the crucial issue of a ballot, we remained silent for far too long. Arthur Scargill continued to make speeches which ended, 'Get off your knees and act like men' – exhibiting the thoughtless arrogance which did his members so much harm. Our sin – Neil's and mine – was not cowardice but sentimentality. That too damaged the miners' cause.

I broke the line when the strike was more than six months old. *Newsnight* celebrated the passing of the half-year mark with a special programme. The producer sent me a last-minute invitation to appear whilst I was on my way to Manchester, where I was to receive the last gold medal to be presented by the Boiler-makers' Society – a craft union which David Basnett had absorbed into the General and Municipal. I am not sure why I was the unlikely recipient of the award. Perhaps Neil was the first choice but felt that, because of the strike, he must remain in London rather than travel to the city in which the Society had been founded, and therefore wanted to end its days. But, whatever the reason, it was another piece of good fortune. David Basnett and I spent the early part of the evening regretting that we had not spoken out for union democracy. So, when the BBC's invitation came, it seemed as if fate was offering a belated opportunity to do the right thing. David and I gave each other the courage we both needed. I accepted *Newsnight* and he offered himself to *News at Ten*. It was, I decided, one of those occasions when the simple truth was best. So I said that, 'Were I a miner I'd be out on strike, but I'd still be agitating for a ballot.' Apart from one or two whispers from the thoughtless left, the change in the leadership's position was assimilated into Party policy without complaint. The strike went on – without a ballot or the support of the Nottingham Region – for another six months. Then the miners lost.

The strike had been over for nearly ten years before Arthur and I talked without the inhibitions of official agendas and accompanying assistants. Then we met in what I still thought of as the union's 'new headquarters' in Sheffield. The vast building had become a mausoleum – an anachronism with an inaccessible front door which hovered ten feet above the ground because the steps that should have connected it to the street below had never been built. Visitors approached through the neighbouring NCP car park and basement garage. The offices were virtually deserted and Arthur's room was filled with files which, he told me, were rebuttals of the *Daily Mirror*'s allegation that Libya had financed the long ended strike. I thought of Citizen Kane alone in Xanadu. Much to my surprise I felt sorry for him – even though he said that Neil Kinnock had been responsible for two election defeats.

There is no doubt that Neil Kinnock came to the Labour leadership determined to make the Party electable again. Though, in the early eighties, he still had to learn that the policy of unilateral disarmament guaranteed political defeat as well as intellectual discredit. But from the start he was determined to dispose of what he called the 'illegitimate left'. Action had to be postponed during the full length of the miners' strike. So a year was lost. But, in the autumn of 1985, the Militants who dominated Liverpool gave him the perfect opportunity to clean up the Party.

The Trotskyites who ran the council had misgoverned the city for years and the Labour Party had responded with a series of embarrassingly feeble initiatives. Although the five members of the *Militant* editorial board had been expelled, a real assault on the infiltrators was inhibited by the formula which Michael Foot had invented to justify their expulsion. It was an offence to 'organise a party within a party'. But no one could be excluded from membership for supporting a philosophy which was in direct conflict with democratic socialism. I believed in 'a broad church', the other cliché of political ecumenicism, but I had never thought it reasonable to welcome bogus converts who, in truth, worshipped a different god. If socialism is a coherent and consistent philosophy, socialists have a right to defend their ideological frontiers against invasion by parasites who, were they to try separate existence, would not survive. I was therefore not heartened by David Blunkett – then a member of the National Executive though not an MP – setting off to Liverpool with the intention of persuading Messrs Hatton and Mulhearn to be reasonable, but I was immensely encouraged by Neil Kinnock's speech to the Bournemouth Party conference in 1985. In effect it declared total war on the Militant Tendency.

I doubt if the speech would have been made that year if Militants had been content to bankrupt Liverpool slowly. But they could not wait to pull the Town Hall down around their heads, and when they literally ran out of money, in Neil Kinnock's words, they 'committed the obscene folly of hiring taxis to deliver redundancy notices to good trade unionists', whose only offence was working for a council which believed that it was running a city in Albania. Kinnock, much to his credit, seized the moment and made the best speech of his life and began to nudge the Labour Party back into the mainstream of politics. For the speech – brave and brilliant though it was – did no more than begin the long and painful process of expelling the Liverpool Militant leadership, one by one.

In those days, Labour's constitution required each expulsion to be approved by the full Party conference after an examination by, and on recommendation of, the National Executive. For too much of the following spring, I was part of what amounted to a highly unjudicial tribunal. The whole Executive – sitting in its usual pattern of trade unionists at one end of the table and the self-designated 'left' at the other – listened to Larry Whitty, the new general secretary, charge individual members with political conspiracy. But we could never quite reproduce the solemnity of the court room. During one all-day sitting we adjourned for fish and chips, which were shared between defendants, witnesses and jury. The accused Liverpudlians waited for sentencing in a room with a window which overlooked the road. They held impromptu press conferences and acknowledged the cheers of the demonstrators who had travelled from Merseyside to support them. The best moments of farce, however, took place during the actual proceedings.

Sam McCluskie, who had bitterly opposed my attempts to become Party leader, was no longer my sworn enemy. Indeed in a strange way the general secretary of the Seamen's Union and I had become at least allies. In one of our conversations I had said something about Shakespeare and the following week Sam saw a three-volume edition of the Collected Works in a junk shop. He bought it as a gesture of friendship. Perhaps unwisely, he presented it to me during one of the meetings at which we examined candidates for expulsion.

It was a magnificent Victorian edition – gilt-edged pages, tooled leather binding, marbled end pages. It also contained 'a memoir and essay on Shakespeare's genius' and 'illustrated with engravings on wood and 100 steel plates, portraits of eminent actors etc'.

At first, I piled them by my chair. Then I lifted them, with some difficulty, on to my desk and from time to time I sneaked a look inside them. For there was something irresistible about line drawings of Mr H. Marston as Hotspur and Mrs Glynn as Constance from *King John*. Unfortunately, Eric Heffer noticed and raised an immediate point of order. 'Who', he demanded to know, 'has supplied the deputy leader with law books? Were they equally available to every member of the Executive? Has he been obtaining surreptitious legal advice? If so, who has paid for it?' When I told Eric the truth he refused to believe me. Worse still he complained that I did not even have the courtesy to invent a plausible lie.

At the next meeting, we considered the case of Councillor Harry Smith. The Party members who appeared before that strange tribunal were entitled to bring with them either a lawyer or what, in the language of trade union disciplinary procedure, was called 'a friend'. Councillor Smith brought George Nibbs, and introduced him as his 'pen-friend'. The Executive laughed like drains, leaving me in no doubt that, whatever the evidence against him, one defendant was not going to be expelled. His introductory statement was a combination of lovable Scouse humour and ingratiating reminiscence. The Executive loved it. Asked (I fear by me) why he had spoken so often at Militant meetings, he replied that he was 'easily taken advantage of' and added, 'My school report says that if I had given more attention to detail, I might have been a brain surgeon.' Sides almost split. Of course we acquitted him. As he left the building, he told the waiting reporters that he was in total support of the comrades who were being persecuted by the witch-hunting Executive.

The comrades who were convicted ended their Labour Party membership ingloriously. Only the conference could expel them, so they were each entitled to make their case against the Executive recommendation to the whole annual assembly. Their public personae – Derek Hatton, the cheeky chappie, and Tony

Mulhearn, the heroic worker – led some newspapers to announce that they would turn up in Blackpool and challenge the claims of the leadership and the might of the block vote. That always seemed an unreasonable expectation. But I did expect them to turn up rather than be expelled *in absentia* after their names had been read out to hoots of derision from delegates. Suddenly the Party realised that Militant were only tough when they were backed up by a guaranteed majority.

It is difficult now to understand why none of us ever drew attention to Militant's undoubted racism. It was not that we were reluctant to make race a political issue. I spent much of the eighties drawing attention to the innate prejudice on which the government's immigration and nationality policies were based. But although I unhesitatingly – and quite rightly – accused the benign Willie Whitelaw of tolerating discrimination, I never accused the malignant Trotskyites of actually promoting it. And promote it they did. They hid their dislike of the Black and Asian British behind the claptrap of class war. Difference in race, they claimed, would be forgotten after the continuous revolution had created a dictatorship of the proletariat. I have some sympathy for the view that race and class are related issues – the ethnic minorities are prevented from emerging from poverty because of prejudice against their race and rich Blacks and Asians can buy their way to a respect which is denied the White poor. But a young man who is refused promotion because he is a Muslim, Sikh, Hindu or Afro-Caribbean finds very little comfort in the knowledge that it will all be better at the millennium. I wanted 'positive discrimination', and, believing that fear of the language leads to retreat from the idea, I was prepared to call it by its proper name rather than invent something more emollient. The Militant Tendency was opposed to what it described as tinkering with capitalism. To my embarrassment, however, its members supported my opposition to 'Black Sections' –

special groups within the Labour Party which were limited to members of the ethnic minorities.

Apart from the distasteful problems of definition, which required the world to be divided between Whites and the rest, Black Sections seemed likely to separate rather than unite the races. I wanted the Black and Asian British to make their way in the Labour Party itself – as they did in Sparkbrook, where five of the nine Labour councillors were Kashmiris and one was a Sikh. And I took it for granted that my successor would be from one of those races. What is more, I had little doubt that the Black Section 'movement' was really a vehicle for promoting the parliamentary ambitions of metropolitan, middle-class professionals. Black Sections had little to offer the unemployed Khans and Singhs of Birmingham. It was making the class point that got me into most trouble.

The attacks began at the 1985 Party conference, where a reference to 'my Asians' was denounced as the language of possession, rather than an indication of connection and commitment. That allegation was easily seen off. At the end of the speech in which I opposed the idea of political apartheid, I asked how many delegates spoke of 'my football team, my family, my party'? But the argument rumbled on and Black Section shock troops from outside the West Midlands mounted a raid on Sparkbrook. Their poorly attended meeting provoked a massive response from Muslims who, as well as supporting me, were culturally and theologically opposed to being amorphously classified as 'Black'. They arranged a counter demonstration at which I agreed to speak. When I arrived – about ten minutes before it was due to begin – a dozen men were standing on the steps outside the Sparkbrook Centre. That is a usual feature of Islamic events. But one of them told me that they were hanging about with a purpose. There were no seats left in the hall and the young men who were on their way from the mosque had to be ushered carefully into the aisles and the space beside the platform. Then I saw, and heard, the approach of the anticipated reinforcements. A column of Kashmiris, Punjabis and Pathans was half walking and half running down the Stratford Road. 'What', I asked to my subsequent regret, 'are they chanting?' He told me, ' "Death to the Black Sections and those who support them". Don't worry,' he reassured me, 'most of them don't mean it.'

By the time that the general election came, one or two Muslims – described, according to taste, as fundamentalists, extremists or Conservatives – had been persuaded that I was not doing enough to promote the cause of Islam. The Tory tabloids called them 'Muslim Leaders' – which was not a total invention, as that was undoubtedly what they called themselves. Since, at most, they led half a dozen members of their own families, I was not unduly worried by the newspaper prediction that an Islamic abstention would lose me the seat. In any case, all the worrying of which I was capable was concentrated on taxation. On my advice, Labour had voted against the two per cent cut in the standard rate with which Nigel Lawson had prepared floating voters for the general election. What was worse, Labour was forced to concede what, in the end, the Party is always forced to concede. To improve public services, we would have to increase taxes. By the time the concession was made, I had persuaded Neil to add Tony Blair to my team. Not only was he outstandingly articulate. He agreed that, since the issue of taxes could not be side-stepped, it was best to face it head on.

In the beginning of what we assumed to be election year, Labour lost the Greenwich by-election. The candidate – an unapologetic supporter of the far left – was attacked by the newspapers for her political associations, her appearance and her husband, who had been a hospital shop-steward during the winter of discontent. Denis Healey and I both spoke at the final press conference. As an implied rebuke to the press for 'personalising' the campaign, Glenda Jackson, after some persuasion, agreed to hand the candidate a bunch of flowers before the formalities began. The attempt to win the sympathy vote was not helped by Glenda looking into the television cameras and saying, 'I think this is a naff idea, but they asked me to do it.'

After the press conference, Denis and I toured the constituency in the Party open-topped campaign bus. He and I stood at the front shouting slogans about foreign and financial policy. The inspector from *On the Buses* stood at the back, in full uniform, crying, 'Any more fares, please?' and, 'No more room inside.' Denis was so carried away with enthusiasm for his subject that, as we passed along a tree-lined road, he failed to duck as a branch swept at head height over the top deck. He neither flinched nor cried out but a long cut appeared on his forehead and blood began to trickle down his face. He refused to pause for first aid.

After a mile or so, the blood began to coagulate in his eyebrows. By the time that we stopped at a row of shops it was cake-hard. Reassured that the bleeding had been staunched, Denis stormed into a ladies' hairdresser which was offering concessionary perms and sets to pensioners. Asserting that he was over sixty-two – and forgetting the bloodied brow – he pushed his head under hair dryers and demanded to know if his famous eyebrows could be trimmed for half price.

The old ladies who were not struck dumb screamed. I cowered in the doorway hoping that nobody would realise that – being Deputy Leader and Shadow Chancellor – I was in some way responsible for what was going on. A tiny pensioner, dressed in black from head to foot, cowered beside me. Denis noticed her and observed, 'You don't seem very happy.' She told him, 'I'm not.' When asked why she confessed to being a Conservative. Asked to justify her choice of Party, she replied, 'I've got a bit of money in the bank.' Denis grinned fiendishly under his matted eyebrows. 'Meet Roy Hattersley. He's the man who's going to take it off you after the general election.'

The 1987 campaign got off to a good start. The opening press conference was held in the Queen Elizabeth Conference Centre and, as part of the theatrical staging which had already become part of Labour's political trademark, Neil and I walked to the podium side by side through the ranks of the assembled journalists. We were both wearing identical blue suits with matching red roses in the buttonholes of our lapels. Michael White in the *Guardian* said that the whole event looked like a gay wedding, but the odd couple gave the right answers about taxation. 'Nobody', we said in turn, 'who earns less than £25,000 a year will pay more in tax under a Labour government.' That pronouncement had the advantage of being more or less true as well as simple. The calculation of individual tax liabilities is a complicated process. And there were undoubtedly some exceptions to our general rule. But the promise was as complete and genuine as any one-line policy statement can ever be. Day after day Neil Kinnock and I – as well as Bryan Gould, who was Shadow Chief Secretary – were cross-examined about the details of hypothetical tax tables. For almost a month, we repeated with dogged determination the formula which we had all agreed.

We knew that we could not win the election. But we were proud of the way we had fought a losing battle and, with the Liberal-SDP Alliance collapsing around the joint leadership of David Owen and David Steel, we were determined to underline our status as the only possible alternative to the Tories. We all agreed that the Cambridge rally was the right time and place at which to make our appeal to the legions of the lost who had defected from Labour to the SDP, for Shirley Williams was the Social Democrat candidate in that city and the Guildhall had been booked for the last Saturday of the campaign. Early on the Thursday morning, Neil asked me if I would replace him as principal speaker. He had decided that the deserters were more likely to identify with me than with him. I was not sure that it was a wholly complimentary judgement, but I welcomed the chance to invite their return. David Hill and I worked most of the Friday on an appropriate form of words. In the end we decided on a phrase which I had used at the Birmingham rally four years earlier. It was not even original then, but was inspired by a slogan which George McGovern had almost patented – in a quite different context – during his 1972 presidential campaign. 'Come home, America' became 'Come home to Labour'.

The Guildhall was packed and my invitation – 'Come home to Labour' – was greeted with rapture by several hundred Labour Party members who were particularly attracted to the slogan because they had never left. To emphasise the essentially gentle nature of our appeal, my speech was followed by a classical guitar recital by John Williams. He was playing an Elizabethan madrigal when David Hill crawled on to the platform and announced, 'We've cracked it. The BBC have sent an outside broadcast van. You're going to be live on the nine o'clock news.' We crawled off the platform together. As we tiptoed out into the night, David repeated what I already knew. 'It's just what we need.' Then he added the equally unnecessary advice, 'Look straight into the camera and say "Come home to Labour". Say it whatever he asks you.'

Martyn Lewis was the evening newscaster. Whilst a recorded account of the day's campaigning introduced the extended item on election news, he thanked me with unnecessary gratitude for 'taking the trouble to come on the programme' – a phrase which I should have recognised as boding no good. Then there was a brief glimpse of my Cambridge speech, which I thought an admirable introduction to the appeal which I was about to make. Mr Lewis smiled and asked me, 'Is it true that no one who earns less than £25,000 a year will have to pay more taxes under Labour?' I told him that it was and then he asked me the same question again. Speaking with what I regarded as admirable restraint I asked why so much air time had been wasted. We had all confirmed that was the position, time after time, during the previous three weeks. So, Mr Lewis said, 'Bryan Gould was absolutely right to say it again today?' In the circumstances, it was totally reasonable to reply with an assertion followed by a rhetorical question. 'Nobody on less than £25,000 will pay a penny more. Why do you keep asking the same question?' Because, Mr Lewis said, 'early this afternoon, Neil Kinnock said it was wrong.' He had said that some people earning less than £25,000 a year would pay more.

The rest of the broadcast is just a blur in my memory. But I do recall David Hill leading me back to the Garden House Hotel, where I immediately telephoned John Smith. I had barely said hello when he told me, 'I know why you've telephoned.' And I asked him, 'Was it as bad as I think?' John, who was not a man to soften the blow, said – irrationally but I fear accurately – 'Worse.' He then added what he offered and I accepted as a genuine compliment. 'If it's any consolation, you did all that a professional politician could do. You abused the interviewer.'

Christopher Andrew, the Cambridge historian with whom we stayed the night, was equally supportive. He hid behind his hedge the 'Vote Shirley Williams' poster which had been displayed on a pole in his front garden. I think that he was motivated by sympathy rather than a sudden conversion to socialism.

CHAPTER
14

Labour responded to its third consecutive defeat with an organised farce called 'Labour Listens'. The idea of the initiative was
to convince the floating voter that the Party and its members were
neither remote nor authoritarian, and that, in government, we
would become the Great Parliamentary Sausage Machine which
sucked in public opinion at one end and spewed out popular
politics at the other. Students of constitutional theory said that
polling opinions first and writing policy afterwards was a denial of
representative government. But if Edmund Burke turned in his
grave he rotated with amusement rather than outrage. The
exercise proved the importance of politicians saying what they
believed.

The first Labour Listens meeting was held in Brighton. The
sea was so high and the winds so fierce that the waves broke over
the promenade and lashed against the windows of the lounge in
which the politicians met the people. It was risibly reminiscent of
the climax to *Key Largo*, when the typhoon symbolised the
destruction of the criminal conspiracy. The room was packed –
but not with what we patronisingly called 'ordinary people'. By
necessity our guests were representatives of special interests. In

consequence, they shared with their hosts a total ignorance of the views expressed on the top decks of the Clapham omnibus. And of course, they hated each other far more than they hated us. The ex-servicemen's organisations called for higher defence expenditure whilst the Campaign for Unilateral Nuclear Disarmament demanded less military spending. Animal rights activists argued for the prohibition of circuses whilst anglers worried that Labour's opposition to blood sports would be extended to fishing. Environmentalists insisted that atmospheric pollution justified a prohibitive increase in petrol tax whilst representatives of the Automobile Association called for a reduction in the cost of the Road Fund Licence.

And there was another problem. Although everyone who had been invited was an experienced lobbyist, all of them wanted to ask rather than answer questions. The Townswomen's Guild's call for a crackdown on pornography was followed by enquiries about whether or not a Labour government would prohibit the production of 'top-shelf' magazines. When we replied that the object of these consultations was to hear views which we would consider later, they assumed – and said – that we were pandering to the commercial interests of the Newsagents' Association which had explained (much to the horror of the Methodists) that restrictions on Sunday trading were a denial of the liberty to buy and sell.

Unfortunately, Brighton was near enough to London to allow metropolitan political journalists to make a morning visit and enjoy a good lunch before they wrote their stories. Notwithstanding their hilarious accounts of the day's events, we reproduced the fiasco all over the country for almost a year. Fortunately, Labour stopped listening before I totally lost faith in democracy.

At our first meeting after the general election, Neil Kinnock told me that if I wanted a second stint as Shadow Chancellor he would be 'perfectly happy'. At the time, I was not sure if the restrained endorsement was a badly expressed vote of confidence or a hint that, although nobody was going to push me, there would be considerable relief if I chose to jump. One of Neil's most endearing characteristics was his loyalty to colleagues. But it sometimes made him reluctant to tell the hard and painful truth and I could not imagine him insisting that it was 'time for a change' – even if he believed it. I had made up my mind on polling day. Had we won a miraculous victory, I would have had no choice but to go to the Treasury. In the more likely event of a defeat, I would move to a job which I really enjoyed. After four years doing what duty, dignity and the Party leader required, the time had come to suit myself. I said that I wanted to shadow Education again.

For the one and only time during our nine-year partnership, Neil said 'No' – categorically, unequivocally and immediately. I had known him express doubts which he hoped I would tactfully accept as an insurmountable reluctance and there had been a couple of occasions when he initially agreed to a proposal and then sent a message asking me to change my mind as he had changed his. But I had never before had a request denied outright. That afternoon he was categorical for reasons he explained with some passion. If I went back to the job which I had done in 1972, the Tory tabloids would announce that I had been demoted. When I explained that I might just be able to survive the humiliation of being written off by the *Sun* and *Daily Express*, he insisted that anything which diminished the leader or deputy diminished the whole Party. Reluctant to argue with Neil Kinnock and John Donne simultaneously, I accepted that Education would not be mine. I also realised for the first time how much Neil had been hurt by the newspapers.

Despite his 'boyo' image, Neil was a deeply sensitive man – easily wounded by remarks which more brutal characters would have brushed aside. I think that I first realised how easily discomforted he was on the night that he gave a dinner for J. K. Galbraith. I had known Galbraith slightly whilst I was at

Harvard and, admiring him to the point of idolatry, turned up early hoping for a private word. True to his reputation Galbraith was early too and, much to my delight, launched at once into his reminiscences. The great man – in size as well as intellectual stature – drops names in a way which never seems conceited or boastful. For the listener always suspects that, all over the world, persons of great distinction are boasting about having met Ken Galbraith. That night he described his encounter with President de Gaulle. 'Tell me,' de Gaulle demanded, 'what is your philosophy of tall men?' Galbraith (six feet six, like the President) thought of Governor Winthrop's address to the inaugural meeting of the Massachusetts State Senate and replied, 'We are like houses built on a hill and we must make sure that we are looked up to metaphorically as well as literally.' De Gaulle congratulated him but added, 'You have missed out one vital point. It is the duty of tall men to tyrannise small men.' Ken stretched out his arm. At that moment Neil Kinnock entered the room. His fingertip touched the top of Neil's head. I waited for some wholly justified Welsh rugby imprecation. The Labour Party leader shook hands as if he had heard and seen nothing of Galbraith's view of small men.

It was twenty years since Harold Wilson had told me that only zombies felt no pain when viciously attacked by malevolent journalists. And I prided myself that – despite all the jokes about my sibilants, the comparisons with Mussolini during the Winter of Discontent and the accusations that I remained with Labour solely in the hope of reclaiming a ministerial car and red box – I had not, by 1987, joined the ranks of the living dead. But I had grown some scar tissue. That was a protection which Neil was denied. Until he became leader, nobody ever said a critical word about him. 'It's all right for us,' Denis Healey had said after the fiasco of Neil Kinnock's visit to President Reagan. 'We've been up to our eyes in shit for years. He's not used to it.' Adjusting to unpopularity was a painful and dangerous experience. Many of the long answers for which he was so often criticised were unnecessary responses to the nonsense about 'a pass degree in Sociology from Cardiff in a bad year'.

Neil then suggested that I become Shadow Foreign Secretary. But shadowing all three of the Great Offices of State seemed a good deal less distinguished than doing the real jobs, and foreign affairs, although one of politics' prestigious subjects, still held no charm for me. So we compromised on Home Affairs, where I could make a nuisance of myself over immigration and develop policies on law and penal reform. When we turned to the difficult question of who should be my successor as Shadow Chancellor, I began to suspect that his anxiety for me to stay was related to the difficulty of selecting a replacement.

John Smith had already told me that – on the assumption that I was moving – he wanted the job. And it was clear that Bryan Gould, who had become close to Neil during the election, had staked a similar claim with the leader. Gould had been campaign co-ordinator and for a full month had set out the Party's policies and responded to the Tory attacks with real brilliance – a word which is much overworked in politics but the proper description of his performance during the doomed campaign. What was more, his brilliance had been visible on television every night for a month. He was, in consequence, the most popular politician in the Party. Gould – an academic lawyer and ex-diplomat – was one of the cleverest men in politics. He was also a passionate opponent of the European Community and, as his subsequent resignation and return to New Zealand illustrated, highly volatile.

Notwithstanding my admiration for Gould and quite independent of my friendship with Smith, I was sure that John should become Shadow Chancellor. Neil would have agreed at once had it not been for the remarkable popularity which had carried Gould to the top of the Shadow Cabinet poll and was, by securing him first place in the National Executive elections, to provide a double triumph which was unique in Labour history. Kinnock

replied to every argument for Smith with the indisputable assertion, 'But Bryan came top,' and then went on to insist, more
disputably, 'That makes it very difficult.' It was when I reminded
him that John Prescott had come second, and might therefore lay
claim to Foreign Affairs, that he began to accept the limitations of
the Parliamentary Party's beauty contest.

Politicians like and admire other politicians who share their
opinions. Bryan Gould and I held the same view of the basic
ideology which should sustain a socialist government. Back in
1983, he had written a more or less academic monograph on the
relationship between equality and liberty. In the same year, I had
published *Choose Freedom*, which pursued the same idea:

> Socialism is the promise that the generality of men and
> women will be given the economic strength which gives
> meaning to the choices of a free society. It is a commitment
> to organise society in a way which ensures the greatest sum
> of freedom, the highest amount of real choice and, in con-
> sequence, the most human happiness . . . Without equality,
> for a majority of the population, the promise of liberty is a
> cruel joke . . . Liberty is our aim and equality is the way in
> which it is achieved . . . It is time that we made our
> ideological purpose clear.

Although *Choose Freedom* was generally well reviewed, it was
forgotten within months of its publication. It is now reincarnated
three or four times a year in bibliographies of socialist texts and
anthologies of political theory. Naturally, I gave Neil a copy, but I
did not expect that he would have time to read it. However,
during the early months of 1988, he mentioned – more or less
casually – that we were approaching a time when the Party should
prepare a Statement of Aims and Values and that, when it was set
out, it should be built around *Choose Freedom*. I said that I was

ready to write a draft when Neil thought the moment was right. Then, believing that the suggestion was just part of the political gossip which makes up most of the conversation between leaders and deputies, I thought no more about it. In any case, I had other things on my mind.

John Prescott had, for several months, hinted that he intended to stand for the deputy leadership – fighting on the manifesto that the job should not be a consolation prize for failed leaders but the focal point of improved organisation. Six years on, I feel some sympathy for Prescott's view – though I would not want to spend a full Parliament in organising recruitment drives and convincing local parties that they had to keep their canvass records up to date. John really wanted to contest the election on a job description, but the newspapers inevitably saw it as a test of the leadership's popularity and Neil himself had no doubt about the way in which the result would be interpreted. He set about persuading Prescott not to stand.

After days of public and private pressure, and following a comical argument about whether or not Neil had promised an investigation into the deputy leader's role, it seemed that Prescott had decided not to run. Then a meeting of the Campaign Group – the sub-faction of MPs who thought *Tribune* had gone soft on socialism – decided that democracy required a leadership contest. Tony Benn selflessly offered to accept nomination for leader and Eric Heffer – operating in the same high spirit of personal sacrifice – agreed to be his running-mate. The election which followed was one of the turning points in Labour history. For it marked the end of Bennism as a force within the Party.

Benn's power base had always been a group of unrepresentative activists. And in 1988, Labour was in a mood 'to consult the membership'. There was still no formal mechanism for constituency ballots, but the pressure to make a real assessment of rank and file opinion was growing increasingly irresistible. I had no doubt that, however the democratic will was tested, the Party would prefer Kinnock-Hattersley to Benn-Heffer. And I was equally sure that I could see off John Prescott – who, when Benn and Heffer floated their hats into the ring, announced that he was no longer obliged to avoid 'the damaging contest' against which Neil had warned. But although I was sure that I could win, I was by no means sure that I wanted to go to the trouble of fighting. I had signed a contract to write a Victorian trilogy and had hoped to spend the summer quietly composing fiction, not campaigning to keep a job which I had not wanted in the first place. I suggested to John Smith that he should stand and he followed his refusal with moral blackmail. 'Nobody you approve of wants the job. You can't escape. It's either you or Prescott.' I voted for John Prescott as deputy leader in 1994 and he has proved that the deputy's job is best done by a candidate who does not regard it as a consolation prize or is more interested in policy than party management. But, back in 1988, everybody whose judgement I respected thought that his election would be a disaster for the Party. Neil really meant that he would resign if I was defeated. 'The Party', he said, 'will have demonstrated that it is not serious.'

I have never had much time for reluctant politicians. Men and women who see service as a sacrifice rarely do credit to jobs which ought to be a joy. My motives were properly personal. Although it was obvious from the start that I would win, newspapers – working on the principle that 'Incumbent Re-elected' is not news, whereas 'Incumbent Defeated' is – predicted my certain humiliation. And I was not prepared to go with a whimper – even if it was a press invention. Two young MPs, Gordon Brown and Tony Blair, came to offer their support. 'You'll get most of the Tribune Group vote,' said Tony. 'Not just us. Real Tribunites.' He was right. Then Neil, who did not know that I was considering standing down, presented me with a massive incentive to stay on. The time had come, he told me, for me to prepare the new Statement of Aims and Values. He was about to launch a major policy review and thought that it ought to begin with a description of the principles on which those policies were based. At the time, the chance to construct the 'ideological framework', about which Tony Crosland and I had talked so often, was too good to miss. It was not until later that I realised that my noble enterprise had a second purpose: Neil wanted to prevent anyone else producing a description of objectives which might prejudice our election prospects. David Blunkett was working on a text with Professor Bernard Crick – a political philosopher who had reviewed *Choose Freedom* twice, once highly favourably and once in a way which I prefer to forget. The way to avoid accepting their version of socialism was to produce our own. Neil was less an ideologue than party manager.

The way in which my colleagues reacted to the statement which I drafted is a vivid illustration of how much the Labour Party has changed between Neil Kinnock and Tony Blair. Nobody argued about the assertion that greater equality – with the redistribution of power and wealth which it required – was the bedrock of our philosophy. The dispute concerned Labour's attitude towards the market. John Smith and John Cunningham – pillars of sensible moderation – insisted that I had overstated the values and virtues of competition and disputed my view that it was essential to a free society. A joint meeting of the Shadow Cabinet and National Executive which was expected to spend all day examining the statement slid to a halt by lunch-time after the commitment to the market had been watered down. I should not have been surprised. In *Choose Freedom*, I had quoted Dick Crossman's sad conclusion that British socialism 'has lost its way not only because it lacks maps of the new country which it is crossing, but because it thinks maps are unnecessary for experienced travellers'. Certainly, the best people of that meeting – the shadow Cabinet members with a clear ideological vision – thought that, having removed what they regarded as fashionable nonsense about competition, there was nothing to be gained in spending time on theoretical discussion. They wanted to go back to their offices and discuss the details of the following week's parliamentary business with their young research assistants. They *knew* what the Labour Party believed in and they wanted to get on with the difficult business of changing principle into practice.

Seven years later, Tony Blair – in comparable circumstances – wisely avoided the problems of launching a philosophical debate. The Party in the country, not being stupid, knew that the real problem with Clause 4 was not so much its intellectual inadequacy as its effect on Labour's chances of winning the election. And the gap its removal left in the Party's constitution was filled with a declaration of purpose that no one regarded as intellectually taxing. So, in 1995, the danger of having to discuss real ideas was averted. In 1988, we were only spared that catastrophe by default. The Party debated *Aims and Values* at half past nine on the first morning of the annual conference. Half of the delegates were still trying to negotiate their way through the complicated security system which guarded every door into Blackpool's Winter Gardens. Most of the rest were still discussing the previous night's humiliating defeat of Tony Benn and his travelling companion Eric Heffer. That was, I suppose, a philosophic event of sorts. It was certainly as near as most Party members ever got to making an ideological statement. *Aims and Values* being disposed of before coffee time, we were able to turn to the aspects of policy which we most enjoyed – not formulation but presentation.

I was and remain one of Peter Mandelson's greatest admirers. He had worked for me – with great determination – during the 1983 leadership campaign and, when the Party advertised for a new director of public relations, he had naturally asked if I would support his candidature. I thought him an ideal choice for the job. Neil reacted to my lobbying in classic Kinnock fashion – he read out a list of other possible contenders. Pressed for his opinion of

Mandelson, he said he preferred both Dennis McShane (now Member of Parliament for Rotherham) and Nita Clarke (now Mrs Stephen Benn). But a week later, I received a message from his office, saying that the leader wanted Peter Mandelson and that he hoped that, despite my reservations, I would give him my support. I do not know if Neil had forgotten that I had suggested Mandelson to him seven days earlier or if, having been convinced of Peter's merits, he wanted the successful candidate to be his nominee. It may even be that he was less enthusiastic for Peter than his staff made out. For during the interview Neil whispered messages about his irritation with Mandelson's failure to condemn the miners' strike, his generally insouciant manner and his pale blue socks. But Peter was overwhelmingly the best candidate and, in the end, was appointed with the Executive's overwhelming support.

The brilliance of Peter's performance during the 1987 election campaign is established beyond dispute. So is (or should be) his success in forcing Labour's publicity machine to face the realities of modern political life. My criticisms of subsequent presentational excesses are directed less at Mandelson – who left the Party's employment in 1990 – than at those of my colleagues who became intoxicated with his achievement. The 1987 election was, in terms of policy and personalities, a total failure. But it was a public relations triumph. The rational reaction would have been an attempt to remedy our shortcomings. And certainly the 'policy review' produced a manifesto which no longer contained the three great liabilities – unilateral nuclear disarmament, opposition to the European Union and wholesale public ownership. But too often we took refuge in the belief that the publicity was an aim in itself – one thing which, since we did it so well, we should go on doing until it brought us victory. As a result, image often took precedence over the ideas, and presentation, instead of being no more than a delivery system, was regarded as the mighty warhead which would blow the enemy to pieces. I always wanted to decide the policy first and worry about the presentation afterwards, rather than vice versa. And I was irritated beyond endurance by some of the publicity stunts in which I was required to take part.

Delegates to Party conferences always receive a 'pack' of essential documents – agendas, seating plans, resolutions and diaries of events. Usually the bundles are held loosely together by elastic bands and sent through the post in rough brown manilla envelopes. In 1986, the 'pack' was despatched in a tasteful apricot-coloured cardboard box with dainty rosebuds decorating its lid. Neil – not always over-fastidious in his attitude towards publicity material – thought that it must have been originally designed to market teenage toilet soap. It was typical of an approach to politics which was more concerned with appearance than with substance – and wanted sympathetic sounds to match the pastel shades of policy.

Labour, under Neil Kinnock, was always most likely to cause me embarrassment when music was in the air. At the last rally of the 1987 election campaign, the platform party had been solemnly warned by the police that, unless we stopped singing and made our way to Yeadon, we would find that Leeds Airport had closed for the night and our private plane had been grounded until the next morning. That evening Neil had begun his performance by leading the audience in 'The Red Flag' and 'Jerusalem' and had then moved on to what can only be described as a recital from his very considerable repertoire of chart-topping numbers. Each rendition was introduced with an appropriate reminiscence – 'This is a number which means a lot to Glenys and me.'

A less indomitable man would have been put off musical politics for life by the performance of the Silver Prize Band which had contributed to the evening's entertainment. Its technique was beyond criticism. And it led the Party leader into the hall, *con brio*. But it had prepared for the triumphal entrance immediately outside the swing doors at the back of the hall and was clearly audible during the warm-up speeches. So Barbara

Castle's spirited defence of the health service was punctuated by sudden blasts on tuba and trombone which sounded like comments on her conclusions about the need for extra hospital beds. Nothing daunted, Neil followed up 'We Shall Overcome' with 'Blowing In The Wind'.

That night he wore a white rose in his buttonhole as a tribute to Yorkshire. The combination of flowers and music always guaranteed an evening of active goose pimples, so I should have realised that I was in for a toe-curling night. Neil was a genuine extrovert – a gregarious loner who wanted to take solitary decisions and then enjoy himself in company. It was one of the qualities which made him a great Party leader. But his character sometimes made life difficult for a deputy who had his own ideas about policy and prided himself on being anti-social to the point of publicly admitting that he found no pleasure in 'standing with a glass in my hand talking to somebody I've never met before and never want to meet again'. That was not Neil Kinnock's view of life. And *joie de vivre* was a major force in his politics. He often said it with flowers.

The floral tendency was established in 1989. On the Friday before that year's Party conference assembled, I had allowed my barber to cut my hair the way which placed the parting on the wrong side. The idea was not new. Indeed, ever since I was a little boy I had been told that my hair grew in the opposite direction from that in which I tried to encourage it. But in youth I was certainly not going to have my hair done like a girl and in age I was reluctant to change old habits. I cannot account for the sudden aberration. But I do recall that my folly was compounded by Jane Bown who, on the same day, took my photograph. The picture appeared, with an article I had written, in the weekend's *Observer*, so it seemed to me that I had better keep my new style for the grand entrance to the conference which the Labour leadership made on Sunday evening. Waiting to go on stage, Tony Benn peered at me as if he feared his eyes deceived him. 'What's happened to your parting?' he asked. All I could think of to say was, 'Everything is moving right this year.' Before the end of the week, the story appeared in the *Daily Telegraph*'s gossip column. My head was back to normal by the time we assembled at the end of the conference to sing 'Auld Lang Syne'.

That was the Friday on which Neil Kinnock spontaneously picked up the roses from the vase in front of him and threw them, one by one, into the audience. A year later members of his staff distributed bouquets amongst the whole platform party, and instructed us to lob them into the body of the hall. When I overheard a plan for employees with babies to bring them down from the crèche and hand them to the best-known members of the Shadow Cabinet, I ducked behind the lime-green backdrop. But the following year the stage managers cut off my escape route by arranging for the senior members of the Executive to be escorted individually to positions on a second podium – a platform which, I assumed, had been specifically erected to facilitate flower throwing. But, instead of following the ritual singing with the ritual rose bombardment, we all stood about listening to the crackling of the public address system. Then it boomed forth a noise which I later discovered was somebody called Queen singing something called 'We Are The Champions'. At the time of its rendition, I had heard neither of the group nor the hit single. I was not alone in that. But the *Guardian* reported that, whilst other members of the Shadow Cabinet had tried to hide their ignorance, I had stood brazenly detached. The allegation of aggressive dissociation was unjustified. I just did not know what to do. John Naughton – writing in the *Observer* – said that those Friday morning television pictures of the Shadow Cabinet sing-along lost Labour the election. Of course, he ludicrously over-stated the damage that had been done. Perhaps the incident itself did no damage at all. But the attitude which it represented – performance rather than philosophy and image in preference to ideas – did Labour irreparable damage.

My prejudices against razzmatazz were reinforced by my allergies. I suffer from hayfever. So, if one of the young ladies who made up Neil's entourage forgot to bring me a plastic rose, I had to decide how to resolve a public relations dilemma. I could appear roseless and apparently alienated from my colleagues. Or I could decorate my buttonhole and risk weeping during an inappropriate moment in one of Neil's speeches.

I was determined to do neither of those things. For I applied myself, as best I could, to the task of being a loyal as well as an assiduous deputy leader. That required attendance at all sorts of formal gatherings – a few of which I actually enjoyed. I particularly looked forward to a dinner, given by the TUC, for Lech Walesa. The architect of Polish freedom – who might justly be described as the man who began the breakdown of Soviet communism – was immensely tired from his journey and declined to make a speech himself. He was told by Norman Willis, the general secretary, that only two brief ceremonies would delay his departure for bed. Neil Kinnock then expressed the gathering's official thanks, concluding his remarks with an emotional explanation that it had been one of the great days of his life. It had combined lunch with Ben Elton and dinner with Lech Walesa, his two great idols. Norman Willis then took out a box which clearly contained a gift of some sort. At the end of a flowery tribute, 'to a real hero of the workers' cause', Walesa stood up in order to accept the presentation. Willis walked past him and handed the box to Bill Jordan, the president of the AEU. It contained a Mickey Mouse watch. The gift was a joke related to a wage deal that Jordan had just negotiated.

There was one other great trade union occasion during my last years as deputy leader – participation in the annual pilgrimage to Tolpuddle. It is one of the genuinely joyous dates in the socialist calendar, for the pilgrims – one or two invited celebrities and hundreds of rank and file trade unionists – march through the village behind bands and banners, make a U-turn at the end of the street and, as the front of the column passes the rear ranks, there is much hand-shaking and back-slapping between old friends. At one point, Norman Willis, who had been appointed general secretary a few weeks before, was approached by a lady who wished him, 'All the best for his retirement.' He finished the march worrying if she knew something that he did not.

When we got to the churchyard, the ebullience of the marchers quietened into solemn respect. I was the first one to lay a wreath on the martyrs' graves. Willis came next. Rod Todd from the Transport and General Workers' Union third. As he bent down with the dignity appropriate to the occasion, the silver prize band at the church gates struck up 'When You're Smiling'.

Much to his credit, Ron managed to take refuge in the hospitality tent before he broke down into hopeless laughter. I was already there in reluctant conversation with a man who insisted that I had served with the Royal Marine Commandoes during the raid on Narvik. Such confusions were regular occurrences. Survivors of the landing at Anzio often insisted that I had been beach-master on that fateful day and were usually offended when I told them that the soldier they had in mind was Denis Healey and that I had been ten years old at the time.

Fortunately I was able to deflect the ex-commando by introducing him to Ron Todd, who really had worn the Green Beret at the end of the war. The two men had a detailed conversation about their military experiences. Indeed it went on so long that I began to feel guilty about being party to Ron's imprisonment. So I interrupted and began to lead him away. 'Are you a member of a trade union?' the man asked as the old comrades parted. Modestly, Ron said, 'The T & G'. It was the second thing the two men had in common. For the comrade in arms responded, 'I hope they have helped you. They've never done a bloody thing for me.'

In the summer of 1991, when we were all becalmed on a political Sargasso Sea, I was the only member of the Shadow Cabinet who was willing to unveil a poster which depicted three skeletons in the Tory cupboard – health service privatisation, extensions of VAT and cuts in social security payments. We had a single poster to display, but we had it pasted across a prominent site at the southern end of Battersea Bridge. David Hill (by then Peter Mandelson's successor as director of communications at Walworth Road) told the newspapers that I was to launch a new major initiative. He hoped – optimistically, I thought – that they would expect the hoardings of Britain to be soon dominated by Labour's new message. Fortunately – as it turned out – it was a windy day. So when I pulled away the sheet that covered our controversial message, it engulfed me and I stood, much to the amusement of passing motorists, like a corpse in a shroud which was several sizes too big for a self-respecting cadaver to be seen dead in. The spectacle was irresistible, even to the Tory tabloids. So the *Sun* and the *Mail* both published pictures of the strange white shape standing in front of a sixteen-sheet poster which, in normal circumstances, they would have suppressed as submissive Bolshevik propaganda.

The successes, achieved by mistake, were rarer than the errors which we seemed to make almost by design. My personal miscalculation during the 1987 Parliament was attempting to be reasonable about Salman Rushdie's *The Satanic Verses*. After almost thirty years in Westminster politics, I should have realised that arguing for understanding and moderation would only produce universal condemnation.

Although my constituency was home to twenty thousand Muslims, I knew nothing about the Islamic hatred of Salman Rushdie's *The Satanic Verses* until the evening on which the Booker Prize was awarded. I attended the Guildhall dinner as the guest of my publisher and listened to Michael Foot, the chairman of the judges, make a speech about Jonathan Swift – who was not even short-listed – and express his disagreement with the choice of winner. Richard Luce, then Arts Minister, gave me a lift back to the House. When he asked me if the Kashmiris,

Punjabis and Pathans of Sparkbrook were outraged by Rushdie's novel, I first told him that none of them had mentioned it to me and then admitted that I had no idea why they might regard the book as so inflammatory. The Fatwa was declared next day. After that I heard so much about *The Satanic Verses* that I tried to read it.

In other parts of Britain, Muslims called for Rushdie's death. But in Sparkbrook, they remained calm and dignified. No effigies were hanged from the lampposts, the bookshops were not set alight and looted, and the churches were not defiled. We did not even have a decent protest march. A few youths wandered aimlessly along the Stratford Road half-heartedly waving the green flag of Islam and calling for retribution against infidels. But their demonstration was nothing like as long and loud as the demands for better policing which followed the Handsworth riots. It might have been easier for me if they had been homicidal fundamentalists, but the only emotion expressed in the mosques of central Birmingham was distress. My constituents felt hurt. They expected me to defend them and their religion against what they regarded as a campaign of calculated denigration. Each of the many mosques in my constituency arranged a meeting to tell me so.

At the first of my innumerable public meetings, I behaved like a good Western liberal – defending Rushdie's right to publish and be damned, even after a day's hard work with an Arabic scholar who convinced me, by careful comparison of alternative nouns, that the insults to the Prophet and his mother were intentional. The liberty to blaspheme was, I tried to explain, essential to a free society. Challenged to explain why I supported Britain's highly selective blasphemy laws, I replied that I would gladly see them scrapped but did not agitate for their repeal because no one took them seriously. I cited Martin Scorsese's *The Last Temptation of Christ* as part of our Christian tolerance and was in turn asked why contempt for my own religion led me to insist that Muslims treated theirs with equal lack of respect. The argument might have gone on for ever if Saeed Moghul had not said, 'You were always on our side, even when other people were against us. Why are you against us now?'

The question was as unfair as it was illogical. But beneath the moral blackmail, the underlying claim was true. Usually I was proud to be on their side. British Muslims have few friends outside their own community, and I have tried to defend them against the whole spectrum of prejudice – from the filth of old-fashioned racists to inventions of modern female liberationists. It was easy enough for me to be calm about the insults to a god in whom I did not believe. I was not poor and Black. My culture was not under threat from a society which expected minorities to conform to majority mores. Music hall comedies did not make jokes about my funny accent, my avaricious ways, my innumerable wives and my willingness to live off the state. I decided to demonstrate, in my moderate way, that I was still on their side.

So whilst I repeated that publication could never be prohibited by law or prevented by intimidation, I made what I believed to be an emollient suggestion. Salman Rushdie should – of his own volition and as a sign of grace – offer not to publish the paperback. I anticipated being accused of pandering to the primitive passions of my constituents. But I did not anticipate being found guilty of defending every Muslim offence – real and imagined – from female circumcision, through ritual slaughter, to cooking strangely smelling food and keeping their grocery shops open late into the night. There was much sneering about my preoccupation with reselection as candidate for Sparkbrook (which was beyond dispute) and my apprehensions about re-election (which was beyond doubt). Members of Parliament who represent ethnic minorities – unlike their colleagues who sit for prosperous suburban seats – are always criticised for advancing the claims of their constituents. It is part of the racism which afflicts our society.

The Satanic Verses was one of politics' little sideshows. The real inter-party battle of those years was the poll tax – an innovation of such overwhelming and justified unpopularity that it is still difficult to understand how a democratic party became attached to it. Margaret Thatcher's personal commitment to what she sometimes forgot to call 'the community charge' was absolute. Had she remained Prime Minister, the poll tax would have remained also and provided a real chance of Labour winning the 1992 general election. The Conservative Party clearly shared that view. By removing Mrs Thatcher from office, the Conservatives denied Labour's best hope of seizing power. Party leaders always say that their opponents are their greatest asset. Harold Wilson said it about both Alec Douglas-Home and Ted Heath and Ted Heath said it about Harold Wilson. Neither of them meant it. But Neil and I genuinely wanted Margaret Thatcher to survive her second leadership challenge. She was the embodiment of the poll tax and the poll tax might just have been enough to outweigh Labour's electoral liabilities. I did not believe that she would go. When, on the morning of her resignation, a television reporter leaped in front of my car as I drove into the House of Commons, and shouted, 'She's gone! She's gone!' I thought that the young lady had risked death in order to play some sort of practical joke.

When the news was confirmed, Neil and I agreed that our greatest danger would come from Michael Heseltine. We thought of Heseltine as cavalry, as distinct from Douglas Hurd who was artillery and John Major who could hardly be compared with any sort of front-line unit. We assumed that if Heseltine was elected, he would repeal the poll tax and, taking advantage of his four-year exile from government, would promise a new start and call an immediate general election. I was in Neil Kinnock's room when the result of the Tory leadership ballot was brought in. Neil's whoop of delight was spontaneous and genuine. We had a celebratory drink before I left to appear on the 'television special' which had been arranged for that evening.

Television specials are always a bore. For they mark events which the general public does not regard as worth a full hour's television time. The programme producers tacitly accept that criticism, for they recruit a panel of politicians to fill in the *longueurs* between the items of real interest which make up about ten per cent of the broadcast. The panel on the night of the Tory leadership election was Norman Fowler, David Steel and me. We ran out of anything to say halfway through the programme. After all, we were discussing John Major. So we were relieved, as well as surprised, by the diversion of a face pushed up against the window of the portacabin from which we spoke to the waiting world. At first the sight reminded me only of a Victorian orphan attempting to gain access to the warmth of the parish workhouse. Then I recognised the anxious features of David Hunt – Secretary of State for Wales and a man who, according to Nicholas Ridley at a Foyles lunch, was promoted to the Cabinet as a result of a single speech on the poll tax about which Margaret Thatcher whispered to her colleagues on the front bench, 'This young man is a real enthusiast. What's his name?'

David Dimbleby, who chaired our discussion, was in a skittish mood. Unusually, he treated the panel like a workers' commune. Should we, he asked, invite Hunt in? We agreed to be magnanimous and, as soon as our visitor was sitting comfortably, Dimbleby demanded to know what he had to say. The Secretary of State for Wales had a statement prepared. 'John Major', he said, 'will become one of the great Prime Ministers of this century.' I was so surprised by his bizarre judgement that for several seconds I did not realise the particular piquancy of Hunt expressing that view. But when I recalled the events of the morning, I asked him, 'If you believe that, why did you vote for Michael Heseltine less than eight hours ago?' Hunt's reply was a classic of its kind. 'You're just trying to bring politics into it.'

Believing that Margaret Thatcher would survive, we had put down a motion of no confidence in the government which we expected she would continue to lead. The Prime Minister's opening speech has gone down into parliamentary history as one of the great bravura performances of all time. In other words, she shouted across the Chamber with a manic self-obsession which the more sensitive Members found profoundly embarrassing. It was my duty to wind up for the Opposition. All the courtesies of debate required Mrs Thatcher to be in her place to hear my reply. She was not there. I regarded her absence as entirely reasonable. It was her last evening as Prime Minister and I assumed that she was in her room either drinking with friends or weeping alone. Both of those activities seemed more appropriate to the occasion than listening to me trying to score points off her government. Some of my less thoughtful colleagues did not share that view, so my attempts to command the House were consistently undermined by noisy cries of, 'Where is she?' Then they began to complain about the absence of her successor. Their cries for John Major were so loud and constant that I could hardly be heard above the noise. I tried to think of a way to tell my friends to shut up. Then, during a point of order, Gerald Kaufman whispered, 'Major's here, but nobody has recognised him.' I hoped that if I repeated the joke – with appropriate acknowledgement, in case it went wrong – I might persuade my Honourable Friends to quieten down. The trick worked and, after several moments of real and general laughter, I stumbled on. As I went out to vote at the end of the debate, John Major was sitting at the very end of the Treasury Bench, hidden from general view by the Speaker's Chair. The new Prime Minister spoke to me. 'You think you're funny. But I think you're pathetic.' It was the first time, during thirty years in the House of Commons, that I had ever known the rough and tumble of debate translated into acrimonious private conversation. John Major's behaviour that night – even more than the confusion in his first statement between a classless and a mobile society – convinced me that he was not the stuff of which real Prime Ministers are made.

John Major is credited with winning the 1992 general election. The credit is not deserved. Labour were always destined to lose.

Neil Kinnock was the only leader who was capable of pushing the Party back into the mainstream of British politics, but the British public – not least because of the qualities and qualifications which made him irresistible in 1983 – were never going to make him their Prime Minister. And he knew it. It was made painfully obvious to him at innumerable polling presentations. He could not have won the leadership election had he not been a uni- lateralist who distrusted the European Union and believed in wholesale nationalisation. Because he had once held those views (and had not served in the Callaghan government), the party trusted him and accepted his reforms. As soon as Labour again became a real political force, however, Neil was personally doomed. His conversion to collective security, Europe and the mixed economy was real – based as much on a changing world as an adjustment in his own principles. But he was represented as the man who would do and say whatever was necessary to become Prime Minister. It was a cruel caricature, made all the more credible by the one real error of the 1992 election campaign – the decision to discuss proportional representation (and therefore appear to bribe the Liberal Democrats) a week before polling day. The idea that Neil had no firm convictions made him unelectable. He would have become a good Prime Minister. But I knew on the day that the 1992 election was declared that the voters would not have him. That did not change the view which, to general surprise, I expressed at the 1995 Party conference: 'In 1983, the Labour Party chose the right man.'

I suppose that I always expected the general election would be my last hurrah. But I looked forward to the campaign. A couple of weeks before it started, a young lady with padded shoulders came into my office to explain what was planned for me. Although I did not know it, a group of Labour Party officials had already planned my programme. My programme, she told me, included speaking at a great rally which was to be held in Sheffield. She described the event as a spectacular.

At first, I said that I did not want to take part. It was, I thought, not my sort of occasion. Then I learned that every member of the Shadow Cabinet was to be there and pride took over from reticence. If they were all there, I must be there. I accepted the suggestion that I should make the opening speech and, rather to my surprise, was asked if I wanted to book a box for the evening. The price was quoted as five hundred pounds. By the morning of the rally, a couple of boxes remained unsold and I hired one at a knock-down price so that my mother – then eighty-seven – could take part in one more election campaign. Our box had its own bathroom and an ample supply of wine and spirits and savoury snacks. I ate the crisps before the rally began. It must have all seemed very different from politics in the Nottingham-shire coalfields during the 1920s.

Ten minutes before the scheduled starting time, I was led through the dark bowels of the Sheffield Arena and more or less carried up the steps of the platform into the night black auditor-ium. Suddenly a spotlight cut through the darkness and, although I could still not see the audience, they saw me and I was engulfed in the sort of roar which greeted the lions when they padded out into the Coliseum. I spoke for what I believed to be my allotted ten minutes. It was not a particularly good speech, but I stuck to my brief to 'sound confident' and the audience cheered every-thing that sounded like a promise. By the end, they were cheering every time I paused to draw breath – and I was pausing to draw breath a very great deal. When it was all over, I walked, as instructed, to my seat at the far end of the arena. As I passed through the rows of Labour Party members, they pushed and crushed forward to shake my hand, ruffle my hair and pat me on the back. Children gave me sweets. Women kissed me. Men, who believed in victory again, wept. I loved it. It seemed impossible that I had once felt doubts about taking part.

In the pen that housed the speakers and the Shadow Cabinet, I collapsed, overcome by euphoria, next to Barbara Castle. 'Do you know', she asked, 'how long you went on?' I was too exhausted to answer. 'You spoke two minutes longer than your proper time. Neil's got to be on by ten to nine for the news.' She consulted her watch. 'They'd better not try to take the time off me.' Neil shouted his incomprehensible greeting at the appointed time. I doubt if it lost Labour a hundred votes.

Twice during that day, I had believed that Labour might win. On the train, during my journey to Sheffield, I had learned that the opinion polls were moving our way. Then, in the heady atmosphere of the rally, I had thought that nothing was beyond us. During one of the intervals, John Cole came into my box from the BBC's booth next door and told me that it was the most impressive political event that he had witnessed since Edward Kennedy's 'The Dream Has Not Died' speech at the Democrats' 1984 New York Convention. Then, when the rally was over, he came back with the news that the opinion polls had changed again. Instead of pulling ahead we were beginning to fall behind. The dream had died after all. As I left the building I was unwittingly consoled by Peter Hitchens of the *Daily Express*, who was dictating his copy into a public telephone just inside the foyer – 'Tonight in Sheffield, Roy Hattersley redeclared the class war.' So at least one member of the audience had got my message.

Thursday 9th April 1992 was an almost perfect English spring day and even the Stratford Road sparkled in the sunlight. As I walked from polling station to polling station, to perform the pointless candidate's ritual of shaking each presiding officer's hand, I was greeted as if my constituents had never greeted me before. I know now that I was enjoying the affection that usually accompanies long service and benefiting from the instant recognition that always follows a period of almost nightly exposure on radio and television. Early on that bright day I thought, at least for a moment, that I was witnessing the long-awaited resurrection of democratic socialism. In Sparkbrook there was a swing to Labour and our supporters were more enthusiastic for the Party's victory than at any time that I can remember. But Sparkbrook is the home of the urban poor who desperately needed a new government. It was not the same in the suburbs.

My optimism did not survive the lunch-time news bulletin and my fears were confirmed over supper. The exit polls were bad. A message from Neil urged me not to give up hope. The BBC had telephoned him to say that they believed that their forecasts were statistically biased in the Conservatives' favour. I should still be ready to make a swift return for the meeting with John Smith at which the senior members of the new government would save sterling. I packed before the count. But I did not expect to make a dash to London through the night.

At half past ten, we left for the Birmingham indoor arena – the second great stadium in which, within the space of eight days, my life changed. In Sheffield the amphitheatre had been dark and vibrating with excitement. In Birmingham it was blazing with television lights and silent with suppressed tension. All of the counts in the city's twelve constituencies were held on the same giant floor in identical prefabricated booths. They reminded me of livestock pens. The platform, from which each result was announced, looked like an auctioneer's dais and completed the impression of a cattle market. There was a recreation area for candidates, agents and accompanying dignitaries. But my agent, Sir Richard Knowles, was Leader of the Council and had told the city's chief executive that his candidate, who would be deputy prime minister before the night was out, must have a room of his own. We were allocated what had been a communal shower. Its ceiling and floor were, like its walls, covered in dazzling white tiles. The glare was only one of the problems. None of our mobile phones could make contact with the outside world and, unless we sat absolutely still, our metal chairs slid across the room. After my result had been declared (and I had achieved my childish ambition of increasing my majority to ten times the margin by which I had won my first victory back in 1964) I walked out into the cold night, found the driver who had been lent to me by the Transport and General Workers' Union and told him that we were going to London. 'Labour Headquarters?' he asked as we approached Westminster. 'No,' I told him. 'I'm going home.'

CHAPTER 15

I knew, even before the long drive home began, that politics – at least, the sort of politics which I had enjoyed for thirty years – was over for me. There would be four or five more years of Advice Bureaux at the ironically named Cottage of Content, three-line whips in the House of Commons and occasional speeches on the subjects which move me most. But the real battle had ended. And, in the Labour Party which I knew best, the joy of battle was often the compensation for the disappointment of defeat. My belief in egalitarian socialism had, like my interest in political ideas, immensely increased since the day, back in 1964, when I was first elected to Parliament. But so had my contempt for the theatre of politics. The great consolation of the 1992 defeat was no more sound bites, no more photo opportunities, no more buzz words. Before we reached London, consolation had turned into contentment. It was, I knew, shameful to accept our failure with such equanimity. For although 1992 was not a tragedy for me, it was a catastrophe for constituents like mine. Yet, instead of raging against fate, I could not help remembering that to everything there is a season, a time for politics and a time to write. The time to write had come.

Politicians who give up politics before they are driven out by age or unpopularity are expected to be disillusioned, disappointed or, at the very least, disenchanted. I felt none of those emotions. I owed the best parts of my life to the Labour Party and I had far from repaid my debt. But there is a time to plant and a time to pluck up. To drive away my feelings of guilt – indeed, to drive every other thought from my head – I switched on the car's map light and began to write my *Guardian* column.

John Smith telephoned me during my Saturday morning surgery. He was not a man to dissimulate. So there were no courtesies or condolences. He took it for granted that he was my candidate to become the new Party leader and asked what we were to do if Neil Kinnock did not stand down in time for a leadership election to be held in the autumn. I told him that a combination of pride and common sense would guarantee a dignified transition. John was not convinced. In the last year of his life he became a great Kinnock admirer, finally won over by the impeccable loyalty which the old leader showed to the new. But in 1992, the memory of Luigi's – the restaurant in which Neil had speculated to journalists about possible changes in official tax policy – was still green.

I had never doubted that the damaging gossip about relaxing the official tax proposals had been no more than loose talk. But John had believed it to be calculated sabotage and it had taken a couple of days to persuade the Shadow Chancellor to meet the Party leader and resolve their public differences. That day, two or three months before the full reconciliation, John suspected that Neil wanted Bryan Gould to succeed him and would arrange the time of his going in a way which helped his favourite. So he kept asking, 'But what if he doesn't go by the autumn?' I promised that, if necessary, I would tell Neil where his duty (and self-interest) lay.

My only mistake was to under-estimate Neil's anxiety to abandon the leadership. The day after I talked to John, he telephoned me with the news that he intended to announce his immediate resignation. Assuming that I did not want to become leader *pro tempore* until October, he would ask the National Executive to convene the electoral college as quickly as the constitution allowed. It was, in its little way, a moment of history. So it was impossible not to look back. I remembered my desperation, twenty years before, to be part of that apostolic succession. Suddenly I was being offered the chance, albeit by default, to have my name added to the roll of honour. Absurdly, I thought of Mr Chips, after years of failure, being offered the headship of Brookfield because all the young men had gone to the war. Unlike him, I chose to say goodbye. Neil and I went together.

John Smith won Labour's leadership election by a landslide – though I suspect that he was right in his suspicion that Neil Kinnock would have preferred Bryan Gould. I rushed back from the New York Convention of the Democratic Party (and, in consequence, missed Bill Clinton's coronation) in order to be present in the Horitcultural Hall in Westminster when he was enthroned. What feelings of dispossession I might have suffered were assuaged by a suggestion, made to me over lunch a couple of weeks earlier, that I should become Executive Editor of the *Observer*, a post previously held by Conor Cruise O'Brien. When I consulted John Cole and Tony Howard – both, in their time, *Observer* deputy editors – they argued strongly against it. Cole warned that all the job involved was meeting and greeting foreign dignitaries. Howard, ever the professional journalist, said that O'Brien 'was never invited to the Saturday news conference'. I had decided to decline before I got the message that the paper was no longer interested in obtaining my services. But by then the tentative offer had reinforced my belief that there was life after Westminster.

Neil Kinnock and I sat side by side on the platform at the formal meeting of the electoral college. As always, we whispered to each other our often uncomplimentary thoughts about the Labour Party, which was spread out before us. John Smith's triumph by more than ninety per cent of the vote left Bryan Gould – a man of conspicuous talent and four years earlier the darling of the party – very near to humiliated. When he stood up to acknowledge John's victory, the applause was almost as loud and nearly as prolonged as the ovation which had greeted the victor. Neil bent his head towards me. 'The Labour Party', he murmured, 'always loves a loser'. No doubt, somewhere in the body of the hall, Tony Blair was thinking exactly the same thing and longing for the opportunity to make Labour the party of winners.

Thanks to John Smith's influence, I moved into the grand suite of offices which he, as Shadow Chancellor, had occupied. And I began to consider how I would best adjust to life on the back-benches after a quarter of a century in which my speech notes had always rested on the despatch box. It took me about a week to realise that the best way to accommodate to my new role was not to perform it. The party conference had lost much of its charm back in the early sixties when the chance of meeting people like me no longer seemed worth making a journey to Blackpool or Brighton for. But I wanted to hear John Smith give the leader's Tuesday address, so I made a day trip to the home of fresh air and fun. With nothing much to do in the morning I hung around Blackpool's Grand Hotel where, to my delight, Jim Callaghan invited me to lunch. I had already agreed to meet a couple of journalists but I still thought of Jim as my Prime Minister and he thought of me as a junior member of the Cabinet. I cancelled the journalists and walked along the windy promenade. As soon as the pleasantries were over, Jim told me the reason for his invitation. 'I have', he said, 'been thinking about your future.' I suggested that my future was no longer worth a three-course lunch but Jim dismissed my modesty and went on to explain what he had decided. 'You must write a big political novel.'

Political novels have never appealed to me. The most exciting thing about politics is the battle of ideas. And that is the one aspect of politics which cannot be translated into fiction. Poor Plantagenet Palliser, Duke of Omnium, had a political career which stretched, from back-bencher to Prime Minister, over six, two-volume novels. But all he managed to introduce was a decimalisation bill. I explained all this to Jim and added, 'It's just not what I want to do. I wouldn't be any good.'

Jim's reply could not have been more frank. 'I never thought of it being any good. But it would be accurate. You know what goes on – times, places, that sort of thing. In a hundred years' time people would say, "It's not much of a novel, but you learn a lot about twentieth-century politics." That's what I meant.' Despite the deference that I still felt towards the ex-Prime Minister, I insisted that political fiction was not for me. Indeed, though I intended to spend the rest of my life writing, I had absolutely no intention of writing about political fact or fiction. My *Guardian* column would become the inconsequential 'English light essay', I would gladly devote days to unremunerative book reviews and, sooner or later, there would be another novel. But it would have nothing to do with ambition on the front bench, disappointment on the backbench and adultery in Committee Room 15. There are too many of those books already.

It was a full year before I announced that I would not contest the next election. I guessed that John Smith realised that I was going. For on that Saturday after the general election when we had talked about how soon he would take over he had asked, 'What are you going to do?' And when I had drawn breath before answering, he had offered, I suspect purely out of friendship, 'Any Shadow Cabinet job you like.' That morning not even Education had tempted me. So I had admitted that all I wanted to do was write. With a simple frankness that had not always endeared him to his friends, John had replied, 'You're probably right. A clean break is usually best.' So I did not think he sat in his House of Commons room worrying about my future. But I thought that courtesy required me to tell him of my decision before he read of it in the newspapers.

Perhaps John had begun to suspect that my mind was no longer solely concentrated on politics. A couple of years before, he had been witness to a scene which had illustrated the obsession's decline. We were on our way to dinner in Edinburgh when he insisted that we call in at a party that a friend of his was giving. My fears that, having not been invited, I might not be welcome, were brushed aside. 'He wants to meet you,' said John. I recognised our host as soon as he came to the door and in my gushing way I said so. 'You used to run for Great Britain,' I cried. The retired athlete looked delighted and explained modestly that 'that was all a long time ago'. I reassured him that some of us still remembered and proved it by adding details. 'You were a middle distance runner. Indeed, you were captain. You carried the Union Jack at the opening of the games.' Blushing, the old hero called to his wife, 'Come and meet Roy Hattersley. He was talking about my youth.' As she approached us I asked, 'What do you do now?' There was a pause before he told me, 'I'm a Liberal Member of Parliament. My name is Menzies Campbell.'

John and I began to talk after the ten o'clock division and, by midnight, he had not asked me why I wanted to see him and I had not told him. But after two hours of reminiscences and anecdotes, I decided to mention the reason for my visit. If, until then, I had not been sure that I had made the right decision, John's reaction would have removed all doubt. He said that he had hoped that I 'would do two or three years in the Cabinet to see the new government in', but that would not be possible if I were in the House of Lords. I was grateful for his offer. But all I could think of was the sixty-year-old ministers who I had watched act as an experienced transition from opposition to government – Soskice and Gordon Walker in 1964 right up to Maude and Soames in 1979. That was not the fate for me. I had chosen to start a new life, not end an old one. I explained, 'There is a time to sow and a time to reap.' John Smith, a good son of the Church of Scotland, corrected my quotation.

The day after I told Sparkbrook what I had decided, the newspapers printed what read like interim obituaries. Most of them were written by old friends – in *The Times*, Tony Howard, who had commissioned that first never-to-be-forgotten profile, and in the *Evening Standard*, Gerald Kaufman, the deputy who had won our victory over Michael Heseltine. At the weekend, Alan Watkins, political correspondent of the *Spectator* when Iain Macleod had first employed me, performed the almost last rites for the *Independent on Sunday* and John Cole, who had saved my political career by refusing to sign me on for the *Guardian* until the whole Labour government was formed, marked my political passing for the *Telegraph*. Brian 'Citizen' Walden had me on his television show purely for Auld Lang Syne. When I mentioned the arguments of twenty years before, he patted me on the knee and said, 'Not twenty. Not thirty. Forty, my old son.' I went contentedly to my premature grave.

There was one unhappy moment when I coincided on a radio programme with the Beverley Sisters. The twin who had graced my first Sparkbrook campaign performed like a proper trouper and we reminisced about old times which neither of us remembered. After the show, the producer told me, 'It was marvellous. But a pity you kept calling them the Andrews Sisters.' By way of apology I explained it was all a long time ago.

I did not say – though I certainly thought – that I was right not to remember every detail of the last thirty years. The Labour Party had a future again. I would not be part of it. Or at least I would be no more than one of those card-carrying party members who enthuse about socialism without feeling any obligation to go out on rainy nights to canvas on behalf of socialist candidates. But in those days, between the announcement of my political quietus and the newspapers' discovery that it was a matter of no coincidence,

I did believe that the hopes of a political lifetime were about to be realised. John Smith would support some policies with which I disagreed – every Labour Prime Minister had done the same. Indeed I disagreed with the Labour Party leadership even when I was part of it. But I had no doubt that we had beaten the challenge both from the mindless left and from the complacent centre. I could go off with my dog to the Peak District, secure in the knowledge that, after the next general election, there would be a real Labour Government.

I gave that assurance to the Sparkbook Labour Party after I told them that I would not again seek nomination as their parliamentary candidate. We all behaved with admirable restraint and instead of expressions of regret on both sides, we went to the usual pub and had the usual drink. 'No chance of changing your mind?' asked Councillor Baghat Singh. Councillor Sir Richard Knowles (my agent in the 1987 and 1992 elections) said, 'We'll miss you'. I made a rough calculation in my mind of what would happen if a resolution, embodying those sentiments, was debated by my constituency party's general management committee. I decided that it would be passed by a substantial, but not quite unanimous, majority.

Next morning the directors of the Royal Opera House, Covent Garden, were on the train which bore me back to London. It was the age of scandal. So when we arrived at Euston and photographers jostled to take my picture, Sir Jeremy Isaacs and Baroness Tessa Blackstone, both old friends, formed their colleagues around me in a protective phalanx. To their surprise, I accepted the offer of a BBC invitation to drive me to Broadcasting House. It was Jim Naughtie's last day before his elevation from *The World at One* to *Today*. There was a great deal of champagne about. As a result, I announced, 'When I grow up, I want to be George Eliot.' The *Daily Telegraph* – no doubt as the result of genuine error – interpreted my hope as the prophecy that I would become the *next* George Eliot. And it expressed considerable doubt about the chances of my ambition being realised.

The *Independent* sent a car to drive me from the BBC to the House of Commons, where (taking advantage of my gratitude) the photographer persuaded me to pose for the sort of picture which I normally despise. Next day a particularly romantic colour portrait appeared on the front page. It showed me standing on Westminster Bridge, looking out across the parapet as if life had not anything to show more fair than the House of Commons. I sent a copy to my mother and when, the following weekend, I made my usual phone call home, asked her what she thought about the picture. She told me that I needed a haircut. It was half a century since I had pushed those first Labour Party leaflets under the doors in Shalesmoor. And it was reassuring to know that some things had not changed.

EPILOGUE

On the morning of 12 May 1994 the *Daily Mail* – a paper which seems to have a tame porter in every major hospital – telephoned me at just after nine o'clock. John Smith, they told me, was dead. The cold professional message ended with a cold professional request. Would I write a thousand-word appreciation? Perhaps the sudden shock of the news numbed its full emotional impact. Whatever the reason, I responded professionally – conscious as I began to write that I was doing my calm duty by John's memory, his family and my contract to the *Daily Mail*. Then I heard the official announcement on the BBC news bulletin and my hands began to shake. Notwithstanding my sudden palsy, I agreed to record a memorial tribute in the studios on Millbank. I was perfectly composed as I walked across Parliament Square but, after my third unsuccessful attempt to record something coherent, the young producer sensibly suggested that I should give up and go home. Jack Cunningham, a tough politician from the north-east, was in tears in the foyer. Tears, at that moment, were respectable.

Even on that desolate first day, I had no doubt that Tony Blair should succeed John Smith as leader of the Labour Party and putative Prime Minister. He would not, I knew, have been John Smith's choice. We had discussed the shadow cabinet during our long last talk together and what I remembered most vividly – after John's complaint that my views on Harriet Harman were 'pure intellectual snobbery' – was our assessment of the rival merits of Blair and Brown. Gordon Brown, the Shadow Chancellor, was at the lowest ebb of his popularity. He had just invented and announced the 'windfall tax'. All of his colleagues agreed that it was a brilliant idea about which they had not been properly consulted and *amour-propre* took precedence over all other consideration. I said that Tony Blair was doing exceptionally well and that, if there were to be a contest for leader that week, he would win. It was not a tactful observation to make to an incumbent who had suffered a heart attack a couple of years earlier. John had the grace and confidence to agree. But he added, 'Fortunately, it isn't going to happen. When the time comes, it will be Gordon'.

The history of the next couple of weeks has been rewritten several times. The truth is that the campaign to make Tony Blair leader began within twenty-four hours of John Smith's death. It must, however, be said in fairness that Peter Mandelson did not take part for several days. He took a whole weekend to decide which candidate was likely to win. When I telephoned Tony Blair, scarcely seventy-two hours after John's death, he told me of MPs who were already pledged to him. He then added, with what I have never doubted was absolute sincerity, that he was worried about the effect of his candidature on his old friend Gordon Brown who had 'always wanted and expected the leadership'. I told him what I later wrote, in slightly more emollient terms, to Gordon. Labour history is littered with politicians who have hoped for, but been denied, the party leadership and gone on to live fulfilling lives. It was rumoured, apocryphally no doubt, that Denis Healey sent the same message but for 'politicians' substituted 'better men than you'.

By the time of John Smith's funeral, it was taken for granted that Tony Blair would run and win – even though everybody paid lip service to the need for a 'proper period of respect'. I sat in the

Edinburgh church next to Gerald Kaufman who, much to my
surprise, sank to the floor of the pew as the coffin arrived. When
the service was over, I asked him if his obeisance was a Jewish
ritual and he told me that he was afraid that his mobile telephone
– in his topcoat, under his seat – was not switched off. He also said
that Tony Blair already had the look of a Prime Minister in
waiting. I heartily agreed.

Jim Callaghan – Lord Callaghan by then – attended the funeral
as the Queen's Representative. A couple of days later I received
an apologetic note: 'Sorry we couldn't gossip on the aircraft on the
way up. So goes the last of the three I expected would one day
produce the leader of the party from the Cabinet of 1976–79 –
David Owen, you and John. Such is the uncertainty of politics.'
By then, nothing could rekindle the regret of 1983. Indeed, it
seemed incredible that I had even aspired to lead the party. I used
idly to consider how we would have felt – not just Jim Callaghan's
chosen three, but equally Bill Rodgers, Eric Varley and Shirley
Williams – if, back in 1979, we had realised that our ministerial
careers had come to a sudden end in our mid forties. But I always
put the speculation aside. No one with an inclination to agonise
about what might have been ought to spend their life in politics.

My most important contribution to Tony Blair's election was
the advice that he should not make Mo Mowlam his campaign
manager. But there were other little items of assistance. One day,
a young man from his office came to see me to ask if I possessed
(and he could borrow) a book called *Choose Freedom*. 'It is', he said,
'all that Old Labour rubbish about equality, but we've got a letter
about it. So . . .' The subject did not warrant him bothering to
finish the sentence. I was able to oblige. For I possessed several
copies – the direct (if slightly narcissistic) result of being *Choose
Freedom*'s author. I sent one to Tony Blair. As far as I can make
out, my closely argued critique of T. H. Green's analysis of the
Second Irish Land Act did nothing to undermine his faith in the
justice, as well as the efficiency, of the market economy.

I was slow to realise that, like me, Tony Blair was entitled to only half the description 'Christian Socialist'. So, when he delivered his acceptance speech to the electoral college, I was not one of the people who, according to his own slightly insecure joke only voted for him because he seemed likely to win. I was taking my seat when I was given a message from the *Independent*. Harold Wilson was close to death. There followed another request for a thousand words about his life and work. I scribbled away as Blair spoke. Then I remembered that I worked for the *Guardian* and I telephoned them with the news – and agreed to write another thousand words. Back in my office, I took a call from the *Daily Mail*. There was a rumour going around that Harold Wilson would not last the night. I wrote a third version of my threnody. On the way home I saw Harold Wilson out for a walk in Victoria with his wife.

For the first few months of Tony Blair's leadership I hoped for glad confident morning. Then David Blunkett, the Shadow Education Secretary, published a policy document with a title which was almost indistinguishable from the Conservative Government's white paper and proposals which were also a reflection of the Tory's programme. Tony Blair assumed that I had joined the critics of his decision to send his son to a school outside his natural catchment area and wrote to me to explain his decision. In fact I had never regarded the Blair's family affairs as any of my business. And I will still gladly defend, as I did at the time, a father's right to do what he thinks best for his son. I was interested in policy. And Labour education policy epitomised all that I found distasteful about New Labour – as illustrated by the week of 'Read My Lips'.

Labour, on the threshold of power, held its annual conference in Brighton. And the retreat from the old ideas – including the protection of the one hundred and sixty-four grammar schools it had promised to absorb into the comprehensive system – was on the agenda. At first I intended to do no more than watch from the sidelines. I always hated the anxiety that speaking at conference induces – jumping up and down to catch the chair's eye, the long walk to the front of the hall and the even longer walk back if the carefully prepared speech has lasted beyond the allotted time and the red light flashing on the rostrum has prompted opponents to begin a slow handclap. But my educationally inclined friends convinced me that I had made so much fuss in the newspapers that silence would be interpreted as a failure of nerve and will. So I worked for days on my five-minute rebellion.

A couple of days before conference began, I received an invitation to a party at which Tony Blair was guest of honour. It was hosted by a couple of newspapers to celebrate an educational broadcasting initiative but a hand-written note explained that Leo Blair, Tony's father, would be there to celebrate the announcement that he had at last joined the Labour Party. Leo Blair was the cause of my permanent embarrassment. When Tony worked for me he had brought his father to meet his boss. And I had predicted that – given hard work and the avoidance of temptation – my young assistant might do quite well in politics. The urge to tell Leo Blair what an ass I felt was irresistible.

My friends said I should resist it. Half an hour into the party, they predicted, Tony Blair would lead me aside and urge me not to rock the boat with a speech demanding support for comprehensive schools. He would, they were sure, talk of the old days when we worked together, express his gratitude for my help and ask for one more act of loyalty and friendship. The result, they had no doubt, would be collapse of stout (and sentimental) party.

Part of the prediction came true. I was actually talking to David English – editor of the *Daily Mail* and the grammar schools' most passionate supporter – when Tony Blair asked, 'Can you spare a minute?' He led me from the drawing room of the hotel suite into the bedroom and we sat, facing each other, on the two single beds. Before he said a word I had not only worked out my concession statement, I had decided how I would justify capitulation to my friends. But, to my astonishment, he did not appeal to my better nature. Instead he asked me if I had ever thought that selective schools might provide a ladder on which bright boys could escape from deprivation. I had thought of it for years and resisted a theory of education which accepted that some children should escape while many more remained prisoners. I could not have held out against a plea for help in winning the imminent election. An argument in favour of selective secondary schools was easy enough to resist.

So I made the speech and David Blunkett, replying to the debate on behalf of the party leadership, told the conference 'Read my lips. No selection by examination or interview'. And I believed him. Even when he tried to change the record to 'no more selection', I still believed him.

Labour won the election with a majority of almost two hundred seats, governed with mixed success for four years and then faced the country again. My mother died in the week that Parliament was dissolved. She was cremated on the first Friday of the campaign. There was no ceremony, just the silent disposal which she demanded. David Blunkett – whose affection and devotion continued long after she had ceased to be a power in Sheffield politics – was amongst the half dozen mourners who were allowed to witness the strange ceremony. Later that day he appeared on *Any Questions?* – a programme which helps 'the team' to relax by giving them supper before the broadcast. The funeral was still on his mind. 'Roy', he told one of the other participants, 'will never forgive me'. Then he added, 'But he must realise that I had to make that promise, otherwise we would have lost the vote.' I did understand and that is why it is unlikely that I shall forgive him.

It was Donald Dewar, my old and much missed friend, who persuaded me that I should become a peer. My elevation would, he said, provide another vote for the abolition of the Upper House. I postponed taking my seat for as long as I could and then set the tone of my membership by inadvertently going through the elaborate initiation ceremony with my tricorne hat back to front. The moment that I ceased being a commoner was captured on television and it is the habit of the Lords' authorities to present new peers with a video of the occasion as a memento. When I took mine home to Sheffield to show my mother, it produced a picture of a violent snowstorm. I suspect that she thought I had invented the story of my elevation in the hope of pleasing her.

Shortly before she died she did concede, 'I've never thought much of our Roy but, I must admit, he does look after his dog'. She would have been astonished to learn that Lord Longford thought my life was worth a biography. He took me to lunch at the Gay Hussar and explained that a lady of his acquaintance had asked him to approach me with a request for my cooperation. 'She would be', she said, 'the perfect candidate for the job. She has written two books already: an account of bringing up an autistic child and a description of nursing her fatally ill mother through her dying days. She is just the person to write about you'. I declined with thanks. If life's joke was on me, it was better to tell it myself.